P9-DTP-309

"*Frank Sinatra, from Hoboken, New Jersey, has forced his presence into American social history; when the story of how Americans in this century played, dreamed, hoped and loved is told, Frank Sinatra cannot be left out. He is more than a mere singer or actor. He is a legend. And the legend lives.*"—Pete Hamill, New York Magazine, *1980*

Legend

FRANK SINATRA
AND THE
AMERICAN DREAM

Edited by
Ethlie Ann Vare

BOULEVARD BOOKS
NEW YORK

PHOTOGRAPH CREDITS
Shooting Star Archives: i, xviii, 16, 26, 44, 60, 70, 86, 94, 120, 150, 218; Yoram Kahana, Shooting Star Archives: 130, 185, 201; Jim Britt, Shooting Star Archives: 172.

See pp. 219-221 for the list of original sources for the articles that appear in this collection.

LEGEND: FRANK SINATRA AND THE AMERICAN DREAM

A Boulevard Book / published by arrangement with the author

PRINTING HISTORY
Boulevard trade paperback edition / November 1995

All rights reserved.
Copyright © 1995 by Ethlie Ann Vare.
Book design by Rhea Braunstein.
Cover art by Alan Reingold.
This book may not be reproduced in whole
or in part, by mimeograph or any other means,
without permission. For information address:
The Berkley Publishing Group, 200 Madison Avenue,
New York, New York 10016.

ISBN: 1-57297-027-8

BOULEVARD
Boulevard Books are published by The Berkley Publishing Group,
200 Madison Avenue, New York, New York 10016.
BOULEVARD and its logo are trademarks
belonging to Berkley Publishing Corporation.

PRINTED IN THE UNITED STATES OF AMERICA

10 9 8 7 6 5 4 3 2 1

for Russell,
the coolest kid on wheels,
and Martin, the warmest man

ACKNOWLEDGMENTS

*T*he talents and generosity of many people made this book possible. I would first like to thank my loyal assistant, Kimberly Ball, for efforts above and beyond the call of duty. Also indispensable was Geneviève Van de Merghel, a most able researcher.

Thanks to Bob Merlis, Alisse Kingsley, and all the helpful folks at Warner/Reprise Records, as well as Sujata Murphy and the good guys at Capitol Records.

I cannot say enough about the excellent resources at the Margaret Herrick Library of the Motion Picture Association of America and its fine staff. I am also indebted to Gary L. Doctor of the International Sinatra Society of Lakeland, Florida, for a peek into the world of fandom and for his outstanding collection of memorabilia.

It was my longtime agent, Madeleine Morel, who inspired me to this project, and I am grateful. And it was Madeleine who put me together with a dynamic editor, Elizabeth Beier, who has remained in my corner throughout.

I want to thank all the authors included in the collection—especially my mom, who has never written on spec in her life—for their words, their insight, and the foundation they established for a generation of journalists . . . like me.

CONTENTS

CONTENTS

CONTENTS

INTRODUCTION
by Ethlie Ann Vare

J have never known a world without Frank Sinatra. When I was five, and the only record I owned was a recitation of Prokofiev's *Peter and the Wolf*, I knew Frank Sinatra. He was that skinny canary in the Warner Brothers cartoons, the one with the floppy bow tie that made the girl parakeets with the big shoes faint. I wasn't sure why, exactly, but I knew it was important. And I was right.

By the time I was a teenager, Frank Sinatra epitomized everything I was rebelling against. He was an archrival of rock 'n' roll—called it "noise" when he was feeling charitable, unprintable epithets when he wasn't. His sound—the cloying strings, the slapping bass, the shuffling snares—was the antithesis of the electric guitar/Fender bass/double-kick drum sound that was the heartbeat of my generation.

Worse, his lifestyle represented everything those of us who trusted no one over thirty rejected. He was a "skirt chaser" and a "booze hound" when my peers were discovering feminism and marijuana. He was, above all, worshipped by our parents, and that was reason enough to despise him.

Of course, the first time I saw Frank Sinatra would have been in 1965, when his television special "A Man and His Music" aired. The first Sinatra hits I ever heard on the radio were "Strangers in the Night," "That's Life" and "Something Stupid." All three topped the charts in 1966 . . . this from an artist whose prime was in 1944.

It's rather like listening to Paul McCartney and Wings's 1979 *Back to the Egg* LP, and finding the Beatles wanting.

To baby boomers, Frank Sinatra was The Enemy—if for no other reason than he committed the unpardonable sin of growing old. How dare he put on a blue velvet Nehru jacket and sing with the Fifth Dimension? How dare he have *jowls*!

Times change, and change back. Suddenly, a new generation—Generation X, if you will—is clutching Frank Sinatra to its collective bosom. Everything old is new again, and the original hep cat is hip. They say grandparents and grandkids bond so well because they have a common enemy.

Is Frank Sinatra the hero of the slackers because they know the choice will surely piss off the fortysomethings?

I thought so, until I listened to Ol' Blue Eyes sing a duet with U2's rock god, Bono Hewson. And though it pains me to admit it, my first thought was, "That old guy is blowing Bono right off the stage."

The thing is, when he exploded on the scene, Frank Sinatra *was* Bono. He was Bono and the Beatles and Elvis rolled into one. His fans were fourteen and fifteen and sixteen years old; he won the *Billboard* magazine *college* poll . . . making him Madonna and R.E.M., as well. He was reviled by the establishment of his day: Columnist Elsa Maxwell said his success was "the glorification of musical illiteracy and the power of synthetic publicity." The *Los Angeles Times* was aghast when he sang with the Washington Symphony, calling it "a disgrace to the nation" that the symphony would "lend its name to entertainers of this type." *Stars & Stripes* looked at the commotion and smirked that "mice make women faint, too."

This "jazz music," the school principals said, could lead teenagers into juvenile delinquency.

When Frank Sinatra graduated from New Jersey roadhouses to national radio—when he had a twenty-nine-inch waist, when RKO was still known as Radio-Keith-Orpheum—there was no such qualifier as "superstar." There had been Rudy Vallee, and there had been Bing Crosby, and then there was Frankie. The Voice. Swoonatra. He wasn't just another million-seller in a world where twenty major-label albums are released each week; he was a bleeding mountain in Kansas. His closest competition in popularity polls was movie star Van Johnson. In 1946, there were *two thousand* Frank Sinatra fan clubs in the U.S. Sales of bow ties increased 400 percent in eighteen months. And yes, girls wearing white ankle socks really did faint dead away . . . perhaps because it was not unusual for them to stand in line unfed overnight to get into a theater, and then sit through seven consecutive shows.

This was before Casey Kasem's *American Top Forty*. This was not only before MTV; it was, for all means and purposes, before *television*. No one knew how to make a pop star; the formula hadn't been invented yet. Frank Sinatra was a totally new phenomenon. Ed Sullivan once remarked that the odds on his stardom were about the same as for throwing four consecutive double sixes in dice: 1,679,615 to 1 against.

Frank Sinatra's first million-seller was in 1943. His last—no, make that his *latest*—was in 1994. In a world where fifteen minutes of fame is optimistic, name me someone else with a fifty-year pop music career. Frank Sinatra doesn't sing standards. He makes standards.

The story of Frank Sinatra is the story of America coming of age. It starts with first-generation Italian immigrants, Democratic ward-heelers and the docks of Hoboken, New Jersey. It starts with a scrappy kid making three bucks a night singing in saloons and going for the brass ring on *Major Bowes' Amateur Hour*. It starts with crooning for carfare on the Mutual Radio Network.

It ends with immeasurable riches and untold power . . . and some of the most memorable music ever committed to acetate, vinyl, or digital audio tape.

When he was a teenager, Frank Sinatra was nicknamed Slacksey because he usually had a pressed pair of pants. Today, there's a boulevard in California named after him. And if that isn't the American Dream, I don't know what is.

It starts out so innocent. In the 1940s, articles about Sinatra had to explain to the readers what an agent is, and why he's entitled to a percentage. What a recording contract is all about. Who gets to make a disc or sing on the radio, and why.

But soon the dollars got bigger, and the stakes got higher. The war was over. The nation was getting fat and comfortable . . . and so was Frank. Frankie Goes to Hollywood, and then Frankie Goes to Washington. The handlers got savvier, and so did the readers. The press became sophisticated. Now the articles are more jaded, ripe with innuendo.

Money is power, power is politics, and you can never be naive twice in the same lifetime. The same Frank Sinatra who fought, often at real personal cost, for civil rights has moved from New Deal Democrat to Trickle-Down Republican. The guy who once escorted Jackie Kennedy to her husband's inaugural ball later (according to a best-selling exposé) played footsie with Nancy Reagan in the White House. No more picket fence in Hasbrouck Heights, New Jersey. Now it's a guarded compound in Palm Springs, California. And the articles can be irreverent, dismissive . . . downright mean.

The story of Frank Sinatra coming of age, and of America coming of age, is also the story of pop journalism coming of age. The fifty years of Frank Sinatra's career also span the entire life of contemporary music criticism. Sure, there were fan magazines before there was Frankie, but they were sycophantic and devoted to movie stars. The arc of Frank Sinatra's life and career is also the arc of my profession.

"He is the most investigated American performer since John Wilkes Booth," said author Pete Hamill, and Hamill is one of many who have investigated him. Some remarkable writers have put down their thoughts about this cultural icon over the past five decades. Adela Rogers St. Johns, doyenne of American journalism, covered the Lindbergh baby kidnapping trial for Hearst and covered Sinatra for *Cosmopolitan.* Gay Talese, before he wrote the bestsellers *Honor Thy Father* and *Thy Neighbor's Wife*, wrote about Sinatra for *The New York Times.* Budd Schulberg, Oscar-winning screenwriter of *On the Waterfront* and the author of the classic Hollywood tale *What Makes Sammy Run* wrote about Sinatra for fun.

Included in this collection are pieces by novelists Christopher Buckley (*Thank You For Smoking*) and William Kennedy (*Ironweed*); by diarists Pete Hamill (*A Drinking Life*) and Mikal Gilmore (*Shot in the Heart*); by essayist Barbara G. Harrison (*Foreign Bodies*), and biographer Jon Wiener (*Come Together: The Life of John Lennon*.) There's also a remembrance by my mother, Shirley Kelley, and by my twentysomething college intern, Kimberly Ball. Each brings to the table a perspective, a moment, a piece of the puzzle.

Yes, Frank Sinatra is a puzzle. The Voice That Thrills Millions once called himself "an eighteen-karat manic depressive," and said he "lived a life of violent emotional contradictions." So it seems. Tough and tender. A lover and a fighter. A loner and a glad-handing Rat Packer. A friend of presidents and a crony of gangsters. A brilliant stylist and a lazy singer. A sloppy actor who won't take direction, and an Academy Award–winning performer.

None of the above. All of the above. Reading stories about Frank Sinatra over the span of his incredible career gives an overview of the most complex, contradictory, mysterious, and private public figure around. At the same time, it's an oral history of popular culture. From sustaining radio broadcasts to fiber optic technology. From bobby sox to Doc Martens. It's what we listened to, it's how we thought, it's what we wore, it's what we hated, and what we loved.

Here is America looking at Frank Sinatra, the man who lived the American Dream.

Legend

FRANK SINATRA
AND THE
AMERICAN DREAM

The Forties:

THE VOICE THAT THRILLED MILLIONS

FRANK SINATRA: BIOGRAPHY

from the desk of George B. Evans, press and personal representative, circa 1942, on a manual typewriter . . . complete with typos.

"*T*he wheel of fortune spins—round and round she goes, and where she stops nobody knows." Frank Sinatra's wheel of fortune started spinning that night when he won first prize on *Major Bowes Broadcast,* several years ago. It has begun spinning him to heights that have made him the greatest singing phenomena in years, and it is still spinning for him for each week he is soaring to even greater popularity.

The lastest popularity poles held by the two leading musical trade papers *Downbeat* and *Metronome* have elected him as "America's favorite male vocalist," the position held by Bing Crosby for the past eight years. The Scripps-Howard Newspapers annual pole topped that off with their voting him "America's greatest Singer." Almost every other popularity pole have picked him as there favorite singer making that unanimous.

A cub sports reporter on the *Jersey Observer*, Frank Sinatra walked into the city room one day and gave his notice to the bewildered editor. The reason? Well he had just taken his best girl Nancy (now Mrs. Sinatra) to see Bing Crosby at the neighborhood theatre and he was convinced that he wanted to be a singer more than anything else in the world. And from that time on he exerted every effort towards that end.

Sinatra was born December 12, 1917 in Hoboken N.J. an only child whose parents dreamed of his studying to be a Civil Engineer. He attended Demarest High School in Hoboken and participated in all sports. He was on the championship basketball team, won a trophy in swimming and was an outstanding member of the track team. He sang with his school band at proms and assemblies and helped form the school glee club. He always liked to sing but never fostered any dreams of a singing career until that fateful visit to the theatre where Crosby was appearing. Sinatra earned pocket money after school by working on a news truck of the *Jersey Observer* and had ambitions to become a newspaperman. Upon Graduation he got a job with the same paper as a copy boy and studied short hand and journalism for a year at Drake Institute hoping to further his newspaper ambitions. He finally got a chance in the sports division of the paper when he

3

was promoted as a "Junior Man." His job was to cover all collegiate sports events.

After his decision to start a singing career he applied for an audition with Major Bowes for his popular *Amateur Hour* show and won first prize singing "Night and Day." He was sent out with a "Bowes Unit" headed for the coast but after 3 months was homesick for his family and Nancy. He quit and came home. He applied for radio auditions at New York studios and was soon heard on eighteen sustaining shows over WOR, WNEW, WMCA, and Jersey's WAAT but all the money he received was 70 cents carfare from the Jersey station. He finally got a paying job at the Rustic Cabin in New Jersey but continued his sustaining programs and on February 4, 1939 married his childhood sweetheart Nancy Barbato and then went on a three day honeymoon. They now have a two and a half year old daughter Nancy-Sandra.

In May of 1939 while at the Rustic Cabin, Sinatra started rehearsing with Bob Chester's band although he had signed no contract with him. He gave his notice at the Rustic Cabin and three days before he was to leave, Harry James, his manager and some musicians from the newly organized James band came in to hear Sinatra sing. (It wasn't until many years later that Sinatra learned that James had heard him before and vowed that should he form a band he would hire Sinatra as his vocalist.) James offered Frank a two-year contract and he went on a tour with the band. About 6 months later while appearing in Chicago with James, Tommy Dorsey asked Frank Sinatra to join his band. He did and it was then that Frank Sinatra, the romantic young baritone with the "voice that thrills millions" began to cause such a furore among the music critics and public.

His recordings of "I'll Never Smile Again" "Night and Day" "Stardust," and "This Love of Mine," which he wrote, skyrocketed the Dorsey record sales to the top of all recording brackets. Sinatra became the byward of every male and female musical devotee from six to sixty.

Sinatra made his motion picture debut with Dorsey in the Pictures *Las Vegas Nights* and *Ship Ahoy*. Then came the deluge of requests from promoters theatre managers and radio advertisers for the solo services of Frank Sinatra.

However, it was Columbia Broadcasting who convinced Sinatra that he would be doing the right thing by becoming a solo star and promised to feature him in a series of daily broadcasts. He gave Dorsey eight months notice and it wasn't long after he left the Band that things started to happen, proving that Sinatra had taken a step in the right direction. For two months later he signed the Lucky Strike *Hit Parade* Contract giving him

4

the coveted starring role on radio's most popular musical program. He signed a contract to make several pictures a year with RKO. Columbia Pictures are now releasing his first starring picture *Reveille with Beverly*.

His first theatre appearance on his own was at the New York Paramount Theatre. After the third day of his record breaking eight week appearance Bob Weitman Paramount manager came backstage and re-signed Sinatra for an extended engagement at the theatre in June. He is featured on the CBS *Saturday Night Hit Parade*. In July, RKO will film the Broadway musical *Higher and Higher*, in which Sinatra will be starred in the romantic lead opposite Michele Morgan. This is the first in a series of romantic musicals featuring Sinatra and Miss Morgan.

Personals about Sinatra: He is 5' 10½" tall, weighs 140 lbs has blue eyes and brown hair. He is a sports enthusiast, with swimming boxing and basketball his favorites.

Nancy and Frank are proud of their two and half year old Nancy-Sandra and have hopes of her being a great musician someday, possibly a harpist. Frank's favorite song is "Night and Day." He likes anything written by George Gershwin and anything sung by Bing Crosby. He likes symphonic and concert music and attends Carnegie and Metropolitan recitals regularly. Likes the colors blue and brown, hates evening clothes, prefers sports clothes. Is sentimental especially about Nancy and little Sandra, music and his parents.

HE CAN'T READ A NOTE BUT HE'S DETHRONING BING, AND FRANK SINATRA IS "WUNNERFUL" TO THE GALS

from *Newsweek,* March 22, 1943

*F*rom the ladies who sigh through five shows a day at the Paramount to the pugs and characters over at Stillman's muscle emporium on Eighth Avenue—Sinatra is terrific. This viewpoint is also shared by a growing number of other solid citizens. For two years Frank Sinatra has won both the *Downbeat* and *Metronome* polls as the best popular vocalist, taking away a crown that everybody had considered Bing Crosby's permanent acquisition.

Sinatra also recently finished an eight-week run at the Paramount Theater in New York City, the first time any one performer has stayed there that long since Rudy Vallee was the nation's vagabond lover in 1929. This summer he will make a picture for RKO. When the Petrillo ban is lifted (if ever) he will start making records for Columbia. On Saturday nights he is featured on the *Lucky Strikes Hit Parade.* Last week he made his debut as a Manhattan night-club entertainer at the Riobamba, where he will stay for three weeks.

"O-o-o-o-o-oh," breathed 17-year-old Blanche Karo, who was present at the opening. "This is the most wunnerful thing that ever happened to me. Crosby's not in it with him. I'll never get to school tomorrow." Miss Karo is president of a Frank Sinatra fan club.

Sinatra's vocal style is way over on the sweet side—vaguely reminiscent of a Crosby attack with the b-b-b-boos left out. He is at his best in numbers like "You'd Be So Nice to Come Home To," "That Old Black Magic" or "Night and Day." His Victor record of two such ballads—"I'll Never Smile Again" and "This Love of Mine"—made while he was a featured soloist with Tommy Dorsey, were important beginnings of the current Sinatra boom.

When Sinatra (now 25) left the Dorsey band last September to start on his own, the first thing he did was to take a vacation to get reacquainted with his wife and 2½-year-old daughter, for he had been touring and playing for most of three and a half years. The son of a Hoboken, N.J. fireman, he decided on singing as a career when he heard Bing Crosby. It looked so easy. He still can't read a note of music and has never had a voice lesson.

Outside of his family and his new house in Hasbrouck Heights, N.J., Sinatra's favorite passion is prizefighting. His two greatest friends are Tami Mauriello, the heavyweight contender, and Al Silvani, his trainer. Tami gave him a gold bracelet and Al put 10 pounds on the half-pint Sinatra frame. He's always boxed since his early days with the Hoboken back-alley gang. "If I didn't know how," he recalls, "that was the end. Somebody else always did."

SWEET DREAMS AND DYNAMITE
by Jack Long from *The American* magazine, September 1943

*I*f West Coast youngsters are like New York kids—and I've never heard anything to the contrary—a lot of square-shouldered Hollywood he-men are going to be feeling neglected soon. Because as this is written a new little guy is on his way there, neither tall nor handsome, who does something to the girls that makes them follow him in squealing, cooing droves, forgetting all other males. For a glimpse of him in person they'll pull hair; for a signed photograph it's murder. I've seen them in action, and it was quite an experience.

On the first occasion, I was walking through Times Square one Saturday morning, eyes straight ahead, minding my own business, when I was suddenly picked up by a whirling mass of humanity and tossed off the sidewalk into the street. A mounted policeman trotted up waving his stick. "Get back in line, you"—meaning me. There was another shove, and more shouting, and I was in the street again. This time I caught a red light and made for the other side of Broadway, where I bumped into another cop.

"Look here," I protested; "I'm a peaceful citizen. Whatever this demonstration is, I'm not in it. And, by the way, what is it?"

The cop gave me an unhappy look. "They're opening the doors for the first show at the Paramount Theater. Like this for the past six weeks," he added gloomily.

I looked back and saw a double line that started at the theater entrance and bent out of sight around the corner—a mob of girls in sweaters, with ribbons in their hair, boys in bow ties, long jackets, pegged pants, all pushing, screaming, laughing, as though they were at the biggest football rally in history. Up above on a huge banner was the legend: "Frank Sinatra, In Person."

"Every day he sings, and every day it's like this," the cop explained sadly.

I moved on, but the mystery bothered me for several days. Frank Sinatra. The name was familiar; I'd heard him on the radio without paying much attention. But what, I wondered, was the magnetism that brought five or six thousand youngsters into Times Square on a Saturday morning to hear somebody named Sinatra sing a few songs?

The papers by that time were beginning to write about "Frank Swoon-atra," and referring to his effect on audiences as a "Sinatrance!"

Finally I quit wondering and went to hear him one night, using a few elementary commando tactics to get into the theater. There were soft lights on the stage, the curtains were drawn, and the whole place vibrated to the shuffling of feet, the twitching of restless young bodies, bursts of whistling, stamping, and catcalls.

I was beginning to get a little nervous myself, when the lights went down, the curtains swished back, and a thin, stoop-shouldered boy in a super-drape suit walked out from the wings. A girl sitting next to me stamped on my instep, jumped to her feet, and screamed, "Frankie! Frankie! Here I am! Look at me!" She was drowned out in a hurricane of human sound that lasted five minutes. Then the band played a brassy chord and slid into a rhythmic introduction. The roar of the audience stopped as though a door had been slammed on it.

A whispering, baritone voice began a song I had never heard before, and which I haven't been able to escape from since. "That old black magic has me in its spell," came the words from the microphone. It was nothing spectacular, I thought, just a wisp of a love song from a boy who looked like someone the girl on my right might have come to the show with—an idea I'm sure she shared.

As I left the theater, with the shriek of young lungs still ringing in my ears, I was bothered by a strange discovery—that you could become a public idol simply by looking young, sad, and undernourished, then skimming off a certain amount of your misery and pouring it into a microphone. How did it happen, I asked myself, that the passionate murmur of this underfed boy could make mature women tremble and young ones bleat with ecstasy?

Since then I've been following Frank Sinatra around like a popeyed fan myself, and I think I've stumbled on a few of the answers. For one thing, Sinatra's appearance actually adds to the appeal of his singing. His voice seems to have more solidity than he does, because it's loaded down with feeling, ornamented with trick phrasing which underlines heartbreak and yearning. It goes breathless with longing; it breaks at strategic moments from an excess of emotion. Sinatra's voice is to popular music what Valentino's eyes were to the silent movies—sweet dreams and dynamite.

This is the boy who not long ago was the high-school hep cat with a collection of swing records and a ukulele. Today, without the uke, he's likely to gross an annual half-million dollars from theater appearances, night-club engagements, radio, movies, and records. He is about to make his first big picture—a musical called *Higher and Higher*. That should be a jolt to some of the folks who've been tossing bricks at the jitterbugs, rug-cutters, and other much-berated members of the younger generation. It was these youngsters who discovered Frank, but they share him now with millions of music-mad Americans of all ages.

There are, for example, the millions who bought records of a single sad ditty called, "I'll Never Smile Again." There are the million and a half who came to the Paramount during his 8-week stay, breaking an attendance record hung up by Rudy Vallee in the dear, dead year of 1929. There are the ten million who listen to his Saturday broadcasts every week on *Your Hit Parade*, and the millions more who are going to meet him in several big Sinatra musicals to be made in Hollywood this year.

I decided to investigate the Sinatra charm further. I drove out to Frank's 10-room stone and clapboard house in Hasbrouck Heights, an un-pretentious New Jersey suburb. The door opened, and a chubby-cheeked 3-year-old bolted out and tackled me by the leg. In a moment I was talking to Mrs. Sinatra—or Nancy—who is dark and pretty and as quiet as one of her husband's songs. Little Nancy-Sandra stuck with us, working with con-centrated energy on an apple her mother peeled for her.

I found that I wasn't the first Sinatra fan on hand that day. "Two girls are here who came all the way from Connecticut to see Frank," Nancy told me. "He isn't up yet, but I didn't have the heart to turn them away. They're members of a fan club and want to write something about him for their school paper."

I found out later that there are some 700 Frank Sinatra fan clubs, with from 10 to 100 members, scattered over the country. More of them spring up like mushrooms whenever Frank goes on the road. Their main function is to collect and exchange Sinatra records, clippings, snapshots, and auto-graphs. A rare snapshot taken by a fan in Peoria, even though a little blurred, is worth more than gold on the New York market.

We went into Frank's den, a comfortable, mannish study with leather-covered chairs, a portable phonograph, and two cabinets filled with record albums. Sitting shyly on the edges of the chairs were two teen-age girls, each holding a large scrapbook containing her personal collection of Sinatra lore. One girl had even pasted in a copy of a song Frank wrote: "This Love of Mine."

In a few minutes Frank walked in wearing a blue sweater, a light grey suit, and a wide-winged bow tie. His dark hair was still damp, his face a little pale and sleepy. Just a kid with a big smile and big ears and a good share of charm, I thought—somebody you'd expect a mother or sweetheart to love, but hardly half the female population of the United States.

When the two girls had asked Frank their questions and carefully noted down the answers, they floated ecstatically out of the house, each fortified for the long trip back to Connecticut by a glass of milk and a piece of cake provided by Nancy.

I asked Frank if being followed through every waking hour by an army of worshipful admirers wasn't a little wearing. He gazed around at the room we sat in. "After all," he said, "it was the fans who bought this place."

He admitted, with some prodding, that being public property has its difficult moments, as the time he made his first personal appearance in Philadelphia, which I'd always thought of as the home of a sober Quaker citizenry. On this occasion it resembled Paris on the original Bastille Day. There were some 2,000 people outside the theater after the last show, every one an autograph-hungry fan.

On the sidewalk six cops had cleared a lane from the stage door to a line of waiting taxis. They were big cops, but not big enough. By the time he got to a cab, Frank had lost his hat, his coat, his bag, the buttons on his shirt, and some of his hair. "If it hadn't been for two tough stagehands, they would have snatched me bald," he says. "Two kids got hold of my tie and almost choked me to death."

When he got to the station, a mechanized battalion of fifty jitterbugs was after him in taxis. Frank vaulted over a soda fountain and hid behind a couple cartons of chocolate sirup. When it was over, he told the soda jerker to mix him a stiff Coke.

"Say," was the answer, "you're Frank Sinatra. How about an autograph?"

Though he may look like a tender sprout to impressionable females, Frank was born with sparks in his pants and a genius for finding answers to the question: "What's in it for Sinatra?" This talent for figuring the percentages burst into flower while he was just a skinny, blue-eyed kid at Demarest High, in Hoboken, and earned him a nickname with a distinctly Broadway flavor—"Angles."

Athletics, Frank decided, was one way of getting in the public eye. In his sophomore year he presented himself to the football coach. "I'd make a good quarterback," he announced.

The coach was amused. At that time Frank weighed about 128 pounds (he's added 10 more since). "You'll be sorry you passed me up," he said, and went to see the basketball coach. He made the first team as a forward, and dropped a lot of balls through the hoop for Demarest.

Like everybody else his age, Frank liked popular music, and was among the school's prize rug-cutters. The only singing he did was strictly personal, and for the ears of dark-eyed Nancy Barbato, who thought it was wonderful even if no one else did. Nancy, who today is the mother of little Nancy-Sandra, used to listen to Sinatra serenades during cool summer evenings at the beach at Long Branch, N.J., while the driftwood fire crackled and the marshmallows got beautifully soft inside. Frankie even got to the point, though it hurts to admit it today, of accompanying himself on the ukulele.

His dad, a Hoboken fireman, planned a college education for him and an engineering degree. But to be an engineer you have to sit down and concentrate on things like trigonometry and calculus. "Math murdered me," is the way Frank explains it.

So he handed Papa his Demarest diploma one day, as the highest academic degree he was ever likely to see his son's name on, and proceeded to spend the summer playing the ukulele on the beach. This went on until Papa Sinatra announced that Frank had a job working for the circulation manager of the Jersey Observer, who was a friend of the family willing to help put an idle son on a paying basis.

Frank had no objection to riding a news truck; in fact, tossing the bundles of papers around was a little like basketball. It didn't take him long, however, to get promoted to copy boy, and the minute he learned where the front office was he went in and told the editor he'd make a good reporter. The editor reminded him gently that he was only a copy boy, and copy boys don't know enough to be reporters.

To prove that this was a shortsighted point of view, Frank went to a secretarial school and enrolled for a night course in journalism—studying English, typing, and shorthand. In less than a year the boss gave up and Frank became a cub sports reporter, covering the school games he'd been playing in not long before. "I really covered 'em, too," Frank recalls. "I'd write a thousand words, and the paper would print: 'Demarest beats Union City, 20-14.'"

So, at the damp and tender age of 18, Frank had a career, and even Papa stopped talking about engineering college.

His contentment was fated to be short. One pleasant spring evening in 1935, Frank took Nancy to hear Bing Crosby, in person. They saw a show, they heard Bing, they held hands. When it was over, Nancy knew that something was wrong. "What's the matter with you?" she asked. "You don't look so good."

Frank had to swallow hard before he could answer. "I'm going to quit my job."

When they got off the subway he tried to explain. "When I saw that guy up on the stage," he said, "something happened to me. It was like I was really up there, not Crosby. I've got to be a singer."

Probably a thousand other youngsters who heard Crosby that night painted the same mental picture—themselves in the spotlight, easy as you please, thrilling millions. But Sinatra was the one out of a thousand with the courage to chase the rainbow.

When it came to a question of learning how to sing, Frank did it by singing. He never read a note, never took a lesson. Instead, he went straight to the experts. He bought records and played them till the grooves were worn off; he parked himself in the front row wherever the name bands played; he rigged a headphone radio up by his bed and followed his favorite vocalists around the dial until two or three in the morning.

Bing Crosby's voice and Tommy Dorsey's trombone were his two role models of tone and phrasing. "There was only one thing I had at the beginning," he says, "and that was good taste. I could tell when a singer was lousy and when he was fine, and it wasn't long before I began to see why. I learned that a voice no better than the next one sounded solid to me because of just one thing—sincerity. The guy who put his heart into the song and made it mean something was my guy."

Frank's first problem was to get an audience. He went out and found one close to home, as a performer in neighborhood theater amateur shows, where you could win $10 or a set of dishes. Frank went from one movie house to the next, trailing clouds of Demarest alumni who had once watched him play basketball.

At home, the clouds were strictly stormy. Papa Sinatra began to think of Frank as the worthless wonder, and it was only quarters from Mamma that kept him in carfare. She also whispered to Frank that Papa sometimes went to the theater to hear him and clapped louder than she did, but he always sat in back where Frank couldn't see him.

After winning a prize on *Major Bowes' Amateur Hour,* Frank landed his first professional contract—$25 a week for acting as singer, headwaiter, master of ceremonies, and comedian at a country roadhouse. And just so he wouldn't have any time on his hands, he took a dozen quarter-hour sustaining programs every week over four local radio stations. Cash returns

13

on these enterprises amounted to 70 cents a week for carfare. But people were beginning to hear Sinatra.

In February, 1939, Frank and Nancy were married, and his hours began to present a real problem of domestic manipulation. Nancy worked all day in an office; Frank worked all night and part of the day besides. His favorite song, "Night and Day," began to take on a horrid and sinister significance.

One evening, when Frank had about decided to turn in his dinner jacket and go back to the newspaper business, a lanky stranger walked into the roadhouse surrounded by two or three other strangers who looked very much like musicians. It was, in fact, Harry James, the trumpet maniac, and some members of his newly organized band.

James called Frank over to his table. "I heard you on the air six months ago," he said, "and decided that if I ever started a band you'd be vocalist. Well, I've started a band."

So Frank and Nancy packed up and traveled west with James for a long engagement at the Palomar Ballroom, in Los Angeles. When they got to California, the Palomar was a heap of slowly cooling ashes. Frank suffered perhaps his first and only disillusionment with the discovery that you don't necessarily eat because you've got a contract with a name band.

When the band finally got a job it was at one of the most exclusive— and smallest—nightclubs in town, with barely room on the stand for James' eight brass. "We blasted the soup out of the customers' plates," Frank recalls.

In December, 1939, they played at a musicians' benefit in Chicago, along with every top artist who happened to be within traveling distance. Also present was Tommy Dorsey, Frank's early idol. After the performance Dorsey called Frank over and told him he was looking for a vocalist. Frank's style, he thought, would fit in perfectly with his band. "It should," Frank answered humbly. "I've been trying for years to sing the way you play trombone."

From that day on, the wheel of fortune has never turned up a wrong number for Sinatra. During his three years with Dorsey, Frank acquired the rabid following of young fans that enabled him to branch out last year as a solo artist.

This following was built up largely through radio and record sales. It was also nourished on a soul-testing diet of "one-night stands." When doing one-nighters, a band goes on the road and plays a single engagement, packs up the instruments at 2 or 3 A.M., and travels a couple of hundred

14

miles by bus to the next stop. If they're lucky, the boys catch an hour's sleep before getting up on the bandstand again to raise the roof for the jitterbugs.

All of which may explain why Frank would like to forget about trouping and take a few weeks' vacation before he gets much older. For one thing, he wants to get better acquainted with Nancy-Sandra, who has been known to ask why she doesn't have a daddy who comes home for supper every evening, like the little girl next door. Also, since his income began to grow into a thing of beauty, Frank has been buying Nancy all the things he wanted to buy her when they were married, and would like to see her in some of this finery.

Frank would also like to get in a little golf practice. "If I don't get going pretty soon," he argues, "my score will be just like the title of the picture I'm making—*Higher and Higher*."

Frank doesn't expect to set the world on fire with his acting—he worked hard enough learning to sing. "If they'll just let me be Sinatra," he says, "I think that would be best for everyone."

George Evans, Frank Sinatra's press agent—who has a standing offer to donate $1,000 to the favorite charity of anyone able to prove that "a kid was given a ticket, a pass, a gift or a gratuity of any kind in any shape or manner at all to go in and screech" at a Sinatra show—has upped his offer to $5,000, due to inflation.

On Thursday, Dec. 9, three days before his 26th birthday, Frank Sinatra was classified as 4-F at the Newark Induction Center because of a punctured ear drum. The process itself was singularly uneventful. No mob was present because the singer reported two days before Dec. 11, the much publicized date. After it was over, Sinatra said: "I'm unhappy about it because I've been bragging to friends that I'd get through."

The date does, however, mark a turning point in a career as musically astounding as any in recent times. And the coming year will tell the real story: Will The Voice fade out as a short-lived phenomenon or will it settle down as a national institution?

*L*ike Byron, Frank Sinatra awoke one morning to find himself famous. The son of a Hoboken, N.J., fireman, he decided to become a singer after seeing a Bing Crosby movie. He took no voice lessons then, nor has he since, believing that the words are the real essence of a popular song. "I pick my songs for the lyrics," he explained last summer. "The music is only a backdrop."

As a vocalist with Tommy Dorsey's band two years ago, Sinatra began to accumulate a following of teen-age fans whose fervor encouraged him to strike out on his own. Leaving Dorsey in September 1942, he rested for a while and then played the Paramount Theater in New York for about two months at $1,000 a week. In February he went on *Your Hit Parade*, and in March he opened at the Riobamba, a Manhattan night club singularly dissociated with hepcats and jitterbugs which nonetheless did such business that Sinatra's engagement was extended and his pay upped from $750 to $1,500 a week. It was at this point that the word *swoon* reentered the nation's vocabulary when a girl in his audience fainted because of the heat, and columnists exaggerated it into a vast syncope over his voice (*Newsweek*, March 22).

*　*　*

What Makes Frankie Run? Perhaps nobody ever will find out. As a singer, he can't read a note. There is many a dispute over whether he purposely flats. There is present, however, a certain Something which has, on occasion, been called a boudoir baritone.

As a visible male object of adulation Sinatra is even more baffling. He is undersized and looks underfed—but the slightest suggestion of his twisted smile brings squeals of agonized rapture from his adolescent adorers. To them he seems to be all things: sweetheart, brother, son and buddy. Yet they know he is happily married, has one child already and another coming. To some psychologists all this has been a horrible example of mass frustrated love in wartime. To most mothers with high-school daughters it is life's most inexplicable headache.

Naturally these sighing societies of Sinatra Swooners—who call their pyjamas Sinatra Suits and who sign their letters Sinatrally Yours while languishing in a Sinatrance—have created many a hot spot for their idol. Recently, in fact, The Voice itself had to tell them to shut up at a broadcast. And mothers of one or two frenzied fanatics were asked to keep their offspring at home.

The Wages of Swoon: Financially, the Swami of Swoon's future looks very bright indeed. He was originally owned like some prizefighters—in parts. But last August the Music Corp. of America bought out Tommy Dorsey and Dorsey's manager, Leonard Vannerson, two of the biggest mortgage-holders, for $60,000, so Frankie at last got to eat some of what certainly isn't hay.

His new radio show starting in January over CBS, will bring him between $5,000 and $6,000 a week. Movies for the coming year should come to around $250,000 and record royalties to about $150,000. Best of all, though, is the current personal-appearance tour he now is making in Eastern key cities. For seven shows a day he is getting a $15,000 guarantee against 50% of the gross—the biggest contract of its kind in the history of the business. In one week in Boston alone he made $30,000.

19

THE VOICE AND THE KIDS
by Bruce Bliven from *The New Republic* magazine, November 6, 1944

t nine o'clock in the morning, the Paramount Theatre is full and already the line outside, waiting to buy tickets, goes around the corner. But today is nothing; you should have been here Thursday, which happened to be a legal holiday in New York. On Thursday there were 10,000 trying to get in, and 150 extra policemen totally failed to keep order. Shop windows were smashed; people were hurt and carried off in ambulances. Because the average fan stayed for two or three performances, the trouble outside went on all day. Out of 3,500 who were in their seats when the first show began, only 250 came out when the second show started. Some people were in line before midnight of the previous day. One man said he had tried to buy an early place in line for his daughter for $8, but had been refused. A woman, in line with her daughter long before the doors opened, said the girl threatened to kill herself if kept home.

This, as you have guessed, is the magic spell of The Voice, a phenomenon of mass hysteria that is seen only two or three times in a century. You need to go back not merely to Lindbergh and Valentino and Admiral Dewey, to understand it, but to the dance madness that overtook some medieval German villages, or to the children's crusade. The Voice wields a not inconsiderable power. He can break up a demonstration for someone as important as Governor Dewey, merely by appearing on the sidelines. He needs a hollow square of policemen to protect him anywhere he goes; his telephone calls swamp any switchboard; his mail runs into the thousands per day. So does his income; he averages more than $20,000 a week the year around, and in some busy weeks earns as much as $30,000, which is about $4,300 per day. His admirers send him all sorts of presents, and when he advises them to put their money into war bonds, they try to give the war bonds to him, or one of his children. One girl wore a bandage for three weeks on her arm at the spot where "Frankie touched me." Another went to 56 consecutive performances in a theatre where he was playing (this means five or six performances a day). Merely to see him cross the sidewalk from an automobile to a broadcasting station, young idolaters lined up five hours in advance.

Two girls picked up by police in Pittsburgh had spent their whole savings and run away from their home in Brooklyn because The Voice was appearing in the Pennsylvania city. A soldier who happens to have the same name gets burning love letters by the dozen. When he appeared in public (he resembles The Voice) he was mobbed by feminine admirers who tore off most of his clothes. The Voice's home is invaded nearly every day by young girls who make a pretext of asking for a drink of water, or to use the bathroom. Trained nurses have to be on the premises in any theatre where he appears, to soothe the hysterical (some of those who faint have gone 10 or 12 hours without food, to see consecutive performances). It is something to think about.

At 9:10 A.M., inside the theatre, the over-ornate red and gold decorations, somebody's idea of the last word in luxury, are almost submerged under a sea of youthful femininity. The house is already packed, but the watchful ushers will not let them stand in the aisles, and therefore the many hundreds who are waiting are shepherded behind glass in the lobby. Four-fifths of those present are of the feminine sex and of these, at least four-fifths belong to the bobby-socks brigade, age perhaps twelve to sixteen. Hundreds of them are wearing the polka-dotted blue bow tie popularized by their idol. Although his appearance is still an hour away, they are in a mood to squeal, and squeal they do. The movie which grinds its way across the screen is a routine affair, but the bobby-socksers take it big, with wild bursts of applause in unexpected places.

The electric contagion of excitement steadily mounts as the film ends and the stage show begins. Everything gets twice the reception it deserves. Then, at a familiar bar of music, the crowd goes completely crazy. It is the entrance cue for The Voice, which was instantly recognized by the devout. The shrieks rise to a crashing crescendo such as one hears but rarely in a lifetime. Through the portiers at the side of the stage comes a pleasant-appearing young man in an expensive brown tweed coat and brown doeskin trousers. With gawky long steps he moves awkwardly to the center of the stage, while the shrieking continues. The bobby-socksers are on their feet now, applauding frantically. A few of them slump into their seats, either fainting or convincing themselves that they are doing so. Some of them rush down the aisle to get as close as possible to their hero. (When he leaves the theatre, a double line of police has to fight back the adorers who yearn to touch him, as, in the Middle Ages, victims of disease sought the healing touch of the king.)

Standing at the microphone, he looks, under the spotlight, like a young Walter Huston. He has a head of tousled black curls and holds it awkwardly to one side as he gestures clumsily and bashfully with his long arms, trying to keep the crowd quiet enough for him to sing "Embraceable You." Contrary to expectation, he appears in excellent health, with a face that seems tanned, not made up. A girl sitting by me says, "Look, he has broad shoulders," and her boyfriend replies scornfully, "Aw, nuts! Pads!" Obviously he is right.

Now, having with difficulty created a partial state of order, The Voice performs. Diffidently, almost bashfully, yet with sure showmanship and magnificent timing, he sings five or six songs, with intervals of patter between them. His voice, to this auditor, seems a pleasant, untrained light baritone—a weak one, were it not boosted in power by the microphone. His talk is inconsequential chatter, which I assume was written for him by someone in the entourage that naturally goes with an income of $1,100,000 a year. He complains a little about highbrow psychologists who write articles about him; carries on a routine artificial "feud" with Bing Crosby (who of course is not present). One or two of his songs were evidently chosen to elicit a frantic response from the audience. When he sings sadly "I'll Walk Alone," the child sitting next to me shouts in seemingly genuine anguish, "I'll walk wid ya, Frankie," and so, in various words, do several hundred others. When the song says that nobody loves him, a faithful protagonist on my right groans, "Are you kiddin', Frankie?" Then the whole audience falls into an antiphony with him, Frankie shouting "No!" and the audience "Yes!" five or six times, the point in debate being whether he is popular or not.

Presently he is singing a song—"Everything Happens to Me"—which seems to be a running diary of his recent life. He brings in the fact, skillfully and without offense, that he recently had tea with the President. Frankie is a Roosevelt fan, he and his wife have given $7,500 to the NCPAC and, if his adorers were old enough to vote, he could win the election single-handed. He breaks all rules for romantic heroes by talking about his wife and two children and mentions the fact that another child is on the way. Far from being repelled by this evidence of domestic bliss, his audience seems enraptured. They shriek, even during his songs, until he is forced to take steps. "Shut UP!" he cries, with mock ferocity. The kids see through him; they understand perfectly that he doesn't mean it.

Another song, and he has vanished, amidst a continuing hailstorm of those astonishing high-pitched shrieks. Instantly the orchestra swings into "The Star-Spangled Banner," and twin spotlights center on American flags whipping in the breeze created by electric fans—obviously the only way to avoid a riot.

What is the cause of it all? It is reasonable to suppose that it began as a publicity stunt, with the first swooners and screamers hired by a press agent. (The young man who threw eggs at Frankie the other day admitted that he had been paid $10 a day to do so, by a "reporter.") But today, it is a genuine mass phenomenon, far beyond the power of any press agent to control. Thousands of girls profess to be spellbound just from hearing The Voice over the radio, never having seen him in the flesh. Undoubtedly, just plain sex has a great deal to do with the whole matter. If the bobby-socksers were a little older, much of it might be explained, at least partly, in terms of wartime frustration, with 11 million young men away in uniform. Doubtless the phenomenon has several sources. Partly, it has become a fad now, with girls of a certain age, to join in the hysterics. You go expecting to be overpowered, and if you weren't, you'd feel you hadn't had your money's worth. But it runs deeper than that. Although I am told that devotion to The Voice is found in all classes of society, nearly all of the bobby-socksers whom I saw at the Paramount gave every appearance of being children of the poor. Oddly enough, this fragile young singer has, among other qualities, a sense of strength and power: there is a solidity and sureness about him that are all out of proportion to his physical frailness. I would guess that these children find in him, for all his youthfulness, something of a father image. And beyond that, he represents a dream of what they themselves might conceivably do or become. He earns a million a year, and yet he talks their language; he is just a kid from Hoboken who got the breaks. In everything he says and does, he aligns himself with the youngsters and against the adult world. It is always "we" and never "you."

But my strongest impression was, not that Frankie means so much to the bobby-socksers, as that everything else means so little. Our civilization no doubt seems wonderful to the children of half-starved dictator-ridden Europe; our multiplicity of gadgets is the envy of the world. And yet, if I read the bobby-socksers aright, we have left them with a hunger still unfulfilled: a hunger for heroes, for ideal things that do not appear, or at least not in adequate quantities, in a civilization that is so busy making things and selling things as ours. Whatever else you may say of the adoration of The Voice, it is a strictly non-commercial enterprise, a selfless idolatry which pays its 75 cents at the box-office and asks in return only the privilege of being allowed to ruin its vocal cords. Perhaps Frankie is more important as a symbol than most of us are aware.

23

by Skippy Alvarez—from the fourth anniversary issue
of the *Swoon Times News*

Little bow tie don't you cry
      Because for you there is no sigh
You're a little droopy here and there
      When you were younger I showed you no care.

Together we have stood in line
      To see another tie that wasn't mine
We sat in the theatre show after show
      Just to watch that bow tie come and go.

We pushed and squealed and
      Fought and shoved
But for you little bow tie
      I showed no love.

While that other bow tie
      Hung around my idol's neck
I tugged at you and pulled you
      Till you were a wreck

And when the other bow tie
      Had gone back to its home
I threw you in my dresser drawer
      Old, worn out, and alone.

But little bow tie I realize
      Just what you have gone through
I idolized another tie
      And never cared for you.

24

Yes, you're old and droopy
       But don't you cry
Just think you might have belonged
       To that Sinatra guy!

And bow tie during *his* rise
       You might have been the choice
Above all other bow ties
       Of the one and only voice

And every one would want you
       For their very own
And the voice would show his love for you
       That I never have shown

So don't you worry bow tie
       I truly love you now
To think of what you might have been
       In some way, or some how.

So I make this bed of silk for you
       And lay you gently down
Until Frank Sinatra and his bow tie
       Again shall come to town.

25

Modern Screen

SEPTEMBER
15¢

SINATRA'S
LIFE
STORY!

PHENOMENON

by E. J. Kahn, Jr. from *The New Yorker*, October/November 1946

I. THE VOICE WITH THE GOLD ACCESSORIES

*F*rancis Albert Sinatra, a young man of twenty-eight who sings popular songs to the satisfaction of several million adolescent girls, is a social phenomenon. He has more avowed fans than any other living entertainer, and not only what he sings but everything he does is of greater concern to them than are the actions of anybody else in the world, including President Truman. Sinatra became wildly famous early in 1943, and there are no indications that he is, as they say on Broadway, slipping. A lady whose unenviable duty is to paste up his publicity scrapbooks, each one of which, though large, can accommodate only a thirty day accumulation of published items about him, is now a year and a half behind in her work, and the prospect of her catching up grows steadily worse. . . .

Sinatra has been most successful as an interpreter of slow, dreamy love songs, or what the trade calls ballads. Without ever taking an audible breath, he records twenty-four popular songs a year, enabling Columbia Records to issue one new Sinatra record a month. His records are now selling at the rate of around ten million a year, from which massive output he will derive annual royalties of some two hundred and fifty thousand dollars. He earns about a hundred and fifty thousand dollars a year in the movies. He is the star of a weekly radio program, which pays him nearly a half million, and every appearance he makes as a guest on somebody else's program brings in six or seven thousand more. For performing on the stages of movie theatres, his present minimum is twenty-five thousand a week. This year, he has limited himself to three one-week appearances. One of them was in Chicago, where the terms of his contract called for him to receive, in addition to the twenty-five thousand, fifty per cent of whatever the house grossed over sixty thousand. The theatre's take for the week was ninety-two thousand, so Sinatra's total emolument came to forty-one thousand— an all-time world's record for a week's appearance by any entertainer. Even before Sinatra's voice became quite so splendid an asset, a talent agency that was marketing it optimistically advertised it as "The Voice That Is Thrilling Millions." This sweeping phrase was condensed by a weary journalist to "The Voice," a term the writer applied not merely to Sinatra's voice but to all the rest of him as well. This name, which has resulted in such imitations as The Hat, The Look, The Body, and The Shape, has stuck to him ever since.

The Voice's voice is one of the world's most precious uninsured properties. Every now and then, Sinatra and a few of his business advisers consider inviting Lloyd's of London to issue a policy on it, but they have taken no action, perhaps because they think that Lloyd's appraisal of its worth might not concur with Sinatra's. His principal advisers fear laryngitis much as other people might the bubonic plague, and they had a bad scare a couple of years ago when an affectionate fan grabbed Sinatra's necktie during an otherwise routine stage-door mêlée and bruised his throat, inside and outside. Publishers of popular music and their song-pluggers are among the most abandoned admirers of his voice; he is one of the few individuals who can make a song a hit merely by singing a chorus of it. He regards his voice as an instrument without equal, and though he tries scrupulously to be polite about the possessors of other renowned voices, he is apt—if the name of a competitor comes up abruptly in conversation—to remark, "I can sing that son of a bitch off the stage any day of the week."

In the past three years, there has been a flourishing revival of a sentimental type of singing originated, mainly by Rudy Vallee, in the Twenties. This is known as "crooning," and is largely dependent on mechanical amplification, in the early days by megaphone and now by microphone. . . . The most relaxed and most successful of all contemporary singers is Bing Crosby, who sometimes sounds as if he were falling asleep in midsong. Crosby began singing with bands in 1922, when Sinatra was four. Since Sinatra has grown up, he has occasionally imitated Crosby; at rehearsals, he sometimes shows up wearing a yachting cap and a florid sports shirt and clutching a pipe—all equipment for which Crosby is noted. The two singers, who are casual acquaintances, get along well enough, but their supporters have been known to clash. A twenty-seven-year-old lady admirer of Sinatra had to be taken to a hospital after her roommate, a Crosby fan, had stabbed her with an icepick during a debate. Many of the radio stations that rely almost entirely on recorded music have tried to give a certain variety to their fare by calling any joint recital of Crosby and Sinatra records a Battle of the Baritones or something else equally bellicose. Listeners are often asked to indicate which of the contestants they favor. Crosby wins the majority of them. Sinatra's most noteworthy triumph was beating out Crosby, in one of the larger polls, 571,978 to 533,211.

Crosby's rise to fame was gradual; Sinatra's, after a slow start, was meteoric. . . . A search of the newspapers reveals that within the space of a single year a number of entertainers who had adequate names of their own were henceforth to be known as the Mexican Sinatra, the Russian Sinatra, the Filipino Sinatra, the Hungarian Sinatra, the French Sinatra, the Indian Sinatra, Canada's Frank Sinatra, the Sinatra of South America, the South of the Border Sinatra, the Bowery Sinatra, Sinatra in Technicolor, the Sinatra of Grand Opera, the Chocolate Sinatra, the Sepian Sinatra, the Older Girl's Sinatra, the 77-Year-Old Sinatra, the Ageless Sinatra, the One and Only Hank Sinatra, and San Francisco's Chinese Sinatra, a singer named Soo who has also called himself Soonatra. . . .

II. THE FAVE, THE FANS, AND THE FIENDS

According to George Evans, his press agent, who likes to say that his association with Sinatra has brought him, Evans, more publicity than most other singers' press agents get for their clients, there are forty million Sinatra fans in the United States. Evans estimates that there are two thousand fan clubs, with an average membership of two hundred, and he has further estimated (by means of logarithms and a press agent's intuition) that only one per cent of the Sinatra fans have yet bothered to join a club. These calculations may be imprecise, but there are unquestionably millions of Sinatra fans, mostly young women in their middle teens. The adulation they have been pouring, like syrup, on their idol since early in 1943 is not without precedent. When Franz Liszt played the piano, every now and then some woman listening to him would keel over. Women kissed the seams of Johann Strauss's coat and wept with emotion at the sight of Paderewski's red hair. In 1843, when the Norwegian violinist Ole Bull, who had long, golden hair and a striking build, gave some recitals over here, his feminine followers unhorsed his carriage and pulled it around town themselves. Then there was Rudolph Valentino's funeral. The astonishing affection lavished by some women on men to whom they have never been introduced is, as a rule, not entirely platonic. Few of Sinatra's fans, however, seem to have designs on him. Of the five thousand letters they send him every week, not many are as amorous as one from a young lady who wrote, on stationery smeared with lipstick, "I love you so bad it hurts. Do you think I should see a doctor?"

STAR-SPANGLED OCTOPUS
by David G. Wittels from the *Saturday Evening Post*, August 1946

How MCA acquired Frank Sinatra—even though he was under contract to someone else—in a deal that was fantastic even for show business.

*J*n the fairy tales of our time, which may be found in publicity releases and the fan magazines, stars are often created overnight, springing full-blown out of fortuitous circumstances. It may be a chance meeting with an angel in disguise, a prince of a producer in the audience or the magic touch of a talent agent's wand. These are lovely fairy tales; it's really too bad they aren't true. They overlook the blood from the cut throats and stabbed backs, the anguished sweat of begging for a chance, the previous sneers from those very same agents. They also skip the financial shenanigans that go into the making of a star, the cutting up of talent into pieces which are haggled over, bought and sold, like potatoes on the produce exchange.

There is, for example, the real story of the rise of Frank Sinatra, a young crooner who proved that the knack of causing young females to shriek and swoon *en masse* can be a highly profitable art. It is perhaps the most spectacular success story of our time—the story of how a skinny kid from, of all places, Hoboken, New Jersey, went from fifteen dollars a week to $25,000 a week in five years. He cannot read music and his voice won't carry without a microphone, but his recording of such songs as "I'll Never Smile Again," "Day by Day," and "Oh, What It Seemed to Be," sold more than 1,000,000 copies each. He used to sing on eighteen radio programs for seventy cents a week; today he gets $15,000 for a half hour radio show. But no benevolent sorcerer of an agent plucked him out of obscurity to this stardom. The bobby-soxers caught on long before the Broadway wise-acres did.

Today, when he is grossing more than $1,000,000 a year, Sinatra is featured among the star-studded clientele of the biggest agents of them all, the Music Corporation of America. But MCA, which handles and sells between $40,000,000 and $50,000,000 worth of amusement talent a year, had nothing to do with his spectacular rise. When he needed guidance the most, no agent would bother with him. To get his chance, he had to pledge 43⅓ percent of his earnings to a band leader and manager who had him under contract. After literally hundreds of thousands of people knew about him, an agency finally took him on. Then, when pent-up public demand at last exploded him into stardom, MCA took him away from the first agency.

Frank Sinatra was nineteen when he first was fired by his ambition to become a crooner. He had sung with the high-school orchestra, but upon graduation he decided to become a sports reporter. Despite his frail appearance, he was a wiry youngster, fairly good at sports and handy with his mitts; and he was a sports fanatic. He got a job as a copy boy on a Jersey City newspaper, and had progressed to the point of being allowed to write one-paragraph leads with box scores appended, when one night he took his girl, Nancy, to hear Bing Crosby in person. They saw Bing saunter into the spotlight, hitch up his pants, open his mouth and tear the house down. They saw him make a huge crowd whistle with delight, listen so wistfully they scarcely dared breathe, then set the place rocking with rhythm. They heard thousands cheer the man with the bat ears, thinning hair, an incipient paunch, and a wonderful frog in his throat.

That did it. That night, as the skinny boy with the Adam's apple walked her toward her home through the moonlight, he told Nancy he had decided to be a crooner. "Gee," he said, "but that guy Crosby is wonderful. You know, Nancy, most people think he's just a crooner—just a buh-buh-buh guy with funny tonsils. But they're wrong. You know what he is, Nancy? He's a troubadour. He sings friendly-like. He tells a story in every song. He's relaxed, but he makes you feel like he's singing just for you. I bet I could sing like that, with more practice. I bet I could. Do you think I could, Nancy?"

"Yes, Frankie," she said. "Sure you could."

If that sounds corny or as if a facile press agent made it up, remember that she was eighteen and he was nineteen—the age of dreams.

That was in 1936. In pursuance of his dream, Sinatra organized a quartet to which he gave a name which at least had the merit of simplicity: The Hoboken Four. They confined their activities to parties given by friends and to an occasional dance or fireman's ball—Sinatra's father was a fireman in Hoboken—until finally they landed on the late *Major Bowes' Amateur Hour* in 1937.

The Hoboken Four, with Sinatra singing the lead, won first prize and a tour of third-rate amusement spots with a Major Bowes unit. This was in no sense a touch of the magic wand, for touring with a Major Bowes unit meant meager pay, a grueling grind and being made the butt of jokes.

32

Sinatra stood it better than most; he got all the way to California before he gave up and came home.

"You know, Nancy," he said, "there was no class to that. What they wanted you to do was to sing loud and funny, for laughs. Or else Mother Machree stuff. You know what I think I ought to do? Get on the radio. If I tried something different on the air, some big shot might hear it and give me a break. Then, boy! I'd knock them dead. What do you think, Nancy? Should I try it?"

"Yes, Frankie," she said. "Sure you should."

He got on the radio easily enough, but getting paid for it was something else again. He worked sixteen hours a day singing on eighteen sustaining programs a week for various stations in Jersey City, Newark and New York; and all he got for it, besides perhaps invaluable experience, was the seventy cents Mutual gave him for carfare each week.

After a while people were beginning to ask why a twenty-one-year-old lug like him wasn't making a living like other fellas. Besides, he wanted to marry Nancy very much. So, in 1938, he took a job at fifteen dollars a week as a headwaiter and singing M.C. at the Rustic Cabin, a roadhouse near Hoboken. In a few months he was raised to twenty-five dollars a week; and so, early in 1939, he and Nancy were married.

On the side, he kept singing on a few sustainers. Though he didn't know it, and no talent agent took note, a few stay-up-late musicians who heard him on the radio during the wee hours of the morning were beginning to discuss him. Some said he stank. "Why does he drag out those notes so long?" But others said, "Wonder who this guy Sinatra is? The monkey's got something."

Among those who heard this talk was Harry James, a trumpeter in Benny Goodman's orchestra. James was planning to start an orchestra of his own, and was hunting personnel, particularly a vocalist. He traced Sinatra to the Rustic Cabin on a night in June, watched him in action, and signed him up the same night. Later, Sinatra woke Nancy out of a sound sleep. "Seventy-five bucks a week!" he howled. "And featured singer with a band! Boy, will I knock 'em dead!"

Sure, said Nancy. Sure he would.

James was an MCA client. MCA experts listened carefully to the band and its vocalist, but none of them, apparently, was impressed by the kid with the big bow tie and the down-to-earth Hoboken rasp in his voice. James played various spots around the country; then, some six months later, was booked into the Palimar, in Los Angeles. But the Palimar was closed by a fire. MCA then booked the band into Victor Hugo's, an ultra-swank

33

place in Beverly Hills, but the owners decided the band was too loud for the clientele and canceled it out.

It was disaster for James, the band and Sinatra. He was broke. Nancy was pregnant. There came a day when he didn't have a dime to buy her something to eat. He scurried around collecting empty soft-drink bottles, and turned them in at the grocery store for enough pennies to get her a meal. But a break came almost immediately. Tommy Dorsey was playing in the area and needed a new vocalist. He had heard Sinatra sing, and he offered him $150 a week. Sinatra was under contract to James and went to him for permission to leave.

"Hell, kid," said James, "it looks like I've got nothing to offer you, anyway. Here." And he tore up Sinatra's contract.

With Dorsey, Sinatra started to roll, first as part of the famous Pied Pipers Quartet, then as a soloist. One night in Dallas, Tommy noticed that when Sinatra did a glissando from one note to the next, holding the first note for all it was worth and then sliding, through trick breathing, into the next, the young girls in the front seats closed their eyes and sighed out loud.

"What are you doing to these kids?" Dorsey demanded. "A skinny, funny-looking guy like you?"

Sinatra has a full-fledged sense of humor, as witness his uninhibited kidding of himself later, but at this point he had a single-track mind about his singing. "I got it all from you, Tommy," he replied earnestly. "You know the way you breathe and slide that trombone to get that sweet tone, the old schmalz that gets them? Well, I worked out a way to do that in singing."

For a gag, Dorsey instructed the band to lay down its instruments and sigh in unison when Sinatra hit one of those glissando effects. That is the sole basis for the legend that the sighing and swooning over Sinatra was started and shrewdly fostered by smart press agents. Sinatra had no press agent until after he became a star. Even when Dorsey told the band to lay off the gag, the female small fry sighed and shrieked just the same; and the boys, though they jeered manfully, flocked to hear him and scoured haberdashery shops for bow ties like his. They couldn't find any, because Nancy made them for him to hide his big Adam's apple.

Sinatra used this singing technique on Victor recordings he made with the Dorsey band of "I'll Never Smile Again," "Star Dust" and "Everything Happens to Me," and each one was a runaway best-seller. Tommy Dorsey raised his pay to $250 a week, but nothing much else happened. Dorsey, too, was an MCA client, but again MCA missed the ball on The Voice.

Nor did any other agent lure him with the traditional come-hither: "You sign with us, kid, and we'll make you a star!" The smart boys apparently chalked him off as one of those freaks, riding briefly on the popularity of a band.

There was one exception, Emmanuel (Manny) Sacks, vice-president in charge of talent for the Columbia Recording Corporation. He heard Sinatra in California in 1940 and then watched the reaction of the audience when Sinatra sang with Dorsey's band in the Earle Theater in Philadelphia in 1941. Sacks somewhat resembles Sinatra, and on that day he was wearing a bow tie. When he first left the theater, scores of young girls, screaming "Frankie! Frankie!" almost literally tore his clothes off. Bernie Woods, of *Variety*, saw this happen.

Sacks became convinced that Sinatra was destined to become the greatest hit in show business. "You're terrific," he told Sinatra.

"Would you record me as a soloist?" Sinatra asked.

"Any time you're free," said Sacks.

Sinatra was crestfallen. "But I may have passed my peak by time my contract with Dorsey runs out."

Sacks put a hand on his arm. "Kid," he said, "you'll be going big when these bobby-soxers are bouncing their grandchildren on their knees."

Sinatra left Dorsey, after two and a half years, early in the fall of 1942. He talked it over with Nancy, and she agreed it was time he tried his luck on his own. He was so eager to get going that, in return for release from his contract, he pledged one third of his future gross earnings to Dorsey, and another 10 percent of his gross to Leonard K. Vannerson, then Dorsey's manager. He did not stop to think that since this percentage was before expenses and taxes—what the trade calls "off the top"—he might wind up with practically nothing for himself.

That was no immediate problem because nothing happened right away, anyway. He haunted radio stations, night-club operators, theater managers and movie studios, but he got either vague half promises or outright refusals. Some said, "What's the use of taking a chance on you? The Army might snatch you." Sinatra knew, from his own doctor, of the punctured ear-drum which later caused the Army to reject him, but the few times he mentioned it he was laughed at. Sacks, however, kept his word and signed him to a recording contract.

To keep him in eating money until the royalties started coming in, Sacks called William Paley, head of the Columbia Broadcasting System. "Bill," he said, "I've got a kid here I think is going to be the hottest thing

35

that ever hit. How about putting him on a sustaining program until he attracts a sponsor?"

Paley put him on the air five times a week, at $150 a week, in Songs by Sinatra. One month later he was singing on the *Hit Parade* at $1000 a week.

That was good, but not sensational, as radio goes. The *Hit Parade* contract was a short-term one, and Broadway and Hollywood, insofar as they paid any attention to him, kept their fingers crossed. A few recognized that "the nibble was on." In Broadwayese, that means "the public was showing interest," but without knowing how hard the public might bite, they were taking no chances.

At about this time, Sinatra finally acquired an agent. Michael Nidorf, then vice-president of the General Amusement Corporation, remembered Sinatra from his Dorsey days. "I always figured Dorsey was a great picker and developer of talent," said Nidorf, "and when I found out Sinatra was loose, I signed him up." One of the first jobs General Amusement got for Sinatra was singing at the Mosque Theater, in Newark, New Jersey.

A few days later, Harry Romm, a General Amusement booker, called on Robert M. Weitman, executive director of the Paramount Theater, New York's top showplace for bands and singers. Romm was highly excited. "Bob," he said, "you won't believe me. You'll figure it's a sales talk. But take a chance and come over and look for yourself. It's the damnedest thing you ever saw. A skinny kid who looks strictly from hunger is singing over in Newark and the kids are yelling and fainting all over the joint. You've got to see it to believe it."

Weitman went over, took one look, and promptly booked Sinatra for four weeks at $1000 a week. "I still don't know exactly why I did it," says Weitman. "I had *Star-Spangled Rhythm* as the picture for those weeks, and that certainly didn't need extra attractions. I had booked Benny Goodman and his band for those four weeks, and he could pack the house himself. But there was something about this kid—"

The first four weeks there was no way of applying the final pragmatic test—box office receipts—to how good Sinatra was. The picture plus Goodman would sell tickets anyway. Weitman kept Sinatra for four more weeks, with a lesser band. The drawing power of a picture should lessen the second month, but the Paramount remained jammed. Weitman was convinced. He and Sinatra had become friends meanwhile, making the rounds of the bars after the last show, and working out in Weitman's private gymnasium between shows.

At the end of the eight weeks Sinatra said, "Look, Bob, did I do all right for you? Are you going to want me back again?"

"Sure, kid," said Weitman. "How much will you want on two options?"

Sinatra had been coached by Tommy Rockwell, head of the General Amusement, but he drew a deep breath. "Is four thousand a week all right for the first option, and forty-five hundred for the second?" he blurted.

"Okay with me," said Weitman. And it was a deal.

It was perhaps the best deal Weitman ever made. When he invoked the first option and called Sinatra back five months later, in May, 1943, he paid Sinatra a bonus of $7500 a week over the sum agreed upon. For in those five months the nibble had turned into a terrific bite—hook, line and sinker—and Sinatra had exploded into what Sacks had predicted—the hottest thing in show business.

In March, for instance, he had gone into the Riobamba—now the Embassy—a smart night club in New York. He went in for only $750 a week, because the wise boys were saying, "Okay, so the bobby-soxers scream. How long will that last? What can he do against real competition or when he gets in front of a sophisticated, show-me crowd? They might laugh him out of the joint."

When he went into the Riobamba, Walter O'Keefe, veteran top-flight master of ceremonies, was billed above him. When O'Keefe's engagement ended, April 9, 1943, O'Keefe made the following farewell speech to an audience of New York's most hardened night-club habitués and show people.

"When I came into this place," said O'Keefe, "I was the star and a kid named Sinatra was one of the acts. Then suddenly a steam roller came along and knocked me flat. Ladies and gentlemen, I give you the rightful star . . . Frank Sinatra!"

The critics raved. After Sinatra's opening night, Paul Ross, one of the hard-boiled editors of *Billboard*, a show-business journal, wrote a notice which caused his superior to accuse him of having been drunk. Ross dragged him to the Riobamba. The next day the superior ordered full-page headlines on the Sinatra story. When Sinatra returned to the Paramount, it made the front pages of the daily newspapers because traffic on Broadway was tied up by crowds which swept aside the police and broke down the doors to get in.

Now, at last, the Music Corporation of America caught on. The orders went out to sign up Sinatra. The fact that he was under contract to a rival agency made no difference. "Get him anyway!" There is a saying in the business that "MCA has several vice-presidents-in-charge-of-making-other-

37

agencies'-clients-unhappy." They went to work on Sinatra, and they did a magnificent job on him.

MCA's night-club man made it a point to meet him at Toots Shor's. "What're you getting at the Riobamba?" he asked. Sinatra told him. "What? That's murder! You're being robbed! If we had you—"

The theater man met him at the Stork Club. "What's your option with Weitman call for? What? You're crazy! Why, we would get you at least twenty thousand!"

The radio man nailed him in Lindy's. "What are they doing for you in radio? What? You? Why, you belong in Bing Crosby's spot."

The movie man got him at Sardi's. "How's your picture deal? . . . You mean RKO is giving you only twenty-five thousand for a picture, with two options? I can't believe it! You're kidding me. You're worth a hundred thousand dollars a picture, at the least! Boy, are you being taken for a sucker ride!"

Sinatra was very unhappy. It was true that he now was worth more money than the deals General Amusement had set up for him, but those deals were made before he clicked so sensationally. He might have chalked this off as hard luck for the time being, except that he had several other reasons for being unhappy. Nidorf, on whom he had come to depend as his personal agent, was in the Army by now. Sacks was away. He felt alone, harassed, gypped.

Above all, there was the matter of 33⅓ percent to Dorsey, 10 percent to Dorsey's manager, and now 10 percent to the booking agents. That made a total of 53⅓ percent before taxes—not counting what he was paying a press agent, writers and Alex Stordahl, a crack arranger who had left Dorsey to follow him. The money was rolling in beyond his wildest dreams, but he was practically broke.

In June, 1943, he met his idol, Bing Crosby, for the first time. Contrary to expectations in some quarters, the two crooners promptly became friends. Sinatra poured his troubles into the prominent, sympathetic ears of the older, more experienced troubadour.

"What would you do in a spot like this, Bing?" he pleaded.

"There's only one thing to do," Crosby replied. He pointed to his throat and whispered hoarsely, "Tell 'em that all those tie-ups make you so nervous you can't sing any more."

To a certain extent, that's what Sinatra did. He turned difficult. He refused bookings which General Amusement lined up for him. He snapped at his agents for the early deals, citing what MCA men had told him they would have got for him. At the psychological moment, MCA struck. There is a legend on Broadway—which always believes there's a hidden ball some-where—that MCA secretly owns half of General Amusement, ostensibly its bitter rival, and that at the proper moment MCA merely took over what it already half owned. The legend has no foundation in fact. Actually, MCA shook the big stick. "Look," it said, in effect, to General Amusement. "You've got an unhappy client. He's acting up and might refuse to work any more. If you don't make a deal with us, we'll start booking him, even though we don't get commissions. But we'll make the bookings, and then Sinatra will be able to go to AGVA and show that you're not doing any-thing for him and win his release from you."

AGVA is the American Guild of Variety Artists, which polices the en-tertainment business for performers. Sinatra, incidentally, is a confirmed union man. A few hours before he was to open at the Riobamba, Matt Shelvey, national director of AGVA, phoned him that the night club had refused to sign an AGVA contract covering chorus girls' wages.

Sinatra promptly called the owners. "My union says you won't sign," he said. "If it has to call a strike on you, you'll have to get yourself another boy, because I won't show up." The club signed within an hour.

General Amusement was caught in a tight spot by MCA's ultimatum. AGVA rules did provide for freeing a performer whose agents did not get him ample work. If Sinatra complained, it might lose him outright. Even if it won the threatened AGVA case, it would still have to contend with a client who might refuse to work. General Amusement hollered murder, but capitulated and turned Sinatra over to MCA.

It didn't get such a bad deal out of the forced transfer, however. In return for relinquishing its client, General Amusement gets half of MCA's 10 percent commissions on Sinatra until November 30, 1948, the expira-tion date of the old contract. If Sinatra signs again with MCA after that, General Amusement is to get one quarter of MCA's commissions as long as he remains an MCA client. Without further headache or overhead, and with MCA's crackajack sales organization at work, it might make more than it would if it had kept Sinatra.

MCA, which had muffed Sinatra so often before, was happy too. A new voice in his affairs, it was able to thump its corporate fist and force reopening the short-priced deals made before Sinatra skyrocketed, and have them adjusted upward. Besides, MCA needed Sinatra's drawing power so much that it was glad to have it on almost any terms. To maintain its position at the top and its exclusive booking contracts with talent buyers, it had to be able to produce top performers. And in producing Sinatra, it could also sell some of the lesser talent it had in its stables.

Tied in with this deal was one to free Sinatra from Dorsey and Van-nerson. After protracted haggling, the price of the 43⅓ per cent hunk of him which they owned was set at $60,000. MCA advanced Sinatra $35,000 of this, and Sacks got Columbia Recording to put up the remaining $25,000. Sinatra was so happy that he sent Sacks a check for $10,000 as a Christmas present last year. Sacks returned the check with a note which said in effect: "Dear Frank: It's my job to find talent. Thanks just the same." This gesture, described as "throwin' ten grand out the winda," had the trade buzzing, with frequent significant tapping of foreheads.

As far as is known, nobody at MCA was hauled on the carpet by Jules Stein, its president, for having missed the boat on Sinatra earlier. Stein never cries over spilt milk, and besides, he often has argued the theory that no man can spot talent until it has ripened. Once, discussing bands with Guy Lombardo, he said, "Bands just happen. You can't make them." He has told others that nobody knows what makes a good performer. The job of a good agent, he contends, is primarily one of making the most money possible for his clients after they have shown they have what the public wants.

40

THE LITTLE THINGS: AN APPRECIATION
by Jane Harris from *The Fog Horn,* newsletter of the
Frank Sinatra Fan Club of Staten Island, February 1948

My love for Frank is made up of so many little things,
the way he smiles, his hair, his voice, and the happiness he brings,
the raising of an eyebrow, laughter no one can replace,
the way he shrugs his shoulder, the structure of his face,
the fullness of his mouth, the certain sternness of his chin,
his blue expressive eyes, his frown, his boyish grin.
His neatness in appearance, his tall and slender frame,
his sparkling sense of humor, and what he endured for fame.
His frankness, his sincerity, his love for every creed,
the help he's brought to many who are troubled or in need.
The many things he's done to give the little guy a break,
the way he has of stressing you should give instead of take.
The great air of self-confidence shown plainly in his walk,
his head held high, his manly stride, his soft and friendly talk.
The times he seems bewildered by the ridicule he takes,
his faults and his confusion, his temper, his mistakes.
His many moods, his habits, whether they be right or wrong,
the way he has of making fans feel that they belong.
His affection for his family, this devotion to his friends,
his faithfulness and loyalty to the flag which he defends.
His immeasurable talent for putting on a show,
the many times that he's gone on although his health was low.
His singing voice incomparable, his personality,
the ordinary things he does, his versatility.
the gratefulness which he's displayed, his family so ideal,
his warm and pleasing manner, his charm and his appeal.
That warm and generous heart of his, as big as earth and sky,
the many things he undertakes for such a little guy.
So you see, it's not that he's a star, or his popularity,
It's the little things about him that mean so much to me.

MEMORIES OF SINATRA
by Shirley M. Kelley

*F*rank Sinatra's songs and person are woven into the fabric of my generation. He was more than a singer—he was a friend. Over the years, I was pleased and proud if the press wrote nice things about him, and embarrassed when the reports were bad. It was as if a family member had misbehaved.

After all, Frank Sinatra was part of my very first big date.

It was 1941, and we had been at war since 1939. I grew up in Montreal and, after my mother died, I grew up in a hurry. I worked afternoons in a local store; we sold cigarettes, magazines and made malts and shakes at the soda fountain. Most of the neighborhood dropped in at some time.

Lorne Greene reported the nightly radio news of Dunkirk, the Spitfire battles over England, Roosevelt's Bundles for Britain, and the streams of young men in uniforms of khaki, navy and air force blue. Some of these boys would drop by the store when on leave, and one day one of them asked me to go out with him. Tommy Dorsey was coming to the Forum. Wow!

My wardrobe was small: two school uniforms—dark blue jumper over white blouse—which I covered with an apron at work; some skirts and twin-sweater sets for dress-up. Styles didn't change much—clothes had to last. For this special date, I found the money for a new dress. I can still picture it: maroon crepe, slim, fitted through the midriff—a copy of the style that Wallis Simpson, the American Duchess of Windsor, made popular with her wedding dress a few years earlier.

I was 15. I had long wavy blond hair, worn in a pompadour, and a good figure in that tight dress. My date was polite, somewhat shy and reserved. He wore the stiff wool Canadian battle dress, proud of the two stripes signifying he was a corporal. We took the streetcar downtown.

The evening was electric. A couple of thousand of us went to hear Tommy Dorsey's orchestra for good music and dancing. The band was good, as expected, and the girl singer was pleasant and friendly. But there was something added: a male vocalist, this skinnymalink who stepped up to the mike and knocked us silly.

He was rail thin; we expected a reedy tenor. But this skinny kid, who seemed little older than I, stood up there and sang a ballad and the dancing stopped. The way he caressed the song, phrasing the words so that each of us felt "He's singing to *me*." Half hypnotized, we paused and we swayed, drawing closer to the stage and to him.

This was before the days of screaming fans, before we all knew the name Frank Sinatra. I had not been psyched up by the publicity to come. I was psyched by the vocalist himself. Fifty-some years later, I still cannot evoke anything I felt about the young man who took me dancing on my first big date. When I try, what I remember is the powerful charisma of a young Frank Sinatra.

The Fifties:
THE COMEBACK KID

THE NINE LIVES OF FRANK SINATRA
by Adela Rogers St. Johns from *Cosmopolitan*, 1956

*L*ess than five years after everyone said he was washed up and a New York newspaper suggested that his name be filed under *things that no longer matter*, Frank Sinatra again has become the Mr. Big of Show Business, one of the hottest properties in the world of entertainment, one of the few living five-threat performers. The same public that turned its back on him in 1952 how falls all over itself to see and hear him in the movies, on TV, radio, and records, and in personal appearances. The panic is not as tumultuous as it was in the early Forties, when hordes of raving bobby-soxers attempted to tear off his clothes whenever he showed his emaciated face and angular figure, but it is still, as panics go, impressive indeed. Sinatra will probably earn around $1,500,000 this year and, judging from past performance, will do his best to spend it all—which will not matter too much, since there is a good chance he will earn even more in 1957.

The Voice has never been better off—as far as his career is concerned, anyhow. "That Frankie," says his friend the restaurateur Toots Shor, "he's like a cat. He always lands on his feet."

Shor is not Voltaire, but the simile is apt. Sinatra does have something of a cat's lithe grace, plus a catlike intensity and ferocity, as well as the restlessness of a cat and, indeed, the ravenous appetites—for women and often for fighting—of an alley tom. To carry the comparison further, in his forty years Sinatra has, like a cat, lived the legendary eight lives . . . with the ninth yet to come.

Nancy Sinatra (his daughter): "My greatest ambition in life is to measure up to what Daddy wants of me. Above all things now he wants me to get an education—to finish high school and then go on to college. I'm always very proud of him, and of course I want him to be proud of me, too. I would like to travel with him when he goes on trips; but for now, anyway, I can please him more by staying home and tending to my homework."

THE CAT TRIES HIS CLAWS

The setting for the first life was highly appropriate for a back-street brawler: the gloomy, rubbish-strewn dockside city of Hoboken, New Jersey, where Francis Albert Sinatra was born on December 12, 1915. "I am convinced," Sinatra wrote years later, "that I might have ended up in a life of crime if it hadn't been for my great interest in music." And so he might. Hoboken in Sinatra's boyhood was the spawning ground for scores of hoodlums who later made their marks—black and blue ones—on the bodies of victims.

Sinatra's father, Martin, fought in pork-and-beans bouts, then became a saloonkeeper, in which he was assisted by his wife, Dolly, who also worked as a practical nurse. She later became even more practical as a ward politician, ran for minor offices, and got a fire department job for her husband. Young Frankie was the apple of his parents' eye, but only a part-time apple. Dolly Sinatra saw to it that he was neatly dressed but permitted him to run loose in the deserted streets, where he learned to defend himself with rocks, bricks, broken bottles or anything handy, including bicycle chains—one of which, swung by a playmate in a fight, broke an eardrum and later kept him out of the armed forces when it was time for him to report.

There was not much music in his life in those days, but there was enough trouble—and what he couldn't find, he created so successfully that his ability to mastermind neighborhood capers earned him the nickname of "Angles." His movie heroes were Edward G. Robinson and Paul Muni, and their pictures must have been heady, hypnotic stuff for a belligerent, antagonistic teen-ager whose blood was never far below the boiling point. Their influence was enduring. To this day, the way he wears his elegant and expensive clothes, the way he moves about at the head of an entourage composed of those who serve him plus hangers-on and friends, his long stride with its hint of swagger and menace, the angle of his hats—all testify to the accuracy of a remark his friend Bing Crosby once made about him. "I think that he's always nurtured a secret desire to be a 'hood,' " Crosby said, but he added, "But, of course, he's got too much class, too much sense, to go that route—so he gets his kicks out of barking at newsmen and so forth."

Sinatra has said, "We kids had no one to turn to but each other. All I knew was tough kids on street corners, gangfights, and parents who were too busy trying to make enough money for food, rent and clothing."

48

He knew the police, too—and hated them. He still does, not just the way an ordinary man dislikes a cop after he gets a ticket for speeding, but with real hatred that stems from an incident that occurred when he was around fifteen.

Nancy Barbato Sinatra (when asked by a close friend why she didn't go out with some of the men in Hollywood who are always asking her): "After Sinatra?"

HE LEARNS TO HATE AUTHORITY

Despite the pleas of his mother, Sinatra continued to run with his gang. Nor had any of his teachers in school managed to get him interested in his studies—an indictment of those teachers, for the boy had a keen, hungry mind, eager to be awakened (new acquaintances today are constantly amazed at the scope and depth of his reading).

Expelled from high school (for "general rowdiness"), he got his first job, driving a circulation truck for the *Jersey Observer*. He liked his boss, a man named Malloy, because Malloy was the first person in authority Sinatra had ever met who made no attempt to push him around.

With some of his first wages, young Frankie bought new clothes—a new blue suit, white shirt, and black patent leather shoes. Wearing them, he was sauntering along a Hoboken street, his unruly hair slicked down from a visit to the barber. A couple of cruising plainclothesmen saw him and wanted to know where he'd got the clothes.

"Ya, copper, what's it to you?" he said, in effect.

When they got through with him he was a torn, tattered, sodden and bloody mess, ribs cracked, nose smashed, face and body swollen horribly.

From that day on, all authority has sent him a little berserk. Every director who knows and likes him—and most of them do like him—still treads gently while working with him. Directors know that if they ask him to do something, he will be the easiest actor in Hollywood to handle. They also know that if they order him around, the set will blow up.

Last year he walked out on *Carousel* because he could not see the reason for shooting the picture twice—once in wide screen and once in Twentieth Century–Fox's new 55-millimeter process—as the producers were insisting. Walking out is as much a habit with Sinatra as it used to be with the Russians at the U.N. He left his son's christening because the

49

priest would not permit him to have the godfather he wanted—a man who was Jewish.

Sinatra's closest friends say that Ava Gardner's greatest mistake and the deepest reason for their breakup was the simple fact that Ava wanted to be boss. "Nobody," a friend says, "can boss Sinatra. *Nobody.*"

The beating he got from the dicks that time might well have pushed him across the line from punk to gangster. It did not. Over the years some of his companions have been none too savory—to some other friends' astonishment, he once took Joe Fischetti to see a performance by Orson Welles, and another time he openly consorted with Lucky Luciano in Cuba—but he has always made it clear that he is on the side of the law and he has devoted much time to working with juvenile delinquents.

"It's a mug's game," he once told a group of boys. "For half the brains and guts it takes to stay alive and out of jail in the rackets, you can be a big shot, sleep safe at night, and have twice as much."

THE HOWLER STARTS TO CROON

50

Sinatra's second life began when he met and began dating another Italian-American product of Hoboken—Nancy Barbato, his first girl.

"I was a poor, lonely, and discouraged kid when I met her," Sinatra later said. "In Nancy I found beauty, warmth, and understanding."

They went to a Jersey City vaudeville house one night in 1933 to see Bing Crosby, who was making a personal appearance there. Afterwards Frankie came up with the words that were to change his life and Nancy's. "I could do that," he said. "I could sing like Bing Crosby."

"Sure you could," Nancy said.

He had never had a singing lesson. He had sung occasionally with school dance bands, but had never thought of singing as a career. His parents strongly advised him to abandon his dreams and look for a job with a salary. But the pull of music was stronger than anything else in his life. He managed to wheedle sixty-five dollars out of his mother to buy a microphone and a loudspeaker in a rhinestone case, and began working lodge dates, club dates, any dates he could get, for three dollars a night.

He won a *Major Bowes Amateur Hour* contest in 1937 and traveled all the way to the West Coast with a quartet, the Hoboken Four. Back home and broke, he was not discouraged, he continued to take jobs wherever he could get them. He sang on New Jersey radio stations for car fare, and for a time his total weekly earnings amounted to seventy cents.

His parents were still urging him to quit, and so were some of his buddies. Not Nancy. "Sure you can, Frankie," she had said, and now she said "Sure, I'll marry you and take a chance." So when Frank was twenty-four they were married in the parish church by the parish priest. He was then singing, for $25 a week, at a New Jersey roadhouse, the Rustic Club.

The little white house they took on a side street in Hoboken, where a year later Nancy, Jr., was born, was hospitably open day and night from the moment they moved in. Then, as now, Frankie would spend his last dime on anything he wanted—beer, cheese, a new phonograph record. There was always, literally, spaghetti on the stove, for the oft-repeated line "Sinatra will eat spaghetti for breakfast" is not a gag. There was a piano and Sinatra often brought pals home for all-night sessions.

To be Frank Sinatra's guest then, as now, was to be offered everything he had. He is at his best as a musician, next as a host. Friends or even casual acquaintances leave his house laden with expensive radios or portable phonographs, with a magnificent Chinese lamp or a modern picture right off the wall.

Generosity has become as much a part of the Sinatra legend as his old trademark, the drooping bow tie. Sinatra sends fabulous Christmas presents to all his friends; one year he spent $30,000 on last-minute purchases alone. During the second World War, hearing that the boys on a Navy P.T. boat had named it "Oh Frankie," he sent a gold St. Christopher medal to every member of the fifteen-man crew. Every child born to any of Sinatra's close friend receives a bond at birth.

Celeste Holm: "A woman doesn't have to be in love with Frank Sinatra to enjoy his company. I wasn't and I did. He's a stimulating talker about any subject: books, music, cooking, his children, whom he quotes oftener than most fathers, and sports—baseball is his specialty, but he knows something about most of the others, including fencing."

THE SHIRT OFF HIS BACK

To Sinatra, nothing matters as much as friends. He will do literally anything for them. Rags Ragland, the comic, died just before he was to open at a New York night club with Phil Silvers. Sinatra flew East to play the opening night as a tribute to his pal. Another time, on a Christmas Eve, he called Toots Shor from Hollywood and told him that a mutual friend was all alone in Hollywood. "Please call him up—it'll cheer him," Sinatra said.

"If Sinatra is your pal, and you need dough," says Toots Shor, "he'll dig it up even if he has to go out and borrow it."

But in the early days, Sinatra had trouble getting food and rent money for himself and his wife. The first break did not come until he had put in almost a year at the Rustic Cabin. Benny Goodman's star trumpeter, Harry James, had decided to take out a band of his own and needed a singer. He heard Sinatra and hired him.

After six months, Tommy Dorsey hired Sinatra away from James for a starting salary of $110 a week. Dorsey taught him a good deal, Sinatra says; he tried to do with his voice what Dorsey did with his trombone. Dorsey says, "I used to tell him over and over, there's only one singer you ought to listen to, and his name is Crosby. All that matters to him is the words, and that's the only thing that ought to matter to you, too."

The odds against Sinatra's becoming a singer had been high in his second life. Now in his third—the Dorsey phase—they shifted in his favor. Dorsey admits that at first he did not realize the vast potentiality of the undernourished kid he hired. The first time the bobby-soxers began scream-ing, the boys in the band thought it was a joke, or something that the band's press agent had instructed the kids to do. Later Sinatra did have an expert press agent, George Evans, who did his share of planting fainting shills in the audience—but in the Dorsey days, the swooning was authentic. Every time the kids swooned, Dorsey had his musicians stop the music and swoon right back at them, "This inspired the girls to go one better," Dor-sey recalls, "and the madness kept growing until pretty soon it reached fantastic proportions."

FRANKIE FEVER BECOME EPIDEMIC

Two of Sinatra's records in this period, "I'll Never Smile Again" and "There Are Such Things," sold over the million mark. It was not long before the crowds were turning up not to hear the bandleader but his vocalist, and Dorsey, realizing that he had a gold mine on his hands, signed him to a long-term contract. It was also around this time that the girls began turning up—not merely to swoon, but actively to pursue. The hag-gard face, the heartfelt meaning Sinatra gave to the words, caused them to write him such things as "I shiver when you sing just like I did when I had scarlet fever." One girl, in 1940, wrote him that unless he met her for a date, she would kill herself.

Sinatra had trouble leaving Dorsey. First, his emotions were in the way—the night he left, in September, 1942, the band had, in Dorsey's words, "quite a ball" and after it was all over "Frank was literally crying on my shoulder." Dorsey did not permit his emotions to interfere with his hold on Sinatra's contract, however. Before Sinatra went out on his own, he had to pledge one-third of his future gross earnings to the trombonist, plus 10 per cent to Len Vannerson, Dorsey's personal manager. (Time and again it had been reported that Sinatra really belonged to Willie Moretti, a gangster. Nancy Sinatra has said, "That's silly! I was there; if that had been true, I would have known about it. Nobody helped us. Frankie did it himself.")

It finally cost Sinatra $60,000 to buy his freedom. Manie Sacks, then of Columbia Records, persuaded his firm to advance Sinatra $25,000 of this sum. The next Christmas Sinatra remembered Sacks' kindness with a typical gesture—he sent Sacks a check for $10,000, although Manie didn't accept it.

Kim Novak: "I think every girl who has ever worked with Frank has been much affected by his personality. Maybe it's a crush at first—but in the end, the crush becomes friendship, as mine did. His honesty is so outstanding that I can't see why everyone isn't his friend."

53

FOURTH LIFE: FREEDOM AND FLIGHT

Once Frank was on his own, he encountered a major problem of his fourth "life": he was mobbed every time he appeared, and was followed everywhere by shrieking girls. Struggling, yelling mobs of teen-agers jammed the theatres where he appeared and caused traffic jams in the streets outside. Psychologists and sociologists made an effort to explain the phenomenon, but never completely succeeded. Nobody could decide whether the mass reaction was pathetic or horrifying, whether the singer was an authentic Pied Piper, whether the girls in their new liberty had become potential sex maniacs, or whether the tension of the war years was twisting them out of shape.

I, as a woman, understood what it was. There was something disturbing and heart-twisting about the girls' reaction. Many of them were unkempt, wistful, neglected, awkward and shy, starved for love and affection—

and Sinatra's great gift was then (and still is) that he seemed to be singing for each girl alone. For a few enchanted moments, each girl in the audience imagined she was his.

Undeniably there were outside interests, passing fancies in Sinatra's life. But Nancy was *Mama,* the mother of his child. She minded her own business, attended to the family, and took care of her husband's checkbook and clothes.

The Swoonatra craze continued. He had an audience with the Pope ("I'm sorry my wife isn't with me. This would mean so much to her"). He was received in the White House by President Roosevelt (all Sinatra could do, says Toots Shor, who was present, was stand in quiet awe). He began to dabble in left-wing politics more actively than ever before. In 1944 a son was born (named Franklin for Roosevelt), but he was spending less and less time at home. That same year he signed an M-G-M contract and moved his family to California into a big, roomy old house in the San Fernando Valley.

HOLLYWOOD MEANT HARD WORK

Later Sinatra said that 1944 was also the year that he and Nancy began quarreling a lot. Sinatra was working harder than ever. Never having danced a step, he worked long and exhausting hours getting ready to do a number with Gene Kelly. He brought a coach out from New York to work with him on his songs. Boxing every day kept him in physical condition.

Whatever was between Lana Turner and Frank began when he was on the M-G-M lot, where Lana was a top star. It probably ended when, years later, an irate Sinatra threw Lana and his wife, Ava Gardner, out of his Palm Springs house one night when the girls had been sitting over a friendly Martini and talking to each other, as girls will, about a boy they both knew named Frankie Sinatra. (They also had Artie Shaw in common, both having been married to him.)

Lana was the first girl to penetrate Nancy Sinatra's guard.

Overnight, Hollywood knew that there was trouble between the ideal couple. Presently they separated, with announcements in the press. In a furious temper, Sinatra went off to Las Vegas, but it was apparent that this had rocked him badly. Actually, from the first moment of his career he'd never had to do without Nancy.

Then one night he was at a table at Slapsy-Maxie Rosenbloom's when Nancy came in. She deliberately avoided looking in Frank's direction. He began to sink lower and lower in his chair. Suddenly he said to his friends at the table, "I'll be back," and, conspicuous as usual, crossed the floor. Everybody turned to watch, and in a moment the Sinatras were dancing together.

Frankie never went back to his table. He and Nancy left together. Soon afterwards he paid a quarter of a million dollars for a house on Carolwood Avenue with a walled and cobbled court, swimming pool, and gardens. There another daughter, Christina, was born.

Sinatra has said and still does that Ava had nothing to do with his separation from Nancy. The first time he asked Ava to dinner, he said, she gave him a dark look and said, "I'm not interested in married men." She continued to refuse him dates until he told her that he and his wife had obtained a separation.

Sinatra has said, "I was on edge and constantly irritable, and Nancy and I found ourselves getting into terrible arguments about trivial matters. I knew our misery would surely affect the children. My health started to go bad and my work began to suffer."

By 1947 he had entered the fifth life, that of the has-been crooner. Reviewers were saying his voice was going flat. His movie contract was canceled. He was finding it more and more difficult to get jobs. By 1951, he was all but finished.

A close friend has said, "Frank shouldn't take all the blame for the failure of his marriage. Nancy didn't grow with him. In the early Hollywood days he had to go out alone a good deal simply because she didn't like parties. If she had stayed closer to him, she never would have lost him. Also, there was one time in the romance with Ava when he would have gone back to Nancy, but she locked the door on him."

Debbie Reynolds: "Being on a set with Sinatra is wonderful. I'm married to a singer myself, but Sinatra ranks a close second with me."

THE SIXTH LIFE WAS SHORT

Sinatra's sixth life began when he signed a three-million-dollar contract with CBS, and ended when it was canceled. He did not work at it. He was chasing every girl who caught his fancy—when he wasn't chasing Ava. And with her began the seventh life.

When he asked for his freedom, Nancy gave it to him. But she amazed everyone by asking for it in the form of separate maintenance—and if there was one thing upon which it seemed Nancy could count, it was Frank's fabulous generosity to her and the children. In 1944 alone he had given her four fur coats. He had bought her a $162,000 house in Palm Springs where they could spend weekends with the children.

THE DOLLARS LANDED EVERYWHERE

Possibly it was this very generosity that bothered Nancy; she had always tried to keep a check of some kind on Frank's crazy spending: a cortege of courtiers and attendants; huge sums given away to any and every organization that was to better the lot of the common man; jewels, furs, gold and platinum cigarette cases for every friend; unsecured loans to anybody who pitched him a hard luck story; diamond bracelets for women in his companies; more suits than he could count; and all the jewelry and luggage he could want for himself.

Actually, in those days Frankie didn't have that kind of money, and it evaporated like an open bottle of costly perfume.

In court, breaking into tears as she answered the judge's questions, Nancy got a settlement of $2,750 a month temporary alimony for herself and the children, the Palm Springs house, the Bel-Air house, three cars, and an agreement regarding a future deal of 33 per cent of his earnings (which at that time were low for him—only between half a million and a million a year, before taxes). "She took him for nearly everything," a friend says.

LIKE CAT AND DOG

Once the separation was accomplished, Ava was on the stage in nothing flat, and from then on they were seldom apart. They had begun to build up to the headlines which said Go Away Frankie and Ava and Don't Come Back.

Was Frankie in love with Ava? A friend of his has said, "I'd called it *possessed*. At the time of this tempestuous romance Frank's weight was down to 118 pounds and he was having hemorrhages when he finally dug himself out from under."

They spent a vacation together in Acapulco. Frankie went to sing at the Shamrock Hotel in Houston and Ava went with him. They were openly, defiantly, wildly, passionately enamored of each other. They couldn't keep their hands off each other; it was a flagrant case of one of those violent attractions that have throughout history wrecked lives and caused disaster.

Ava had come to Hollywood as a raw country girl in her teens, and had been pursued by Hollywood's wolf pack from the day she arrived. She had been married to Mickey Rooney and Artie Shaw, two experiences not calculated to bolster a girl's confidence in men, and she was so disillusioned that although she was capable of falling insanely in love, she resented it.

Her resentment was evidently nothing compared to that of Nancy, who steadfastly refused to give Sinatra a divorce. Before long, witnesses say, he did not know what he was doing half the time. He contemplated desperate measures.

Eventually Sinatra confronted his wife and asked her for a divorce. She gave her consent—oddly enough, in the minds of Sinatra's friends, this was a serious mistake. They said she should have stuck it out, that he would have come back.

Sinatra and Ava were married in Philadelphia on November 7, 1951, at the home of a friend—Ava in ice-blue, a seven-tiered cake on the table, and Dolly Sinatra standing by. The press was barred from the ceremony, which gained Sinatra no new friends. Nor did his behavior during his frantic, transcontinental transocean pursuit of his bride. There were a few placid, tender scenes, including the time Ava was making *Mogambo* in Africa with Clark Gable and Grace Kelly. Sinatra flew there, laden with gifts for his wife and the cast. That was the pattern—the pursuit, the momentary reconciliation, and then another bitter battle.

Grace Kelly: "Frank has a sweetness and charm as a person and as an actor that is very endearing."

DESCENT OF A STAR

It was the nadir. He was sick, just about broke—reduced even to borrowing from Ava. Finally his friends became concerned and attempted to get him to pull himself together. His career was a shambles and his personality was close to it. Toots Shor, Hank Sanicola (his accompanist and perhaps his best friend), Jimmy van Heusen, "Beans" Ponedel (his makeup man), and countless other members of the Sinatra clan all talked themselves hoarse trying to argue him into getting hold of himself.

As it turned out, Sinatra himself, and the indomitable alley-cat spirit in him, saved Sinatra. He had read James Jones' *From Here to Eternity* and knew that the part of Maggio, the tough little Italian who refused to be broken, could have been written with him in mind. He went to see Buddy Adler, the Columbia Pictures producer, and asked to be tested for the part.

"Frankie," Adler said, "that's a big acting part—and you're a singer."

"I can act that part better than anyone alive," Sinatra said.

Adler was dubious. He was testing five actors. He told Sinatra that if none seemed right, he would give him a try. Sinatra told his agent, "I'll play that part for fifty dollars a week."

Sinatra was in Africa with Ava when word came that Adler was dissatisfied with the other actors he had tested. He flew back in two days and astounded everyone.

"First take, we knew we had it," Adler now says. "Cold, that morning on the set, we knew it was going to bring an Academy Award."

Janice May (M-G-M publicity woman in charge of Sinatra's unit): "The first day I ever walked on a movie set, Frank Sinatra saw me hiding in a corner shaking. He called, 'Hi, baby, what's your name?' When I told him and explained that I was the new girl in the publicity department and that my first assignment was to write newspaper items about him, he grinned and said, 'Don't worry, kid, anything you want, just ask me. I'll give it to you. I don't like to see girls scared. The big lesson in life, baby, is never be scared of anyone or anything.' He's never let me down once."

58

"THE VOICE" IS HEARD AGAIN

Sinatra earned eight thousand dollars in the picture and, a friend says, spent ten thousand chasing Ava. But that life was gradually drawing to a close. *Eternity* came out and started the comeback, the eighth life. Within a few months he was back on his feet, making *Guys and Dolls, The Tender Trap, The Man with the Golden Arm,* and singing better than ever on records and in personal appearances. Three records—*Young in Heart, Learnin' the Blues,* and *The Tender Trap*—were in the million-copy class.

He and Ava have long since publicly announced their agreement to disagree. He no longer pursues her, although he recently shipped a Cadillac to her in Spain. Some think he will go back to Nancy; he has been spending more and more time with her and the children, and only recently, when a reporter asked Nancy a question about him, she said "I'll have to ask Frank when he gets home to dinner."

It is clear that Sinatra has found himself at last. He is more mature, more calculated about his career, less hot-headed, and less prodigal in expending his emotions and money. In his eighth life, he seems to have arrived at some kind of philosophical understanding of himself, his talent, and his relationship to the world.

As for the future, only Sinatra can say what that will be. He will make no predictions. He says, simply, "I'm going to keep working." *High Society,* with his old idol, Crosby, and Grace Kelly, is awaiting release. *Johnny Concho,* his first Western film, is being shot as this is written. Capitol Records has just released another long-playing album, *Songs for Swinging Lovers,* that is destined to be a hit. NBC has offered him a multimillion dollar write-his-own-ticket television contract, and there have never been more offers for high-priced personal appearances. Whatever he does, wherever he goes, one thing is certain. In the ninth life, he'll land on his feet.

FROM HERE TO ETERNITY
production notes, Columbia Studios, June 2, 1953

*C*ulminating more than two years of preparation since the purchase of James Jones' best selling novel, *From Here to Eternity,* Columbia's film version of the brilliant and powerful story of soldiers and soldiering has been brought to the screen with a star-studded cast that rivals any in Hollywood history.

As Prewitt, the independent and unregimented G.I., Montgomery Clift draws a role which every important male star had coveted. Burt Lancaster is seen as Warden, the First Sergeant who manages his company with the dedication of a saint while engaged in a love affair with the commanding officer's wife, Karen Holmes, played by Deborah Kerr, who was selected for the part after almost every other top Hollywood name had been reported as seeking it. After more than 50 contestants tested for the envied role of Alma, Prewitt's girl friend, Columbia contractee Donna Reed won out for the part. Frank Sinatra's persistence in applying for the off-beat role of Private Maggio to the extent of traveling 27,000 miles from Africa and return for a screen test, got him the part of the tough little Italian-American who is violent and funny and sour.

For the role of Fatso Judson, the sadistic sergeant of the stockade, stage and screen actor Ernest Borgnine, who recently appeared on Broadway with Helen Hayes in *Mrs. McThing,* was signed. Philip Ober, stage and film actor who has been a familiar figure on Broadway for more than 20 years, plays Captain Holmes, the pompous commanding officer whose infidelity causes his wife (Kerr) to seek romance with the sergeant (Lancaster). Barbara Morrison, British actress whose classmate at the Royal Academy of Dramatic Art was Charles Laughton, plays Mrs. Kipfer, the well-upholstered *grande dame* who operates Honolulu's New Congress Club where Alma (Reed) works as a hostess when she meets Prewitt (Clift).

The drama depicting the emotional pressures that fill the vacuum of life in the pre-Pearl Harbor Army has been faithfully adapted for the screen by Daniel Taradash, for the millions of readers who expect an accurate translation of the novel. Just as the book was not involved with an elaborate symbolism, the screenplay gives the essence of a soldier's life rather than symbols. It is the eloquent virtue of *From Here to Eternity* that the authors make the characters believable, from the brass hats to the brass checks. They are human within the subhuman anonymity of the military machine.

Upon completion of the filming of the interiors in Hollywood, the cast and crew of about 100 persons flew via chartered planes to the Hawaiian Islands where all of the exteriors were photographed at the identical locale of the novel, with approximately three weeks of shooting at Schofield Barracks, the Royal Hawaiian Hotel, Waikiki Beach, Diamond Head and the Waialea Golf Course.

Inasmuch as *From Here to Eternity* was produced with the cooperation of the Departments of Defense and Army, Col. Kendall Fielder and Warrant Officer William Mullen served as technical advisers on the picture. Since the period of the story involves the transitional Army uniform and weapons between World Wars I and II, wardrobe and prop problems had to be licked in order to insure strict authenticity.

Old-style Army clothing for 400 men such as canvas leggings, campaign hats, blue two-piece fatigue outfits with pullover top and out-of-date cap, and flat steel helmets had to be packed and shipped to Hawaii for the picture's featured players and the bits and extra that were cast on location. Also, 400 1903 Springfield rifles, 20 Thompson sub-machine guns, 20 BAR's, 15.45 pistols and approximately 55,000 rounds of ammunition were shipped. A total of 800 soldiers from the Hawaiian Infantry Training Center appear in the film.

In addition to the wardrobe and weapons, tons of equipment such as generators, cameras, lights, reflectors, cables, sound trucks, etc., left by boat several days before the personnel flew out from Hollywood in order to arrive in time for immediate shooting.

One of the most exciting action sequences ever filmed for the Hollywood cameras was the strafing of Schofield Barracks by Japanese "Zeroes." This re-creation of a phase of the sneak-attack on Pearl Harbor, in which the Army installation was riddled by machine gun-fire as the Japanese pilots made their bombing run on the Navy ships, was photographed at the locale of the disaster as described by novelist Jones.

A group of planes of the 199th squadron, Hawaii Air National Guard, bearing the familiar red "meatball" insignia of the Jap fighters, participated in the simulated attacks in the mock battle scenes featuring all of the featured players and the men of the Hawaii Infantry Training Center.

It is significant that the stars in *From Here to Eternity* are playing roles that are unusual for their accepted screen personalities. Burt Lancaster, a war veteran of three years' service with the famous Fifth Army, plays an Army man for the first time in 17 starring films. Although his roles have covered a range of portrayals, this is his initial film role as a soldier. Despite his Army service, he had to learn to use the outmoded equipment of the pre-Pearl Harbor Army as though he were a recruit.

Montgomery Clift, as the individualistic Regular Army soldier, is a boxer, bugler and romantic figure. Under the tutelage of former welterweight champ Mushy Callahan, Clift did roadwork, boxing and worked out on punching bags and other body-building devices to develop his muscles. He also spent several hours each day with a Master Sergeant who taught the actor drilling, the manual of arms including the break-down and assembling procedures of the rifle, the drill and use of the bayonet and close-quarter knife-fighting for a scene in the picture.

Frank Sinatra, who plays Clift's soldier-buddy, underwent the same type of military training for his role which, incidentally, is strictly off-beat for the singer who does no singing in this dramatic part.

Deborah Kerr, who up to now, has been playing "Duchess roles with a tiara," does a complete change of pace in her role as the captain's sexy wife. Miss Kerr's hair was re-styled from her normal ginger red to topaz blonde. Deborah worked at losing her British accent with a voice coach who specializes in this type of voice control. Movie audiences for the first time will see Miss Kerr in a bathing suit and shorts and will find the charming lady's figure a pleasant sight indeed.

Donna Reed heretofore has been established as an actress who is usually seen on the screen as the faithful wife or girl friend of the leading man. But in *From Here to Eternity,* as Alma, Montgomery Clift's girl, Donna plays a completely different type.

George Durning, who wrote the background music for the Rita Hayworth starrer, *Salome,* incorporated in the score of *From Here to Eternity* two songs, "The Re-enlistment Blues" and the ballad, "From Here to Eternity," written for the film by Fred Karger and Robert Wells. James Jones co-authored the lyrics of "The Re-enlistment Blues" which were published in his novel and revised to fit the music.

I remember a Sinatra who didn't pal around with rich Republicans. During the early 1950s, at my Sunday school in St. Paul, Minnesota, one of the highlights of the year was the annual screening of *The House I Live In*, a short film starring a young and skinny Sinatra. In it, he told a gang of kids that racial and religious differences "make no difference except to a Nazi or somebody who's stupid." He sang about "The people that I work with/The workers that I meet . . . The right to speak my mind out/That's America to me." *The House I Live In*, made at the peak of Sinatra's popularity, won him a special Academy Award in 1945. Four years later his career was in ruins, in the wake of charges that he was tied to both the Mafia and the Communists. Forty years later his career is legend, his politics solidly conservative.

At first glance Sinatra's political odyssey from left to right seems to have followed a well-trod path. "Maturity" has been defined by figures as different as John dos Passos and Jerry Rubin as the abandonment of youthful ideals. But Sinatra's case is different. Beaten down as an activist leftist, his career destroyed by the right-wing press, he made a stunning comeback, then found himself snubbed and abused by the liberals whose views he shared. Only then did he sign up with his old right-wing enemies.

The House I Live In was a turning point. The *Cumulative Index to Publications of the Committee on Un-American Activities* (HUAC), a handy list of everyone named as a communist in 20 years of committee hearings, indicates that in the eight years following *The House I Live In* Sinatra was named 12 times. The *New York Times Index* for 1949 contained a single stunning cross-reference: "Sinatra, Frank: See US—Espionage." Sinatra reportedly denied the reports that he "followed or appeased some of the CP (Communist Party) line program over a long period of time."

But once the allegations had been made, Sinatra's image in the press changed dramatically. He was first linked to the Mafia in a February 1947 gossip column that reported he had been seen in Havana with mobster Lucky Luciano and other "scum" and "goons" who "find the south salubrious in the winter, or grand jury time." The columnist's source, and the source of many subsequent Mafia-Sinatra stories, turns out to have been Harry Anslinger, a crony of J. Edgar Hoover. Anslinger served as head of the federal narcotics bureau and was out to get Sinatra because he was a "pink."

"Frank's big nosedive," as the pundits called it, began on April 8, 1947. That was the night he punched Hearst gossip columnist Lee Mortimer at Ciro's celebrated Hollywood night spot. The Hearst papers went wild, running whole pages on the incident, repeating the Mafia story and HUAC charges. "Sinatra Faces Probe on Red Ties," a headline read. Soon gossip titans Hedda Hopper, Louella Parsons, and Dorothy Kilgallen were heaping abuse on him. Overnight Sinatra was transformed by the right-wing press from the crooning idol of bobby-soxers into a violent, left-wing Mafioso.

Sinatra said he punched Mortimer because the columnist called him a "dago." In fact Mortimer had been calling him some other things in print. He wrote about what he called "the crooner's penchant for veering to portside" and reminded readers that Sinatra had been named in HUAC testimony as "one of Hollywood's leading travelers on the road of Red Fascism." Mortimer, nephew of the editor of the Hearst-owned New York *Mirror*, pledged that "this column will continue to fight the promotion of class struggle or foreign isms posing as entertainment"—like *The House I Live In*.

How pink had Sinatra been? HUAC's sources were pretty disreputable. The first to name him was Gerald L.K. Smith, a raucous native fascist. In 1946 he told the committee that Sinatra "has been doing some pretty clever stuff for the Reds." Sinatra was named again in HUAC testimony in 1947 by Walter S. Steele, a private Red-hunter who had once accused Campfire Girls of being "Communistic." Jack B. Tenney, a California state senator who headed a state version of HUAC, reported in 1947 that Sinatra had taken part in a dinner sponsored by American Youth for Democracy, which J. Edgar Hoover had declared a communist front.

Between *The House I Live In* in 1945 and the big 1947 HUAC hearings, Sinatra had in fact moved much closer to organized left-wing political activity. In 1943, when riots broke out in Harlem, he went uptown to speak at two integrated high school assemblies, urging the kids to "act as neighborhood emissaries of racial goodwill toward younger pupils and among friends." Shortly after, when white students in Gary, Indiana, boycotted classes at their newly integrated high school, Sinatra spoke in the school auditorium and sang "The House I Live In." What other star at the top of the charts had thrown himself into the civil rights struggle so directly?

In May 1946 Sinatra issued what *Billboard* called "an anti-Franco blast." The statement was remarkable for two reasons. First, the only people who still remembered the support that Spain's dictator received from Hitler and Mussolini were real leftists. And second, there was Sinatra's Catholic background. The comment caused the Catholic *Standard and Times* of Philadelphia to label him a "pawn of fellow-travelers."

Sinatra moved closer to the Communist Party in July 1946, when he served as vice-president of the Hollywood Independent Citizens Committee of the Arts, Sciences and Professions. Known by its asthmatic acronym, HICCASP had been a broad coalition of pro-Roosevelt liberals and leftists, ranging from Thomas Mann to Rita Hayworth. Sinatra became an officer during a faction fight in which Communists pushed liberals out of the organization and steered it toward Henry Wallace's left-wing challenge to Truman in 1948. Sinatra wrote an open letter in *The New Republic* to Wallace at the beginning of 1947, calling on him to "take up the fight we like to think of as ours—the fight for tolerance, which is the basis of any fight for peace." Within three months headlines appeared linking him to the Communists.

A month later he was fired from his radio show; six months after that his New York concerts flopped. Soon his personal life was falling apart as fast as his career. By December 1949 his affair with Ava Gardner had become an open scandal. Columbia Records was trying to get back the advance they had given him. In 1950 he was released from his MGM film contract, and his own agent, MCA, dropped him. He was a has-been at 34.

After Sinatra's stunning 1953 comeback in *From Here to Eternity*, he remained a Democrat. He sang "The House I Live In" at the Hollywood Palladium at a 1956 campaign salute to Adlai Stevenson. He returned to the political wars with new energy during the spring of 1960. He had two projects that season: working for the Kennedy campaign (Sinatra's version of "High Hopes" was the official Kennedy campaign song) and breaking the Hollywood blacklist that had barred left-wingers from working in the movies ever since the 1947 HUAC investigations.

The second project was announced shortly after Kennedy won the New Hampshire primary. *The New York Times* headline read, "Sinatra Defies Writer Blacklist/Hires Albert Maltz for filming of *The Execution of Private Slovik*." Maltz had written *The House I Live In*. *The Execution of Private Slovik*, a recently published novel, told the story of the World War II G.I.

who became the only American since the Civil War to be executed for desertion. "This marks the first time that a top movie star has defied the rule laid down by the major movie studios" 13 years earlier, *The Times* explained. Sinatra would produce, Robert Parish was to direct. Slovik would be played by a TV tough guy named Steve McQueen.

Sinatra, asked if he was fearful of the reaction to hiring a blacklisted writer, had a defiant, I-told-you-so response. He quoted his own 1947 statement criticizing HUAC's witch-hunt: "Once they get the movies throttled, how long will it be before the committee gets to work on freedom of the air? . . . If you make a pitch on a nationwide radio network for a square deal for the underdog, will they call you a commie?"

A square deal for the underdog seemed to be exactly what Sinatra was after—for underdog Maltz, who served time in a federal penitentiary for refusing to name names, and also for Slovik. According to director Parish, Sinatra regarded Slovik not just as a victim of an unjust system of military justice, but as "the champ underdog of all time."

"They're calling you a fucking Communist!" Harry Cohn, king of Paramount Pictures, shouted at Sinatra. The attack had come, predictably, from Sinatra's old enemies in the Hearst press. Editorial writers for the New York *Mirror* reminded readers that the guy who just hired a Red had once had a " 'romance' with a dame to whom he was not then married." (Sinatra must have murmured, "Hey, that was no dame, that was Ava Gardner!")

John Wayne found Sinatra's Achilles' heel. Asked for his opinion on Sinatra's hiring of Maltz, Duke said, "I don't think my opinion is too important. Why don't you ask Sinatra's crony, who's going to run our country for the next few years, what *he* thinks of it?" Sinatra responded with "A Statement of Fact," for which he bought space in *The New York Times.* In it, he declared that connecting candidate Kennedy to his decision to hire Maltz was "hitting below the belt. I make movies. I do not ask the advice of Sen. Kennedy on whom I should hire . . . I have, in my opinion, hired the best man for the job."

Just as the controversy seemed to be dying down, the Hearst papers ran the banner headline: "Sinatra Fires Maltz." *The Times* and the trades contained a new ad signed by Sinatra, headlined simply "Statement": "Mr. Maltz had . . . an affirmative, pro-American approach to the story. But the American public has indicated it feels the morality of hiring Albert Maltz is the more crucial matter, and I will accept this majority opinion."

In an interview shortly before his death in 1985, Maltz recalled the incident. "Sinatra threw down the gauntlet against the blacklist," he said.

"He was prepared to fight. His eyes were open. The ad firing me was ridiculous. The American people had not spoken; only the Hearst press and the American Legion had. Something had come from behind that caused him to change his position."

Maltz brought out his scrapbooks. Among hundreds of faded clippings was one from Dorothy Kilgallen's gossip column. "The real credit belongs to former Ambassador Joseph P. Kennedy," she wrote. "Unquestionably anti-Communist, Dad Kennedy would have invited Frank to jump off the Jack Kennedy presidential bandwagon if he hadn't unloaded Mr. Maltz." Kennedy's campaign advisors worried also about Sinatra's Mafia aura and expressed the hope that the singer would keep his distance from the senator. But, the advisors said, they hoped Sinatra would help with a voter drive in Harlem, "where he is recognized as a hero of the cause of the Negro."

After the election, JFK asked Sinatra to organize and star in his inaugural gala. The singer proudly escorted Jackie, but Jack was the one he cared about. In a gesture of classic macho deference, Sinatra offered to share a prize girlfriend, Judith Campbell Exner, with the president. Kennedy liked the idea and began an affair with Exner. (Sinatra's hit that year, appropriately enough, was *All The Way*.) Then Sinatra went too far; he introduced Exner to Chicago Mob leader Sam Giancana.

J. Edgar Hoover's ever-present eyes and ears quickly discovered the liaisons. Bobby Kennedy, in the middle of a campaign to crush the Mafia, put a stop to his brother's involvement with Exner. The Kennedys had been planning to stay with Sinatra in Palm Springs. He'd remodeled his house in anticipation of the presidential visit. At the last minute, JFK announced they'd stay instead with Bing Crosby—who wasn't even a Democrat. To the public, it was an inexplicable snub.

Sinatra always was, as *Village Voice* jazz critic Gary Giddins puts it, "a virtuoso at storing wounds." He got even with Bobby in the 1968 California primary by supporting Humphrey. Then he discovered the Humphrey campaign had the same reservations that the Kennedy campaign had had, and he quietly left.

As youth culture flowered in 1966, Sinatra married Mia Farrow; he'd just finished an album he called *September of My Years*. He was 51, she was 21, five years younger than his daughter Nancy. A sixties rebel, Mia cut her hair short and wore pants, and opposed the Vietnam War. Sinatra's friends explained the attraction: "He digs her brain." Soon, however, she was denouncing him and his pals: "All they know how to do is tell dirty stories, break furniture, pinch waitresses' asses and bet on the horses," she said. She left him to join the Beatles in India, meditating with the Maharishi.

*   *   *

Sinatra announced his retirement in 1971. "The principal activity of his retirement years," *New York Times* music critic John Rockwell writes, "was his political shift from left to right." The key moment seems to have come when the House crime committee held a new investigation of Sinatra's Mob ties in 1972. The committee was headed by Democrats including California senator John Tunney, an old Kennedy friend for whom Sinatra had raised $160,000 with a special show. The main evidence against him was the testimony of a confessed hit man who said that a New England Mafia boss had boasted that Sinatra was "fronting" for him as part owner to two resort hotels. The committee called Sinatra. "That's all hearsay evidence, isn't it?" Sinatra asked. "Yes, it is," the committee counsel admitted.

Always a public man, Sinatra explained the shift in his political thinking in a *New York Times* Op-Ed piece he wrote just after he appeared before the committee. His old politics of standing up for the little guy had been altered. Now he embraced the right-wing populism that defined the principal oppressor of the little guy as big government. And he saw his subpoena as a prime example of government oppressing a little guy. Sinatra became a Reagan Republican. "It didn't gall him as much as he had thought it would," reported columnist Earl Wilson.

His turn to the right coincided with a deepened contempt for women and his most offensive public behavior ever. At a pre-inaugural party in 1970, he shouted at *Washington Post* columnist Maxine Cheshire, "Get away from me, you scum. Go home and take a bath . . . You're nothing but a two-dollar cunt. You know what that means, don't you? You've been laying down for two dollars all your life." He then stuffed two dollar bills in her drink, saying, "Here's two dollars, baby, that's what you're used to." He made that kind of language part of his concert routine for several months, to the evident enjoyment of his new right-wing following.

President Nixon invited him to perform in the White House in 1973— something the Democrats had never done. He sang "The House I Live In." Twenty-eight years earlier, he had sung it for students at newly integrated high schools. Now he was singing it for the man who began his career as a member of HUAC from 1946 to 1950, when the committee smeared Sinatra. The president beamed with satisfaction, and Pat Nixon kept time by nodding her head. At the end of the program, for the first time in his public career, Sinatra was in tears.

The Sixties:
THE RAT PACK

 *F*rank Sinatra wishes American scientists, along with their research on nuclear matters and rockets, would investigate the possibility of crowding three or four more hours into every day.

Today the enthusiastic Mr. S. finds himself torn between increasing activity in television, numerous highly rewarding cabaret engagements, a stepped-up schedule of phonograph recording activities at Capitol, and feature film commitments on the major Hollywood lots.

Sinatra's latest picture is a filmization of the highly successful play *A Hole in the Head*, by Arnold Schulman, who also wrote the screenplay.

It was Sinatra who bought the play, took it to famed Frank Capra to produce and direct, and formed with Capra a partnership for its production under the banner of Sincap Productions, which is a compilation of their names.

A warmly ingratiating comedy, with dramatic overtones, *A Hole in the Head* has Sinatra cast as an improvident dreamer, a widower, faced with the problem of raising a 10-year-old boy, Eddie Hodges, amidst the hurly-burly of Miami Beach and its (to say the least) colorful characters.

Frank Sinatra is as unusual as his career is unique. If you set out to duplicate his success you'd probably have to start as he did—as a Hoboken kid from the wrong side of the tracks. Today he is a man who seemingly just can't miss. No matter what he turns a hand to (Hollywood will tell you), he hits a figurative jackpot. Well, it wasn't always that way. His childhood days were lean days; everything came the hard way.

If England's future wars are won on the playing fields of Harrow, then Hoboken's future wars are won on the vacant lots, alleys and blackboard jungles of the end of town where Sinatra grew up. In addition to being a skinny kid with soulful looking eyes, Frank had the further disadvantage of an adoring mother who insisted on dressing him in sissy clothes. In order to survive he soon had to adopt the military dictum that the best defensive is a walloping offensive, and by the time he was ten he was the terror of juvenile Hoboken. Only the most uninformed strangers ever made the mistake of picking on him.

He used to work on a newspaper delivery truck after school and this gave him the idea that he wanted to be a reporter. After he graduated from Demarest High School (where he had done some singing with the Glee Club) he got a job as copyboy on the Hudson Observer. He chucked this over, however, in 1936 when Bing Crosby's success decided Sinatra to become a singer.

He organized, booked, and sang in a quartet called The Hoboken Four, which got as far as Major Bowes' radio amateur hour. The quartet didn't make it, but Sinatra did with a solo version of "Night and Day." After a Bowes vaudeville tour he did a lot of sustaining programs around New York, and then became singing m.c. and headwaiter at the Rustic Cabin roadhouse. He was hired by Harry James and then Tommy Dorsey, and began recording with the Pied Pipers and then as a soloist. As a featured vocalist on *Your Hit Parade* and as the star of his own CBS radio show, *Songs by Sinatra* he became that remarkable phenomenon known as The Voice.

In the five years between his headwaiter job at the Rustic Cabin and his famous starring stint at the Paramount Theater in New York, when bobby-soxers were swooning in droves at the sound of his voice, Sinatra's income rocketed up from $15 to $25,000 a week—not bad going for the skinny Hoboken kid with the soulful eyes.

In 1943 he added another facet to his career with his first starring appearance in a movie titled *Higher and Higher.* Two years later the Academy of Motion Picture Arts and Sciences gave him a special Oscar for his performance in *The House I Live In,* a short subject devoted to the theme of tolerance for which Sinatra has always been an active crusader.

He has since appeared in increasingly important roles in pictures such as *Step Lively, Anchors Aweigh, Till the Clouds Roll By, It Happened in Brooklyn, The Kiss* [sic] *Bandit, The Miracle of the Bells, Take Me out to the Ball Game, On the Town* and others.

He had proven himself one of the finest actors in Hollywood by 1953 when he won his second Oscar—this time for Best Supporting Actor in his performance as Maggio in *From Here to Eternity.*

It was a non-singing role, as was his role in *The Man with the Golden Arm*, in which he portrayed the tragic Frankie Machine, the golden-armed poker dealer in a losing fight against drug addiction, a performance which gave his career added lustre.

As Nathan Detroit, proprietor of the world's oldest established floating crap game, in *Guys and Dolls*, and in a variety of starring roles in *The Tender*

Trap, Suddenly, and other pictures, Sinatra has steadily solidified his position at the top. With *Johnny Concho* he took on another chore—that of producer as well as star. After his top role opposite Bing Crosby and Grace Kelly in MGM's *High Society,* he was signed to star in Stanley Kramer's *The Pride and the Passion* and followed this with *The Joker's Wild, Pal Joey, Kings Go Forth, Some Came Running,* and *A Hole in the Head.*

Today he is at the top. With unfailing regularity his name repeatedly turns up in the first two or three names in all polls regarding records and movie popularity.

He is five feet, 11 inches tall, with dark brown hair and blue eyes. In 1939 he married Nancy Barbato and they were divorced 10 years later. They have three children. He then married Ava Gardner and they are currently separated.

Throughout his career Sinatra has been a crusader for a better world, and for better understanding between peoples. He has been prominently active in many worthy causes including the national Polio Drive and the National Brotherhood Week observation sponsored by the Conference of Christians and Jews, in addition to the Heart Fund and many other causes.

His Motion Picture Credits (revised April 1964)

Higher and Higher	*Johnny Concho*
Step Lively	*High Society*
Anchors Aweigh	*Pride and the Passion*
It Happened in Brooklyn	*The Joker Is Wild*
Till the Clouds Roll By	*Pal Joey*
Miracle of the Bells	*Kings Go Forth*
The Kissing Bandit	*Some Came Running*
Take Me Out to the Ball Game	*A Hole in the Head*
On the Town	*Never So Few*
Double Dynamite	*Ocean's Eleven*
Meet Danny Wilson	*Devil at Four O'clock*
From Here to Eternity	*Sergeants Three*
Suddenly	*The Manchurian Candidate*
Young at Heart	*Come Blow Your Horn*
Not As a Stranger	*Four for Texas*
Guys and Dolls	*Robin and the Seven Hoods*
The Tender Trap	*None but the Brave* (Starred and
The Man with the Golden Arm	Directed)

I hate "blind items," those nasty paragraphs without names, but with just enough identification, that permit the printing of gossip, rumor and scandal without creating the possibility of a successful libel suit. Not only the guilty, but the innocent suffer. It recalls that old story of ten men receiving the same wire, ALL IS DISCOVERED, and all ten leaving town.

Well, it was in the form of a "blind item" that Frank first began to feel the power of the press in his private life. One columnist wrote, "What blazing new swooner-crooner has been seen night-clubbing with a different starlet every night?" And another wrote, "Wonder if the wonder boy of hit records tells his wife where he goes after dark?"

The item, even the innuendo, had some basis in fact. Frank was on a tear and he was tearing about publicly. It was as if he were daring anyone to make something of it. And, of course, the dare was accepted. But that didn't keep Frank from continuing to parade about town with one glamour girl or another.

By this time I had come to know Nancy well. I liked her and sympathized with her. But I knew enough to keep my sympathy to myself. Just the same I was aware that she was deeply hurt. In a sense, I was almost relieved when I heard that she had separated from Frank.

The relief soon went. Talking to Nancy, I quickly knew that she didn't love Frank any less, that her pain wasn't quieted by the separation; only increased. And, like many others, I was happy when they reconciled.

Nancy bloomed, grew more radiant. Frank calmed down. And little Tina was born.

But this was the calm before the eye of the hurricane hit the Sinatras. Hurricane Ava. Ava Gardner.

When Frank met Ava, it was like atomic fusion. There was a terrific explosion, tremendous damage and long-lasting fallout.

The first effect was the end of the Sinatra marriage. Frank wasn't philandering now; he was deadly serious. A woman can, and has, been able to handle a dozen rivals, but I never knew a woman who could handle just one.

Few affairs involving a married principal have ever been carried out as openly as that between Ava and Frank. Here were two tempestuous people who believed in "going for broke" and didn't care who knew it. Both of them, for lack of a less polite word, were temperamental and didn't mind revealing it publicly.

Frank followed Ava to Mexico, to Las Vegas, to Houston, Texas. The press followed Frank. There was snarling, the hurling of insults, the issuance of threats. Frank, who had invited the public into his private life, was angered because he wasn't getting any privacy. It was childish—and typical. He put himself above and beyond any rules.

Ava went to Spain and Frank followed.

Nancy had reached the breaking point. As she told me over the years, she loved Frank, loved him very deeply. However, she could not condone his public infidelity and keep her self-respect which, she admitted, was already badly bruised. However, there was a religious consideration that she had to deal with. At the end, she decided that much as it pained her to get a divorce, it would be far better for Frank, his children and his reputation if he were a free man.

Nancy got her divorce October 30, 1951. The grounds were extreme cruelty. She was awarded full custody of the three children and substantial alimony, equaling a third of his annual income.

Frank was free. Eight days later he and Ava were married. The wedding was a day late, delayed by another of the violent quarrels that marked their relationship.

No review of Frank Sinatra's life and career can merely mention Ava Gardner in passing. I think she is one of the more tragic figures in recent Hollywood history. If she had never known Frank Sinatra, I think she still would have been one of the more tragic figures.

I think of her—this once beautiful woman—an expatriate in Spain, target of gossip, rude laughter, cheap remarks. I recall that she played Brett Ashley in the picture made of Hemingway's *The Sun Also Rises*, and it seems to me that nature outdid the writer's art.

A wise man once said, "You earn the face you have at sixty." He was saying that each of us mirrors his own life; and chose sixty as the date when the mirror was clearest. But there are those whose faces are mirrors long before they're sixty. And Ava is one.

I recall the excruciating beauty she had when she came to Hollywood from Smithfield, North Carolina; innocent, eager, excited. And I recall the last time I saw her. She had been as profligate of her beauty as she had of her talents. And how much she had of both!

It was soon after she married Frank that she reached the apex of her career. It was at the same time, right after their marriage, that Frank's career started downhill without any brakes being applied.

Frank's pictures had become routine. He was cast as the brash young man who sang songs in picture after picture and his audience was getting smaller all the time. Then came an opportunity for which he had tried very hard; the opportunity to play a straight role, the part of a priest, in *Miracle of the Bells.*

The picture wasn't good. Frank was worse than the picture. It was a blow to his ego and his reaction was to get tougher, meaner, harder to get along with. He needed something to bolster his self-esteem and he chose to throw his weight around. He found that it wasn't much greater figuratively than it was literally. In a short time it was announced that Frank and the studio had parted by "mutual agreement."

If luck had been prodigal in the beginning days, misfortune was also to come to him in heaping tablespoonfuls.

His voice began to fail. It had been his ace in the hole, his sure thing in a world where there were few sure things. He could always go into a studio and cut records that were sure to sell in the hundreds of thousands. He was the kingpin recording artist at Columbia Records and, as far as he was concerned, the kingpin could do as he pleased.

If he had a sudden whim to record at midnight, arrangements were made. Musicians and technicians were rounded up and what did it matter if they received overtime, double time, golden time? Anything Frankie wanted, Frankie got.

But now this too changed. The bearded Mitch Miller, a man well known for his strength of personality, took over at Columbia. Mitch had no patience with Sinatra's peculiar, and expensive, working habits. He let it be known that Frankie, like the other artists recording for Columbia, was expected to come into the studio on time—the studio's time, not his.

Once Frankie might have told Miller to "drop dead." But now he could not. His records weren't doing so well. In recording you're not much better than your last sales statement.

So Frankie reported for recording sessions in daylight. But that didn't help. His voice was obviously in bad shape. The word was whispered more, rather than less, gleefully that he was through. Now there are all sorts of magic that sound technicians can and have done to help a vocalist when his voice starts to go. If they like the singer, as has been proven a number of times, they can keep him going even when his voice is just about gone. But they didn't like Frank.

One of the technicians confided to a friend of mine, "He was one of the meanest———we'd ever known. Nobody wanted to help him out."

Frank and Columbia Records parted by "mutual agreement."

This was the hardest part of his entire life. Of course he had a cushion. He would never be in need of money. And he was married to a beautiful, exciting woman.

But he didn't have the other trappings of success. The hit picture. The hit record.

And he didn't have his home and family. His wife—his new wife—was a star with a world of her own. And pretty much a life of her own.

And he missed the children. The court had awarded Nancy absolute custody and that meant she could prevent Frank from seeing the children if she wished. But she didn't wish that. He was their father. They loved him and wanted to see him. So, when he was in Hollywood, he had that at least.

Frankie, in the words of his own Broadway, started "to press." That meant he didn't think and reason things out, just tried everything. In 1951 and 1952 he was involved in two TV series and appeared in two pictures and all were failures.

The word was out. Sinatra was done. "Snake-bitten" is the term the smart boys use. Frankie was snake-bitten. Stay away from him

There is one phenomenon common to all branches of the entertainment world. More than a phenomenon, it might almost be called a commandment, and it runs, "Ride with a winner and rap a loser." When a star begins to fizzle, when someone at the top starts to slip, the anvil chorus always comes into play.

And the tune it played this time was, "Sinatra's done—finished—*kaput*."

That's the moment when the hangers-on, the stooges and the parasites start looking for another host. That was the moment they deserted Frankie.

For a time it appeared as if even he believed them. For a time, he wasn't Frank Sinatra any more; he was Ava Gardner's husband. He even went along with her to Africa, where she filmed *Mogambo* with Clark Gable and Grace Kelly. When a man starts playing male maid for his wife, it is almost a sign that he has surrendered.

But a lot of us underestimated the skinny infighter from Hoboken. We didn't take into account that while we might believe he was beaten, he didn't think so. We didn't give him credit for a mile-wide streak of—well—guts.

A report came from Africa that Frank had packed up and left. Most people thought this was because of his public disagreements with Ava, disagreements that caused many of the natives to report that Tarzan and his mate were back in the wilds. We couldn't imagine any other reason.

But he had another. He was going to see Henry Cohn, head of Columbia pictures, and try to persuade him that no one but he—Frank Sinatra—could play the part of Maggio in *From Here to Eternity*.

That wasn't too easy. Frank was a has-been. And even though the price was right—Frank was willing to accept $8,000 to play the role and previously had been getting $150,000 a picture—Cohn had his doubts. It took a superb job of acting on Frank's part to sell Cohn. He virtually played his first rehearsal before Cohn.

The rest is now commonplace. Frank got the role. When the picture was released, he got the raves. When nominations were made for that year's Oscars, he got the nomination. And then, of course, he got the Oscar.

I recall that night so well. A peculiar thing happened and I can't explain it. I ran into person after person who said, "He's a so-and-so, but I hope he gets it. He was great." No one had to give the antecedent of the "he."

When anyone tells me the Oscar is a popularity contest, I remind them of Sinatra's victory.

Something happened to Frank when he got that award. He told it best himself in an interview he gave writer Louis Larkin in 1959:

"The greatest change in my life began the night they gave me the Oscar. It's funny about that statue. You walk up on the stage like you're in a dream, and they hand you that little man, before twenty or thirty million people, and you have to fight to keep the tears back. It's a moment. Like your first girl or your first kiss. Like the first time you hit a guy and he went down. I've heard actors kid about the Academy Awards. Don't believe them . . . I don't think any actor can experience something like that and not change."

Certainly Frank did change. Here he had been on an express elevator going down and, suddenly, the switch was reversed and he started up.

His voice came back along with his confidence. He moved over to Capitol Records and his new recordings sold as his old ones had in the days when he was everybody's No. 1 on the Hit Parade.

Producers started clamoring for him. Those who had shouted the loudest that he was snake-bitten now hoped that it was contagious.

Only his private life remained disturbed, unimproved. He and Ava did more fighting than the whole Foreign Legion and did it where it could be observed. After a time they started living apart. Everyone waited for the inevitable trip to Reno. Finally in October, 1953, it happened. Ava took up residence.

She stayed the requisite number of weeks, and ordinarily, this would be followed by the court putting two people asunder. But not so with this pair. Ava, her waiting period over, simply packed and left. Still married to Frank.

But if they weren't legally divorced, they certainly were and have been, in every other sense of the word. Ava's life has been filled with bullfighters in her beloved Spain. There she lives in her isolated home, waiting for twilight, I have been told, before she goes out.

And Frank—well, wasn't there a long-ago countryman of his named Casanova?

He always had the charm that enthralled women. Apparently he has lost none of it with the loss of his hair and the passage of the years.

And he has received fairly extensive press coverage, although as one wag remarked, "You can't tell the girls without a score card."

But, and here again arises the contradictions within this man, he is also a family man. Hold that snicker!

At every opportunity he saw Nancy and the children. Whenever he was needed, he came. And all I can say is he is the most married bachelor I know. He has the full freedom of the home where Nancy and the children live. In every respect but one it's his. He not only seems to have his cake and eat it, but with icing.

In these past years he has been reported serious about only two women. One was Lauren Bacall, widow of Humphrey Bogart. He was a great friend of the Bogarts and very close to them during Bogey's final illness. Afterward he and Lauren ("Betty" to her close friends) were almost continually together.

The second supposedly serious romance had Juliet Prowse, a talented dancer from South Africa, as the party of the second part.

My own hunch is that he has developed an allergy to the word "marriage." Whenever it is mentioned, Frank gets an itch to run. And does.

He goes through life asking, "Where's the action?" and never stays content when he's found it. By now a mythology has grown up around him and his buddies. Their lingo demands an interpreter. When he says "ring-a-ding-ding," he means "action," and when he says "action," he means where the girls are. The habit of adding "ville" to words he began, starting out with "Dullsville," which is defined as boring beyond endurance. A "schmo" is a "square," and a "square" is anyone who isn't "hep"—and this means just about the entire population of the world, except Frank and his cronies. He is said to divide females into "dolls" and "dogs."

He seems to enjoy carrying on his feuds even when, as with me, the other party of the feud doesn't know how it came into being or why it continues.

Whatever else he may or may not be, Frank Sinatra is a good, loving father. And the one person in the world from whom I've never heard a word against him has been his first wife.

Not long ago, Nancy said to me, "There's nobody else in the world as kind and good as he is."

How can you figure a man like that?

I can't.

WATCHING SINATRA TAPE A SHOW
by Peter Levinson from the *New York Herald Tribune*, January 1961

*T*onight, from 8 to 10 on CBS-TV, the music of George Gershwin will be interpreted by the likes of Frank Sinatra, Ethel Merman, Maurice Chevalier, Julie London and Florence Henderson on "The Gershwin Years." The show is produced by Leland Heyward, himself involved in the production of such Broadway musicals as *South Pacific, Call Me Madam, Wish You Were Here* and *Gypsy*. Richard Rodgers, a Gershwin contemporary who needs no introduction, will serve as host for the spectacular.

The current gossip has it that two weeks ago Frank Sinatra, anxious to have Ethel Merman appear at the gala he is presenting for the Democratic party the night before the inauguration, agreed to appear on the show for nothing in exchange for Miss Merman's free services in Washington on Jan. 19. Her appearance for the Democrats necessitated the closing of "Gypsy" for the night at a cost of about $5,000, reportedly being paid for by Mr. Heyward.

Gossip and show biz finance notwithstanding, last Monday afternoon, just before one P.M., Sinatra walked into CBS Studio 52 on West 54th Street to tape his songs for "The Gershwin Years." After shaking hands and talking briefly with Heyward, he took off his overcoat and walked over to confer with Jay Blackton, who was conducting the orchestra. The orchestra had already run through Frank's three numbers—"I've Got a Crush on You," "A Foggy Day," and "Nice Work If You Can Get It"—which had been arranged by Nelson Riddle and sent ahead for the taping.

BRIEF REHEARSAL

Wearing a black hat, blue blazer and slacks, Sinatra rehearsed his numbers with the orchestra, signaling the musicians to stop at certain points with such directions as "When I hit the chorus, bring those fiddles way up behind me" and "Jimmy (Jimmy Nottingham, trumpet player), you come in again right after the end of the chorus and really wail." Several of the musicians such as Nottingham had worked in big bands during Sinatra's tenure with the Tommy Dorsey Orchestra, and he called them by their first names. An audience of about forty persons watched, some in obvious adulation.

The rehearsal was brief, and when it ended Heyward told Sinatra to change his clothes as the taping was about to begin. Ten minutes later Sinatra returned in black tie, stood in the corner of the stage, lit a cigarette and shouted "Ready, Jay?" The orchestra broke into "I've Got a Crush on You" and the tape began to roll. Singing one of his first important recordings, Sinatra gestured with the cigarette to emphasize the romantic mood of the song. He asked if it could be done again. This time he changed his phrasing slightly as well as his gestures. Over the speaker from the control room a voice asked, "Mr. Sinatra, would you like to hear it played back on the set over here, it's a good one, or on the one to the left of you. That one's not so good." Sinatra answered: "I'd rather go to a bar."

ONE MORE TRY

84

Sinatra watched the two renditions on the TV set in front of him, carefully studying his performance, and elected to try it one more time. At its completion, Heyward remarked, "That's good, Frank, we'll use that one." The audience applauded respectfully. Sinatra acknowledged it with a shy grin and nodded "Thank you."

After some more discussions between Sinatra, Heyward, Blackton and various cameramen and soundmen, author-comedienne Kay Thompson popped in for a brief chat with the star and producer. Sinatra then left to change for his next number. Heyward called for all concerned to "take five" which meant a fifteen-minute halt in the taping. Returning in a black suit and round-collar shirt with a plain black tie tied in a large Windsor knot, Sinatra went over to the set which represented an apartment with a party scene complete with bookcases, assorted furniture and the usual piano player on hand. The pianist, Lee Evans, introduced the orchestra's treatment of "A Foggy Day," another of Sinatra's most popular tunes and long considered a Gershwin evergreen. It took only two renditions of "Foggy Day" with Sinatra singing directly to a young couple on the couch before Heyward felt it was done right.

By now, Ethel Merman in a bright red blouse and swirling black skirt had arrived in the studio. She bestowed upon Sinatra the traditional show business hug and kiss greeting and sat down to watch him render "Nice

Work If You Can Get It." Over the loudspeaker, Jay Blackton asked, "How do you want tempo, Frank?" Sinatra replied, snapping his fingers in rhythm indicating a particular beat, "somewhere in there." "Nice Work" was wrapped up in three attempts.

Ethel Merman came on to join him in a duet on "Let's Call the Whole Thing Off." The two veteran performers laughed it up while the cameramen got ready to shoot the scene. Sinatra began to look serious for a moment, which led a cameraman to shout, "Frank, you're supposed to be in a happy frame of mind. Think of something funny." Sinatra broke up Miss Merman and the camera crew as he blurted out, "Ha, Nixon!"

"Let's Call the Whole Thing Off" has a tricky set of lyrics that calls for a precise pronunciation of such words as "potato" and "tomato" in both the upper class and ordinary pronunciations. Miss Merman and Mr. Sinatra sat casually atop a table and began singing.

They rehearsed the number once. On the first rendition of the number for taping, they made several near clinkers that led Frank to sing, "Yeah, let's call the whole thing off—off," this being the sign to stop taping. They started again and breezed through the number with perfect ease.

The three-and-a-half-hour-long taping session was now at an end. Sinatra and Heyward thanked one another and Sinatra said, "I've got about thirty phone messages to answer. Leland, I'll be in touch with you this week. Thanks for everything." He looked over toward the orchestra and yelled, "And thank you, Jay. Good work, men." With that he went off to his dressing room.

*K*omsomolskaya Pravda, the Communist youth newspaper of Lithuania, praised Frank Sinatra in its editorial pages. "He hates only racism, Fascist ideology and coercion," said the Soviet organ. "He loves little children."

Lithuanians hear Sinatra via the Voice of America, as well as German and Scandinavian radio.

PLAYBOY: Do you believe in God?

SINATRA: I think I can sum up my religious feelings in a couple of paragraphs. First: I believe in you and me. I'm like Albert Schweitzer and Bertrand Russell and Albert Einstein in that I have a respect for life—in any form. I believe in nature, in the birds, the sea, the sky, in everything I can see or that there is *real* evidence for. If these things are what you mean by God, then I believe in God. But I don't believe in a personal God to whom I look for comfort or for a natural on the next roll of the dice. I'm not unmindful of man's seeming need for faith; I'm for *anything* that gets you through the night, be it prayer, tranquilizers or a bottle of Jack Daniel's. But to me religion is a deeply personal thing in which man and God go it alone together, without the witch doctor in the middle. . . . It's not necessary for us to make it to church on Sunday to reach Him. You can find Him anyplace. And if that sounds heretical, my source is pretty good: *Matthew*, Five to Seven, "The Sermon on the Mount."

BIOGRAPHY OF FRANK SINATRA
excerpt from a Warner Bros. and Studios bio, April 1964

Frank Sinatra is often, and rightly, called "Mr. Show Business." His popularity as a motion picture star, recording artist and night club entertainer has no parallel. He is consistently on every list of top box office stars and heads almost every public and disk jockey poll on popular singers.

Frank Sinatra is also one of show business' busiest businessmen. He heads his own Sinatra Enterprises, is a special assistant to Jack L. Warner, President of Warner Bros., and is a member of the board of Warner Bros. Records-Reprise Records Co., following the recent merger of his Reprise Records with Warner Bros. Records. Also among his business ventures is the ownership, with Danny Kaye, of a number of major radio stations.

In recent years Sinatra has received much personal satisfaction, as well as worldwide acclaim, for his work on behalf of underprivileged children throughout the world as well as his continuing charitable contributions in time, talent and money in his own country.

In motion pictures, he has proved to be a consistent winner as a star as well as the head of a company which has co-produced films. His most recent show business step is into motion picture directing. He found a story in *None but the Brave*, on which an American and Japanese writer collaborated, that especially aroused his enthusiasm and led to the decision to shape it himself into a film.

Besides debuting as a director on the World War II drama, told through the eyes of a Japanese officer, Sinatra is starring in a difficult, complex characterization. Other stars in the Sinatra Enterprises production for Warner Bros. are Clint Walker, Tommy Sands, Tony Bill, Brad Dexter and Sammy Jackson, plus a group of leading Japanese actors.

Sinatra recently completed *Robin and the Seven Hoods* for Warner Bros. in association with his and Dean Martin's production companies. The Technicolor picture, a satire on Chicago gangland during prohibition, stars Sinatra, Martin, Sammy Davis, Jr., Bing Crosby, Peter Falk, Victor Buono and Barbara Rush. Gordon Douglas directed and Howard W. Koch was executive producer.

89

Currently in release is *Four for Texas,* which his company co-produced for Warner Bros. and released with Robert Aldrich's The Associates and Aldrich and Dean Martin's Claude Productions. Before that he starred in such outstanding pictures as *Come Blow Your Horn* for Paramount and *The Manchurian Candidate* and *Sergeants Three* for United Artists. . . .

The entertainer recently started his own "people-to-people" program when he first went to Mexico City in 1961 to do a show on behalf of the National Rehabilitation Institute which promoted great good will among Mexicans for their big neighbor country. He repeated the Mexican benefit a year later and extended his visit to Acapulco for a children's hospital and followed that with a world tour for the benefit of children's and youth organizations. The projects, which included being accompanied by musicians, a staff and a large amount of equipment, were undertaken at his own expense.

VITAL STATISTICS

Born:	December 12	Where:	Hoboken, New Jersey
Height:	5' 11"	Weight:	155 lbs.
Hair:	Dark Brown	Eyes:	Blue

SINATRA MEANS A JUMPING JILLY'S
AND A LOT LESS SLEEP FOR ANOTHER CAT
AT HIS FAVORITE BAR

by Gay Talese from *The New York Times,* July 1965

A one-eyed cat named Joey, the pet in Jilly's saloon at 256 West 52nd Street, usually relaxes quietly at the bar, rarely drinks anything stronger than Dubonnet and does not often run into other cats except when Frank Sinatra is in town.

But now Mr. Sinatra is here and Jilly's, the singer's favorite New York bar, is swinging with rhythm and crawling with celebrities, and Joey is keeping horrible hours table-hopping with the rest.

It is quite a scene at Jilly's after Frank Sinatra arrives. He usually does not appear until after 11 P.M. following his concert at Forest Hills, but as early as 10 P.M. dozens of people are jamming the sidewalks waiting for a glimpse of him.

Inside, another crowd is packed around the bar listening to a lively jazz combo and watching the door, and the headwaiter, a 260-pound former Jersey City Giants fullback named Mike Patrick, is politely trying to keep people from sitting at the table in the back of the room. This is Frank Sinatra's table.

TWO BLUE ARMCHAIRS

As long as he is in New York, this table is reserved on orders from the owner himself, Jilly Rizzo. The table is furnished with two wooden blue armchairs, one for Mr. Sinatra and one for Mr. Rizzo or whomever the singer is talking to; and when Mr. Sinatra is not in New York, these chairs are removed from the floor and stored.

Jilly Rizzo, who looks like a man who has had a few prize-fights although he hasn't, is 48 years old and has been a personal friend of the singer for about seven years. They met in Miami Beach when Mr. Sinatra was performing at the Fontainebleau, and they "sort of hit it off," Mr. Rizzo said.

As a boy, Jilly used to help his father carry ice into various nightspots around New York, and his ambition was to someday own one himself.

After some years as a bartender and manager, Mr. Rizzo did buy a bar on West 49th Street, and in 1958 he moved his establishment to its present address.

Since then, whenever the singer comes to town, his hangout is Jilly's. The very moment he arrives, a sudden electric quality overtakes the place: the drinkers turn, pretty girls smile, and the musicians around the piano really cut loose.

310-POUND BODYGUARD

Mr. Sinatra, smiling, moves slowly towards his table in the back, shaking hands along the way and signing autographs. Accompanying him through the crowded aisle are his New York representative, a gray-haired and bespectacled man named Henri Gine; his bodyguard, a 310-pound former All-American named Frank Pucci; his show business friends (which regularly include Sammy Davis, Alan King, Soupy Sales and Dean Martin when he's in town), and Mr. Rizzo and his wife—an energetic and ever-sun-tanned woman whose hair is dyed light blue.

Seconds after the party is seated, the drinks begin to arrive: Jack Daniel's and water for Mr. Sinatra; J&B's and soda for Martin; Daniel's and coke for Sammy; vodka and tonic for Judy Garland; straight vodka for Soupy Sales; Tanqueray gin (94 proof) for Alan King—and chicken chow mein for everybody.

Sometimes they will sing with the jazz combo around the piano, sometimes they will tell jokes and talk until 4 A.M. and always there is the crowd outside on the sidewalk looking through the window at the table in the back, waiting for the party to break up so that they can get another glimpse of the singer moving through the throng, and then climbing into a limousine and disappearing.

And then after he is gone, Jilly's is back to normal, and Joey the cat catches up on his sleep.

*A*ctress Maureen O'Sullivan announces the engagement of her daughter, Mia Farrow, to singer Frank Sinatra. "Frank is a wonderful person and I know they will be very happy," said Miss O'Sullivan.

The nuptials between 21-year-old Farrow and 50-year-old Sinatra are planned for the end of the year.

NEWS FLASH
—July 1966

*I*n a surprise decision, Frank Sinatra married Mia Farrow at the Sands Hotel in Las Vegas during a civil ceremony of five minutes' duration. The couple's engagement had been announced only last week. Neither the family of Mr. Sinatra or Miss Farrow was present at the event.

This is the third marriage for Sinatra, the first for Farrow.

NEWS FLASH
—November 1967

*F*rank Sinatra and his wife of 16 months agreed today to a trial separation. The 52-year-old singer acknowledges that he and his 22-year-old wife have spent very little of that time together.

SK-620

The Seventies:

THE CHAIRMAN
OF THE BOARD

*F*rank Sinatra announced today, March 23, that he was retiring from show business. At 55, the entertainer says he wishes to spend more time with his family and perhaps write. The performer, who spends most of the year in the New York apartment he shares with his mother, insists that his decision is final.

97

PROTECTING SINATRA AGAINST THE BIG BEEF STORY
by Christopher Buckley from *New York* magazine, 1972

*D*ebbie Reynolds was getting nervous. There she was, talking in whispers with Tom Jones, surrounded by Liberace, Sonny Bono, Joey Heatherton, James Darren, Buddy Hackett, P.R. men, photographers, reporters, and waiters, and there, suddenly, I was, leaning on a ledge four suspicious feet from her tiara, taking notes about the Bacchanal, the private dining hall at Caesar's Palace, Las Vegas. She motioned to Chris Hutchins, Tom Jones's P.R. man. He signaled to someone sitting directly below me. He stood up, put his arm over my notebook, and gave me a stare inducing frostbite. I tried looking him in the eye, and after fifteen seconds, blurted, "Am I making you nervous?" No soap. He stared another five seconds, and then turned to Tom Jones's bodyguard. "Hey, he's taking *notes*," he said. Tom Jones's bodyguard played the title role in the grade C Italian Hercules movies. *Honest.* He is six foot five, prognathous. The buttons on the front of his shirt strain to contain his chest. His forearm, the size of a small log, is suddenly resting across the edge of the notebook. "Hey," he whispers, "they don't like you around here."

But then everyone's nerves were a bit edgy. Tom Jones had just finished a two-week engagement, and the "surprise" birthday party arranged for him by the hotel is missing someone. Someone who would have made the difference. The luminaries toasting Tom Jones are sweating conviviality. But the word is already out: Frank Sinatra is not going to show. He's asleep.

One hour earlier, while Tom Jones was onstage at the Circus Maximus (the auditorium-nightclub at Caesar's Palace), Frank Sinatra sat at one of the blackjack tables dressed in a blue golfing jacket with the word COACH on the back. A crowd of 60 people gathered around him, straining on tiptoe, muttering, "Yeah, it's him," or "Okay, I seen him, now let's get a drink," trying to see over the wall of security men. They wanted just a glimpse. Was he winning? Who was he with? *What was he saying?*

Sinatra grinned—the dealer had dealt him an ace and a king. Then 60 people grinned. "All right, Frank, way to go!" He got up, leaving his handful of $25 chips (his bodyguards presumably retrieved them). Six security men formed a phalanx that juggernauted through the crowd. And so, Frank Sinatra disappeared, silently and efficiently, into the dark recesses of Caesar's Palace. It was 2 A.M. and his two-week show would open tomorrow. As the guards left him at the door to his suite on the third floor, he said, stagily: "Goodnight, sweet prince," and went off—to sleep, one presumes.

So everyone in the Bacchanal, especially the local press, was curious about Sinatra's conspicuous absence. If it turned out to be a snub, it was a Story. Newsstands would quickly shimmer with the show-biz news: WHY FRANK SNUBBED TOM—INSIDE STORY. A reporter from *People* magazine thrust himself between Liberace and James Darren and, like Clarke Mollenhoff going after Nixon, shouted: "Tom, as you know, Sinatra's in the hotel and—" Chris Hutchins cut him off angrily. "Look, if you have any questions, the hotel will be glad to answer them, okay?" Hercules materialized. *People*'s representative sighed off, in the direction of the egg rolls.

A few feet away Don Stubbs, a reporter for *Eyewitness News*, shrugged. "Yup, you can put down in your story that Sinatra's *style* here is to come down to the casino, get smashed, gamble, get surly—and then snub people. But I kinda wish he'd come down. We were hoping to get a big beef on him."

99

Members of the press are always hoping for a "big beef" story on Frank Sinatra. His press agent complains that whenever the singer makes one of his frequent philanthropic donations, the story is inevitably buried on page 79—or wherever—between 4H Club announcements and the shipping schedules. But when Sinatra, so goes the complaint, has someone roughed up in the men's room of a Palm Springs hotel or insults a gossip columnist in a Washington restaurant, the news makes it onto the front page of the nation's dailies. So for newsmen, there is always the hope that Frank Sinatra will step out of line, providing them with meaty copy. And nowhere was this hope more generously fed than in what has become known in the annals of Western history as The Incident at Caesar's Palace. There are several versions of what happened in the casino at 5 A.M. that Sunday, September 6, 1970.

VERSION ONE: Sinatra is playing baccarat at $8,000 a hand and wants to double his stakes to $16,000. His "marker"—a gambler's credit sheet—is up to $450,000. The order comes in to freeze the credit. Sinatra throws a tantrum, and casino manager Sandford Waterman pulls out a .38-caliber pearl-handled revolver. Sinatra storms out. Waterman is in due course arrested by Sheriff Ralph Lamb, who complains to the press that

Sinatra had been "intimidating waiters and waitresses," and vows, "If he gives me any more trouble, he's going to jail."

VERSION TWO: Waterman makes "uncomplimentary remarks." Sinatra responds by hurling chips in his face. A rumble between Sandford's men and Sinatra's men ensues. When Sinatra tries to leave, Waterman slams a door on his arm, an arm still bandaged from a recent operation. Said arm now bleeding, Sinatra punches Waterman in the face with his free arm. Waterman pulls the gun and dares him to strike again. "This gun bull went out twenty years ago," says Sinatra. "I'm leaving. Is anybody leaving with me?"

SINATRA'S VERSION: He wasn't anywhere near the baccarat table. "I just sat down at a blackjack table and hadn't even placed a bet, since the dealer was shuffling the cards. At that point, Waterman came over to the dealer and said, 'Don't deal to this man.' I said to him, 'Put your name on the marquee and I'll come to see what kind of business you do.' And I walked away. That was all that was said."

But THE GRAVEST VERSION OF ALL had an enraged Sinatra hissing to Waterman, "*The mob will take care of you.*" Jim Mahoney, Sinatra's public relations man, said Sinatra wouldn't even dignify that accusation with a denial, and added that he, Mahoney, doubted the performer would ever again return to Las Vegas. . . .

Meanwhile, Jilly Rizzo, close friend, confidant, and constant companion, stayed behind, playing Henry Kissinger between hotel and singer—to no avail. Frank Sinatra still had two weeks left as part of a three-year contract with Caesar's Palace. But he felt betrayed, and said so. And six months later the particular obligations to Caesar's Palace were forever adjourned. Frank Sinatra announced his retirement.

So there was jubilation at Caesar's Palace last November, when "Ol' Blue Eyes" said he would return to Circus Maximus. All of Las Vegas joined in an act of contrition. Sheriff Lamb gave out a story that was summarized in a five-column headline: LAMB DECLARES SINATRA SUPERSTAR. Sinatra, the sheriff explained, had been his "personal friend for twenty years," and the sheriff was "very pleased Mr. Sinatra is coming back. . . . "

So Sinatra returned to the scene of the incident—last January. But after completing only three shows out of eight, Frank Sinatra suddenly left the Palace yet again, for a couple of days, this time complaining of "Vegas throat." When tender vocal chords are exposed to 110-degree heat back-to-back with the icy refrigeration of Caesar's Palace, "Vegas throat" happens. The sharks moved in. Rona Barrett, the gossip columnist, clairvoyantly discerned that it was a "throat hemorrhage." Signals got mixed up. Sid Gathrid, director of entertainment at the Palace, diagnosed it as a "stomach problem."

Two one-week engagements in March were announced. But Jove himself seemed determined that Sinatra would not make it. He postponed, complaining of a "persistent sinus condition." The man who had been billed on his triumphant January return as "The Noblest Roman of Them All" was beginning to look like Brutus-of-the-persistent-stomach-throat-sinus-condition.

Even as Tom Jones sat talking with Liberace and Debbie Reynolds, Caesar's legion of skilled craftsmen were busy removing his name from the colossal marquee outside the Palace. In an hour or so, it was apparent to motorists and pedestrians a mile away that Caesar's had convened an awesome spectacle. There on the marquee, flanked by life-size plastic gladiators and slave women, were the names that would fill the Circus Maximus with 1,200 people a night and the coffers of the casino with many Eisenhower silver dollars:

SINATRA

ELLA FITZGERALD

COUNT BASIE

And His Orchestra

PAT HENRY

After nearly four years, Frank Sinatra was finally rendering unto Caesar that which was indisputably Caesar's.

There is great excitement at one of the tables near the stage. Circus Maximus forks and knives are tearing through tender limbs of sautéed frog-flesh, and the atmosphere inside the airy auditorium is lightly laced with the sudsy smell of just-opened bottles of Dom Pérignon. But at table 127, the silverware is silent for a brief moment and the champagne glasses rest on the white tablecloths. Someone has spotted Cary Grant. "Oh my God, will you look? And he doesn't look a day over 55." The lady, having had her fill of Grant, picks up her chicken Kiev and tells me she is *shpilkes*, Yiddish for nervous, on edge. Waiters, garbed in blue and gold, are running through the aisles carrying trays laden with cocktails. They have two hours to serve 1,200 plates of imperial foodstuffs before the curtain goes up. They may serve drinks during Count Basie, Ella Fitzgerald, and Pat Henry, but when Frank Sinatra walks out on stage, there will be only silence.

When Frank Sinatra descends from the third floor—where he is lodged in one of Caesar's most magnificent chambers—there is no problem with crowds. People do not get close to the man who causes the whole world to fall in love. When he arrived for the engagement, Caesar's Palace supplemented its regular security force of 100 armed-to-the-teeth Wyatt Earps by 25 per cent.

So, should Sinatra desire to have a drink with friends after one of the shows, the 25-man security force, the D.A.'s guards, and Sinatra's own muscle guarantee that no one is going to keep the drinks from flowing steadily from bar to table. No one in fact is going to get within 30 feet of the man. When the dozen or so friends are seated at the long rectangular table in the "Galleria"—Caesar's main watering-hole—a crowd starts to gather. When Jilly Rizzo, Barbara Marx, Pat Henry, and a few friends of the orchestra are congregated, the crowd spots the one empty seat and *knows*.

The whispers begin. "Where is he?" "I think I saw him." "Yeah, he'll be coming out that door there." Two Caesar's Palace guards move in. "Move back. Keep to the rear. Don't block the way, huh." And then, as the recalcitrants are herded back, three men with the sunglasses, the surly stares, and the familiar bulge under the left arm position themselves by the entryway to the "Galleria." This excites the crowd even more. Now they really *know*. Four more guards appear by a rear service door. The door opens a crack, and out comes Frank Sinatra.

The crowd, by now, is 100 strong. Frank Sinatra, surrounded by enough men to guard the President, takes his time sitting down. He does not look in the direction of the throng. That would be . . . acknowledging the people, tantamount to saying, "I see you but I can't come over to say hello." He shouts to Jilly, who laughs, and then, snapping his fingers at a hotel manager, orders Sinatra's drink. And when Sinatra sits down, a full complement of security people moves in, one for every person at the table. They stand behind their charges, arms crossed like so many Colossi of Rhodes, giving everyone within range The Beady Stare. No one is going to mess with Frank Sinatra.

A man sitting next to me at the bar—about 50 feet from Sinatra—looks at the crowd and swears with disgust. "Look at them. Gawking. Like flies on a dead horse's ass." The fellow once played with Sinatra in Allentown, Pennsylvania, in 1942. But: "Do you think I'd be stupid enough, *rude* enough, to walk over and say, 'Hi, Frank, remember me?' That would be the stupidest thing in the world."

One of the captains is himself rather *shpilkes*, because his territory includes tables with Joe Louis, Sugar Ray Robinson, Princess Fatima, Howard

Cosell, Joey Heatherton, and Sonny Bono. So many people are now stopping by for autographs and the usual "Hey! Remember me?" salutations that getting the supply line of Dom Pérignon and Scotch to Jilly Rizzo's table is threatened. Jilly Rizzo is seated near the stage with 50-odd close friends of his and Sinatra's. Jilly Rizzo is a heavily built, blondish-gray man in his early fifties. Behind his orange shades--the kind with the frames that look like silver-plated Erector Set girders—one eye wanders restlessly. Jilly Rizzo is Sinatra's Number One . . . everything. Above all, the supply line to Jilly has to be kept open.

The tables are littered with Sinatra hype literature. A red felt booklet, stamped with Caesar's imperial insigne and the bold name SINATRA in gold, says inside that "When the man sings the whole world is in love." Another slogan conceived, no doubt, in order to give the man yet another new image. When Frank Sinatra came out of retirement, he arrived back on the scene freshly labeled as "Ol' Blue Eyes," a title conjured up by Ed Thrasher, art director of Reprise Records. During the recent sixteen-city tour, the "Ol' Blue Eyes" motif was everywhere: on posters outside Carnegie Hall, painted on large red balloons at the post-concert parties, and on the programs. But here, he is simply Frank. By the time Sinatra got around to his return at the Palace, he and his P.R. people had shed the "Ol' Blue Eyes" chrysalis. A complete round trip: from Frank Sinatra to The Hoboken Kid to The Crooner to The Chairman of the Board to Ol' Blue Eyes—and now, just plain Frank. "Ol' Blue Eyes" was only necessary for the re-entry. "It served his purpose. He's back," says Jim Mahoney. Frank Sinatra has shed another layer of skin.

Cisco, one of the supplementary Sinatra guards, stands by the elevators in the lobby eight hours a day to keep "kids and rip-off artists" from prowling the upstairs corridors. Cisco looks something like an extra on the set of *Gunsmoke*. Sunburned face, a wisp of a white mustache, and wire-rimmed glasses. The paging system calls Princess Fatima. "I think that Princess Fatima must be a cigarette girl—you know, the one with the huge boobs. . . . "

Cisco has one of those six-pointed gold stars over his heart engraved with the words "Special Officer." On the job, Cisco sees "Frankie boy" five or six times a day. "He gives me a pain in the ass," Cisco says. "He's always callin' me 'Pappa.' "

"Ladies and gentlemen, Count Basie and his orchestra!" The house lights go down. The red velvet curtains slide back, and there is the Count, eyes twinkling, pudgy black fingers caressing the keys, smiling devilishly but making no mischief. He takes his orchestra through two numbers while the

audience leans back, letting his beautiful jazz accompany the champagne from mouth to throat. The Count is the relaxer. Now comes the voice that will whet the crowd's appetite to the straining point.

"*Ladies and gentlemen, Miss Ella Fitzgerald!*" Ella Fitzgerald does not walk; she glides. You seldom see her feet; what you see is a large figure dressed in a flowing cobalt-blue gown. She has a little-girl voice when she says, "Good evening! Good evening!" and as she sings the first few measures of "There'll Never Be Another You," eyes close and heads droop. Fifteen minutes later, as she's finishing "Mr. Paganini," a stocky man with the face of a truckdriver is apparently transformed into a sleeping angel. His chin is cradled in the palm of one hand, his eyes are shut, and he must be dreaming of clouds and maidens wrapped in silk and a mirror-calm sea and—his friend across the table winks and points to him. "Hah," he whispers, "will you look at that? Dead asleep. Shoots craps twenty hours a day. Can't stay awake."

Ella Fitzgerald's delivery is breathtaking, but the imminent epiphany of Frank Sinatra holds 1,200 people in the grip of bladder-bursting *shpilkes.* The Question is tonight—the Question every night—is *How long can Frank Sinatra endure?* One man shrugs philosophically: "With Frank, every night could be closing night." But in the event Frank Sinatra were ravaged by Vegas throat or sinusitis, in the event of another conflagration at the baccarat table, causing him to call for his private jet, Caesar's Palace would be covered. Even with the names of Liberace, Wayne Newton, Debbie Reynolds, Joey Heatherton, the Smothers Brothers, and such Las Vegas heavyweights embroidered on other marquees of the strip, Caesar's Circus Maximus would not crumble. Ella Fitzgerald and Count Basie are headliners in their own right.

After the applause for "Mr. Paganini" subsides, Ella Fitzgerald and Keter, her bass man, do a duet, "The Man I love." She and Keter are alone, musically, on the stage as two small spotlights pick them out and pin them to the background. Keter plucks away, be-bup-bup-boom. . . . Ella Fitzgerald glides back and forth across the stage, looking down at the nearby tables through her thick glasses, with her little-girl smile, looking, searching, for *her man. . . .*

The show now moves studiedly from the sacred to the profane. Pat Henry, who has been with Sinatra for several years, spends fifteen minutes onstage mouthing funnies on such themes as (1) "doing tinkle in other people's pools," (2) Italians and blacks, and (3) Golda Meir. The fifteen minutes encompass approximately 50 or so jokes—one-third of them mildly funny. But the audience is amused, all right.

Some years ago, after Sinatra had befriended a young, blind, and near-destitute musician called José Feliciano—whom people were later to abuse for "disgracing" "The Star-Spangled Banner"—Sinatra, Pat Henry, Feliciano, and his wife were together at a table. Feliciano's wife was giving Henry a hard time, so he turned to her, and with typically feigned lukewarm vitriol, told her, "Look, you don't shut up, I'm going to tell your husband what you look like."

"*Ladies and gentlemen, Pat Henry!*" And out he comes brisk, erect, eyes never moving from their focus on the edge of the stage. He carries a large alarm clock. A few people titter.

"I got fifteen minutes, ladies and gentlemen. That's the way Frank wants it. An' I don't fool with Frank. Christ, he once told Howard Hughes to get lost, and look what the hell happened. So when this goes off, I go off." I began my own countdown. "Frank, one helluva guy." This is part of the hype. "Will ya look at the names he brings in? What names! Fungi Terenazi. Gaetano di Lupidicci. Bananas Scarnalo. There ain't a goddamn fruit stand open in New York this whole week."

He lets the audience digest his witticisms before moving on. "But you know, ladies and gentlemen, Frank—this man is *humble*. I see him get down on his knees every night and thank God for everything. Then he asks God if there's anything he can do for Him." He stoops to pick up a drink from Jilly Rizzo's table. Walking back to the microphone, he peers into the glass. "Heh, an ice cube wit' a hole in it. I was married to one for eight years." A few minutes later (my watch says he has five minutes left) he gets onto Nixon and Watergate: "That whole Watergate thing was a mistake. Look, when you wanna wire a building, you don't do it yourself. You get four Japanese guys. They're great wit' wires. And they're *honorable*, you know? They get caught?—pfffffft—dey kill demselves. Hell, Nixon ain't that bad. He kept us out of Ireland, didn't he?"

He has two minutes to go, and as he explains to us why it was that he never became a priest, Jupiter forbid—Frank Sinatra is cinching his cummerbund in room 365 on the third floor. A few minutes earlier, four or five guards, each carrying Smith and Wesson .38 or .41 caliber revolvers, posted themselves outside his door. Two guards stand by the elevator, and others are positioned at short intervals along the path he will take to the backstage of the Circus Maximus. Ironically, Frank Sinatra must take the service route. When he is ready to leave the room, Pat Henry checks his own watch. Sinatra starts down with his bodyguards, as well as the hotel's and the D.A.'s. They step into the elevator, get out at the second floor, and move like a procession of Presidential Secret Service men down two

105

flights of stairs, through the kitchen, and finally onto the backstage. Clock-work. Pat Henry's alarm clock erupts, mercifully preventing him from completing another Golda Meir joke. He—and Sinatra—were not kidding. When it goes off, Pat Henry goes off, blowing several wet kisses.

There seems to be a dramatic plot in juxtaposing Pat Henry and Frank Sinatra. The audience, still limp with Henry's rhapsody of wit, is suddenly caught off guard. For several crucial seconds, people have forgotten what is to come next: the alpha and omega of the Circus Maximus.

No announcement. "*Ladies and gentlemen, Frank Sinatra*!" would be superfluous, offensive. It takes the 1,200 people in the auditorium three full seconds to realize it is *Frank Sinatra* striding up to the microphone. The voice of the crowd starts close to the stage. It ascends, gathering gasps and groans on the way, moving faster and faster over the banks of settees until it hits the back of the Circus Maximus, where it can go no farther. Then it explodes in a unified roar of adulation. Count Basie and the orchestra provide the tempo for Frank Sinatra's entrance, playing the introduction to "Bad, Bad Leroy Brown." Sinatra takes the microphone off its claw-hook on the stand. He smiles, and the tremor heightens noticeably. He blows a kiss, and staccato whistles add a treble beat to the bass hum of the crowd. Caesar's Palace is riding the crest of the Augustan age as Sinatra clicks his fingers and syncs his voice into the voice of the band.

Frank Sinatra's voice is raw, as though it were being filtered through a sandy thorax. The lady across from me says, "Well, he's still got his *style*." Style the man has, and when he brings "Leroy Brown" to a close, the roar of the audience begins again. "Thank you, thank you . . . your applause is so nice. I may even come back tomorrow night!" Tremendous laughter. Sinatra has a penetrating sense of self-parody. He bounces off his own foibles. Complaining of the heat, he says, "I haven't been this hot since I went before the grand jury."

After two more numbers, there is rapture in the Circus Maximus. Even the fellow who shoots craps twenty hours a day is wide awake, perched on the edge of his chair, hanging on every syllable that issues from the great throat. Sinatra coaxes the microphone and with a flick of the wrist sends a parabolic ripple coursing through the wire lying the length of the stage. Now he stops to chat. He loves to talk to his people. "I used to sing that one back in 1912. Hah! That was when Mr. Basie was a kid in Red Bank, New Jersey. He used to ride in the back of the bus. Now, he owns the bus, Red Bank, the racetrack, and the state troopers. And you know what I say? I say, *right on*!" The Count smiles in a grandfatherly way. Sinatra eases into "Rainy Day."

The song hits some members of the audience like a shot from Special Officer Cisco's Luger. Milton Berle is there, his hands ceaselessly moving from one pocket to another in search of the cigar he never lights. When Sinatra glided out of "Rainy Day" at his Carnegie Hall concert last spring, there in the third row center was Uncle Miltie, his face in his hands, mumbling, "Breaks your heart, breaks your heart." I happened to be sitting next to him at that concert. When he wasn't fiddling with his cigar, or mopping his forehead with a silk handkerchief, Uncle Miltie was saying, to no one in particular, "Magic! Charisma!"

Uncle Miltie can be a severe critic. When a warm-up act was prancing about the Carnegie Hall stage, he turned to me and said, "Crazy, huh?"

"Well, yeah," I said.

"It's *toute la même chose*," Uncle Miltie explained. "All repetition—they never do anything different. It's *toute la même chose*. You know French? You know what that means in French?"

"All the same thing."

"Yeah, smart kid. Watch the show, will ya?"

Tonight in Vegas, Milton Berle seems more subdued. He does not, as he did in New York, yell up to the stage and command Frank to sing "I Wanna Wabbit," composed by Milton Berle.

Sinatra's voice still has a rasp. There is strength in there, but the edges are slightly jagged. But the little imperfections are of no consequence to the 1,200 people in the Circus Maximus. "It's not easy for Frank. He's fighting," says one. But when the song is ended, the same man stands up and shouts, his own gruff vocal chords screaming, "Good boy, Frankie!"

As the screen behind the orchestra turns a bright shade of turquoise, a morning color that appears over the mountains to the west of Las Vegas just as the sun is rising, Frank Sinatra sits on a stool and whispers, "*This is a lovely song* . . ." The song is called "If." When the lone spotlight frames his face, 1,200 hearts beat together and he sings, "*If a face could launch a thousand ships, then where am I to go?*" The question answers itself. This is the Moment, the same Moment Bob Dylan accomplishes with "Blowin' in the Wind," the Moment the younger Paul McCartney reached in "Yesterday," the Moment of worship Faustus felt when he gazed on the metempsychosis of Helen of Troy. Apotheosis. A few seconds spent in the company of the Sublime. Frank Sinatra's hand reaches out into the cool, blue space of the stage, his sunburned hand caressing air, defining the form of the Dream, creating. Frank Sinatra, 57, with a sandpapery inflection of Vegas throat, is fighting, but for three and a half minutes in the Circus Maximus, he is the center of the universe.

107

A cluster of split-image moons appear on the turquoise screen as Frank Sinatra and his guitarist decelerate. Two seconds lapse before the roar starts up. The audience is more exhausted than he is. After the bows, he clears his throat and says, softly, "That's such a pretty song. I only wish I could do it justice." Michelangelo, putting the final buff polish on the *Pietà*, deploring the abuse of marble. A chorus of maybe 500 screams. "Oh, you did, you did!" Sinatra smiles demurely. "But when you got a split reed there ain't a helluva lot you can do, except say, 'Bartender, another one, *if you please.*'" The message of the Circus Maximus is clear. Frank Sinatra's "split reed" is just . . . beside the point.

Frank Sinatra clears his throat again, this time trying on purpose to sound like Godzilla with laryngitis. He laughs. "You don't know the pains." The audience laughs too, not noticing that beneath the facetious delivery there lurks a note of seriousness. Sinatra's fee for the two-week engagement is one of the most closely guarded secrets in the world. One reporter said the figure was roughly $300,000. But that, too, is beside the point. The point, really, is this: Frank Sinatra works as hard as he did when he sang with Tommy Dorsey. He *knows* the crowd in the Circus Maximus is paying a minimum of $30 a person to hear him. He *knows* they love him, and so, for at least ten minutes during each show, he opens up his life for their benefit.

After "If" and up until he reaches Phase Two of Apotheosis with "My Way," Frank Sinatra descends from Olympus. He jabs at his favorite target, Rona Barrett: "Ladies and gentlemen, I will not talk about Rona Barrett tonight. Nor will I talk about Benedict Arnold, Aaron Burr, Adolf Hitler, Bruno Hauptman, or Ilse Koch—she's the one who made the lampshades . . ."

From levity to hambone pride: "Ladies and gentlemen, I ask you please to raise your glasses in a toast to my little granddaughter, who is two weeks and three days old." It's an emotional home run. There are many grandfathers and grandmothers in the audience; the crowd salutes him with a big "Awwww." "What a kid this is, folks. Why"—with artful mock braggadocio—"she's even more beautiful than I was when I was a kid." He swaggers and sips from a tumbler full of vodka and water. "And I was *some beyoootiful kid.* Hah! Some beyoootiful kid." He strikes a Frank Sinatra/Archie Bunker pose as a man in the audience yells, "You're a grandfather!" "Yeeah," he mugs, "an' I am the swingingest muthah grandfather around."

Minutes later, after talking about his granddaughter, his mother, and after drinking "to the confusion of our enemies," Frank Sinatra clicks his fingers and sings "I've Got You under My Skin." A woman in the Circus

Maximus, recalling the time she got up at six in the morning one day in 1942 to stand in line outside Philadelphia's Earle Theatre—where he would be singing in twelve hours—lets out a devastating "Eeeeeeagh!" Frank Sinatra flicks the microphone wire, humping another ripple along the floor. He stops in mid-lyric, wrinkles his brow with teasing sympathy and says to her, "Where's it hurt ya baby?" Probably where it's hurting everyone tonight. Under the skin.

SINATRA: AN AMERICAN CLASSIC

by Rosalind Russell from *Ladies' Home Journal*, November 1973

What one word best describes Frank Sinatra? "Compassionate," says his close friend Rosalind Russell. In this Journal *exclusive, the distinguished actress writes a frankly sentimental tribute to the man she calls "the performer of the century," as Norman Rockwell, America's most famous artist, unveils the singer's long-awaited portrait.*

His face may never be part of the frieze at Mount Rushmore, but this legendary Italian-American from Hoboken, N.J., is an appropriate subject for a Normal Rockwell study. Because Frank Sinatra *is* an American classic, a man who has had his ups and his downs but who has never been counted out. The performer of the century, however, did step aside in June, 1971, after completing 58 films, 100 record albums, more than 2,000 individual recordings; and I believe that after three decades of concentrated work his decision to retire was a sincere one. (On Nov. 18, Sinatra comes out of retirement to do a television special for Magnavox on NBC from 8:30 to 9:30 P.M. E.S.T.)

That June night at the Music Center when I introduced him and announced his "final" appearance, many people questioned my emotion. It came from the fact that I felt it was sad indeed that this talent was literally being silenced by Frank himself—whose voice was, by the way, never better. I thought of the night I heard him in Philadelphia, where he held thousands of people spellbound for over two hours; of the charities for which he sang his heart out to help so many. (I asked him once if he could count the benefits he had done, and he just laughed.)

We drove back from the Music Center that night to my home. Was he really happy now that it was over? "Rosie," replied the Chairman of the Board, "you can't imagine the relief I feel. I did not start, as many people think, singing at a well-known nightclub in New Jersey. I started as a teenager singing in joints on the Jersey Shore for cigarettes and my dinner." (Note to Mom Sinatra: true, your Frankie was well-fed at home, but when "The Voice" developed, so did the ambition to entertain.)

There were multiple reasons for Frank's retirement. I believe that his father's passing had shocked and hurt him deeply. Then, too, he wanted to pause to think things over, to be without pressure for the first time in his active life.

Three generations recognize Francis Albert Sinatra as Frank, Frankie, or just Sinatra. I have known him since 1940, when he sang "I'll Never Smile Again" to my husband Freddie and me during our courting days; Frank was singing with the Tommy Dorsey Band then. He sang the song again, among others, at the 25th wedding anniversary party he gave for Freddie and me—a three-day festival which no one who attended will ever forget.

To be Frank's friend is like one of his songs: "All or Nothing at All." It is a total, unconditional commitment, a never-fraying security blanket. He has a short fuse when it comes to criticism of friends he holds in high regard, and he is willing to accept the heat and the flak. True, he is sometimes noisy in his reaction to someone else's abuse because his feelings are intense—as is his sense of justice.

He dislikes women who smoke or drink too much or who wear heavy perfume. He dislikes roast lamb, fair-weather friends, green salads, phonies, complainers, and welshers. He enters any public place with trepidation. It is almost a ritual that some man will leave his group, walk over to Frank's table, tap him on the shoulder and ask, "Are you really the lover my wife thinks you are?" Take my word for it, Frank remains patient far longer than he is ever given credit for.

When the *Ladies' Home Journal* suggested that I do this article, the editor asked me to describe Sinatra in one word. Without hesitating I responded "compassionate." I have never seen him refuse a child anything. When Claudette Colbert's husband was critically ill in Barbados, a group of us were at Frank's Palm Springs compound, where he spent the entire night arranging for a plane to fly non-stop to Barbados—complete with medical staff and change of crew (required by law) to pick up Claudette and her husband. After Sammy Davis' serious accident, it was Frank who made him dance again. But most of this rarely reaches the press.

There are several Frank Sinatras. Perhaps this is what makes him both fascinating and controversial. He is tempestuous, tender, searching, indefatigable, unexpected. As a father, he is doting, generous, always involved. I overheard him remark to his daughter on the phone one day, "Yes, Nancy, go ahead, cut your hair if you feel you'll like it." He hung up, shaking his head slightly. "You know, Rosie, I never really left home," he said.

111

The lover? Of course! Marlene Dietrich once called him "the Mercedes-Benz of men."

Then there is Sinatra, the practical joker. One night at the compound, my husband Freddie asked if he could have some cheese and crackers before retiring. "There'll be no night food," said Frank. "Lights out!" A half-hour later, we heard the wildest racket coming from an ear-shattering bell, and there was Frank pushing a serving cart full of food, beer, an assortment of goodies.

He is, of course, the perfect host—a great Italian cook, a knitter-together of people, a constant plate-filler and glass-replenisher. He himself is what I call a "fake" drinker; more times than not he talks more about drinking than he actually imbibes. He needs very little sleep. He lets people believe he is swinging every night in the week, whereas he is often home reading. He is an Eric Hoffer buff, a best-seller addict, and has an insatiable interest in history. He recently acquired a brace of French Impressionist paintings, but as a guess I would say his taste runs from the humor of Hirshfeld to Andrew Wyeth.

Then there is another Frank Sinatra—one he may not like my discussing: Sinatra the loner, the constant observer, a profoundly sensitive man. "My Way" has not always been his way. There have been troublesome times, painful times, which he has harbored within himself and shared with no one.

Then there is Sinatra the American. Some may mock it, as is the fashion today, but deep down he is the original all-American, Fourth of July boy. Maybe it is because his father was an Italian immigrant—a prizefighter whom Frank watched become a respected fire captain. Maybe it is because Frank always knew that he himself could never have happened in any country but this one.

Though his political affiliations may change, his respect for his country does not. He raises and lowers the American flag in front of his house every day. Recently he was invited and welcomed to the White House. President Nixon himself led the applause for Frank Sinatra's after-dinner singing with the comment, "Once in a while there is a moment when there is magic in this room." Excuse me, Mr. President, there is magic in every room, in every life, that Mr. Sinatra has ever touched.

THE WORKS OF FRANK SINATRA
excerpted from a Reprise Records bio, July 1974

SINATRA'S TOP REPRISE ALBUMS

Ring a Ding Ding!
I Remember Tommy
Sinatra & Strings
Sinatra-Basie
The Concert Sinatra
Sinatra's Sinatra
September of My Years
Sinatra: A Man and His Music
Strangers in the Night
Sinatra at the Sands
That's Life
Francis Albert Sinatra & Antonio Carlos Jobim
Cycles
My Way
Ol' Blue Eyes Is Back

FRANK SINATRA: MOTION PICTURE CREDITS

Reveille with Beverly
Higher and Higher
Step Lively
Anchors Aweigh
The House I Live In
Till the Clouds Roll By
It Happened in Brooklyn
The Miracle of the Bells
The Kissing Bandit
Take Me Out to the Ball Game

Some Came Running
A Hole in the Head
Never So Few
Can-Can
Ocean's Eleven
Pepe
The Devil at 4 O'Clock
Sergeants Three
The Manchurian Candidate
Come Blow Your Horn

On the Town
Double Dynamite
Meet Danny Wilson
From Here to Eternity
Suddenly
Young at Heart
Not As a Stranger
The Tender Trap
Guys and Dolls
The Man with the Golden Arm
Johnny Concho
High Society
Around the World in Eighty Days

List of Adrian Messenger
Four for Texas
Robin and the Seven Hoods
None but the Brave
Von Ryan's Express
Marriage on the Rocks
Cast a Giant Shadow
Assault on the Queen
The Naked Runner
Tony Rome
The Detective
Lady in Cement
Dirty Dingus Magee

SINATRA: STILL GOT THE WORLD ON A STRING
by Michael Watts from *Melody Maker* [U.K.], November 9, 1974

MADISON SQUARE GARDEN, NEW YORK—FRIDAY

"*T*he People's Ticket" it read outside Madison Square Garden last Friday. It said the same on the ten-dollar stub I clutched to get inside, way, way up to the mezzanine seats, high in the bleachers, where one looked down on, cut off from, the royal-blue square of stage with its red ribbons and the well-heeled New Yorkers who'd paid 250 bucks for the privilege of being eye-witnesses.

The following morning *The New York Times* said 11,000 people had been at the Garden that night. The *Post* put the figure at 16,000, but then that paper is solidly pro-Democrat, and that, after all, is what the fuss was supposed to be about: a fund-raising rally for the Democratic party, just like those the Kennedys used to hold a decade ago, when Peter Lawford, Sammy Davis, Jr., and Frank Sinatra would be drawn out of the hat to entertain "The People" and nudge the would-be Democratic voters.

Ticket

Funny—did I say Sinatra? Why, you wouldn't know it from your ticket or the announcement outside, but Frankie is indeed back again with the Democrats tonight.

He circles around the imperial eye of the Garden, watched in turn by Representative Hugh Carey, who this week is riding for Governor of the State of New York, former New York mayors John Lindsay and Robert Wagner, the present incumbent Abe Beame, and these 11,000 to 16,000 people (take your pick) who are either Democrats, Sinatra fans, or both.

There was a time when being a Democrat and a Frank Sinatra devotee were entirely compatible, and then there was another time, few years later on, when it was much harder to reconcile the two. What happened?

He had pitched strongly for the Kennedys, this singer from New Jersey, from an emphatically Democratic family, whose mother Dolly Sinatra was a Democratic ward leader in Hoboken.

JFK had even been over to the Palm Springs house, used the red telephone in the study, and slept in the guest room, so it was said.

But there had been sponsorships for "the People's Party" long before that, too. Rallies for Adlai Stevenson and FDR himself, including a speech at Carnegie Hall in aid of Young America for Roosevelt.

Then Sinatra, in the words of the more outspoken Democrats, "went bad." The Kennedy Klan was replaced in his affections by the Terrible Triumvirate of Reagan, Agnew and Nixon. Open a newspaper and there would be photos of him linked with one or the other.

At his Palm Springs home he named a guest cottage "Agnew House." Politically at least, he fell into line behind Duke Wayne, the Republican Whip in the amphitheatre of the entertainment world, even taking Sammy Davis with him, which on Davis' part was an act of devotion beyond the call of duty.

The split between Sinatra and the liberal Democrats has never been truly defined, but it's always been felt that it stemmed from a word in the ear of John Kennedy that alleged that good ol' Frank had unsavoury underworld connections, a remark that eventually brought Sinatra before a Federal Grand Jury a couple of years ago.

And the message-bearer was, it's been said, JFK's brother himself, Robert Kennedy, then Attorney-General. There would be no more guest nights, no more use of the red telephone, after this. Frankie bled, and he trailed his wounds over to the Republican camp.

116

Party

That's the way it's been for years now, until early last month Sinatra met Hugh Carey at a cocktail party hosted by Phyllis Cerf, widow of publisher Bennet Cerf and a close friend of former New York mayor, Robert Wagner.

And Sinatra said yes to the suggestion that was dropped in his ear. He would sing for the Democrats once again, like the old times. Okay, Ol' Blue Eyes would be coming back.

Since more than ever these days the pressman is an object of antipathy in Frank's eyes, the motivation behind this reversal has gone unstated. But remember, the Nixon Era is finally over. In a Long Beach hospital, Nixon has his own wounds to attend to, both physical and psychic, while Spiro has long been banished from the arena of power.

In America politicians and entertainers seem willing and inseparable bed-fellows, for the difference between them is often minimal.

Perhaps Sinatra has suddenly found his own bed chill and empty, and wishes to lie down with an old friend, forgetting the harsh words that have passed and remembering more the once-familiar warmth.

The action is somewhat contemptible, but it's also very human, and it's that quality of *humanness*, both in his life and his singing, which can make Sinatra so touching, so innocent of guile.

Politics

I don't know. I know nothing of Republican or Democratic politics. I see only a guy who himself understands politics on a basic human scale of rights and wrongs and injustices. An eye for an eye, a tooth for a tooth. A guy who swings from one extreme to another. If you're not my friend, you're my enemy.

Besides, one can forgive a great artist his lapses in judgment. Sinatra's apparent need to always be around a winner may be infantile, but one recognizes the emotion.

This sounds already like a defence speech, but it's not meant to be. After all, who's using who? Representative Hugh Carey seemed much more nervous about confronting Sinatra than the other way round.

As Frank strolls about the stage he makes no reference to the Democrats, nor to Carey. His manner is businesslike even, as if he regrets what he agreed upon but has to go through with it now.

He doesn't appear until two and a half hours after the show has begun, long, long minutes of Melba Moore straining to get through "The Long and Winding Road," of Ben Vereen trying to come on like Mr. Bojangles, and of Carol Channing, "Miss Broadway" in silver, black and blonde, singing mercilessly in a voice like rape itself and throwing cut-glass baubles to the front rows while performing "Diamonds Are a Girl's Best Friend."

In between these asininities, the orchestra plays such songs as "Happy Days Are Here Again," just to reassure those voters out there in the bleachers that a new reign is upon them.

But Alan King, the comedian and link-man for the event, understands all that gut-response which wants to be let loose, knows that it's more than a carney, that the crowd is looking for spit and sawdust in its bread and circuses.

He tells jokes about his mother-in-law, but he also says things: "No

117

matter how rich you get, you can never forget what poverty's like." Oh, how they cheered that! And high above the stage the red, blue and white clusters of balloons trembled.

He is also conscious that the show has a double significance that though it's ostensibly for "the People's Ticket," for a new push to the White House in '76, it's also a celebration of the Sinatra myth as iconoclast and outlaw.

Church

"I suppose you all know that Francis is going to be here later," he tells the audience, "and that there was a lotta controversy over politics. Well, I was just in his dressing-room, and I told him: 'even an atheist can come back to his church.' " More, increased cheers.

Then he speaks of the Sinatra virility. He says, "I've known Frank ever since we were kids, and, you know, he's still a sex symbol." Everywhere, tremors shake the hearts and bodies of aging bobbysoxers at what they know must be the truth. Photos still kept in drawers, maybe on the walls in one or two cases, and a dozen albums on the record shelf, next to the kids' Led Zeppelins and Black Sabbaths.

Of course, Carey has to get in on the act, too. He steps onto the square of royal blue, with his wife and what appears to be a dozen kids, in a ploy so crass it takes the breath away.

Words like "passion" and "integrity" spill from his lips in unctuous drool. But he gets folksy. He says he and his wife used to listen to Frank when they were courting—of course—and now—wait for it—"the Republicans have made it so bad that even Ol' Blue Eyes has had to come back to us."

His teenage sons fidget and scratch their behinds in full view, but down in the 250 dollar seat enclosure the patriots are on their feet and applauding.

It's a mere moment, and then the lights dim, Sinatra's name is mentioned in a tone of importance, and six spotlights suddenly fasten on this bulky, grey suit being hustled past the outstretched hands in a flurry of bodyguards and attendants, onto the stage—at last!—and there's Frank Sinatra with a microphone in his hand, and Don Costa and the orchestra, leading us away with "I've Got the World on a String."

Elation

It's an instant that does, in truth, clutch at the heart, a few seconds of elation, as if some Eternal Verity has been briefly vouchsafed to us.

Sinatra's grey head bobs in the spotlights, the orchestra gleams gold and brass, and the inky outer space reverberates, like blue lightning, with the flashing of cameras, attempting to preserve it all for posterity.

Yet there was as much about his short performance—30 minutes, almost to the second—that was as perfunctory as it was elating. Jim Croce's "Leroy Brown" and "The Lady Is a Tramp" tripped easily off his tongue, but without much heart.

Showbusiness songs done in the most showbusiness fashion. He had the world on his string, you'd better believe. No one was gonna make a sucker of him.

He said very little. Once he stopped for a fraction mid-sentence in Paul Anka's "Let Me Try Again" and answered an audible moan of pleasure from a woman in the crowd with "I love you, too," and it felt as if some god, or father-figure, had thrown us all a kind word, a scrap of praise.

His only public pronouncement was to the present Mayor of New York, Abe Beame. In-between songs he told him: "I hadda go on a detour of 48 blocks to get here." He didn't sound as if he was joking.

119

Charm

But when he sang "Violets for Your Furs," I melted into total admiration. "The day I bought you violets for your furs." A great line, a song that throbbed with melancholy. Something tired and old about him, but ageless, too. Then I understood his charm, the infinite layers of his sensitivity.

But he finished with "Tramp," left the same way he'd come in a welter of arms and hands, pausing only to sign autographs for the Carey kids, the same ones who'd been scratching their arses half an hour ago. And I knew, too, that I didn't really understand at all.

But then "the People's ticket" means different things to different people. I wondered what Sinatra's interpretation was.

OH, HOW WE WORSHIPPED THE GODS OF THE FIFTIES
by Barbara G. Harrison from *Viva* magazine, July 1976

I have a snapshot taken on my sixteenth birthday, in 1950: I am wearing black leotards, a flared quilt skirt that ends midcalf in delicious, provocative waves; my feet are shod in Capezio ballet slippers; my mouth is fixed in a Tangee (orange-in-the-tube, pink-on-your-mouth) grin; my hair is tortured in an improbable arrangement that has even less to do with art than it has to do with nature; oversized gold hoop five-and-dime earrings graze my neck. It is my Greenwich Village uniform. But I have never been to Greenwich Village. It is still a country of the mind; and my beauty-parlor perm and my Tangee Natural and my screw-on earrings mark me as ineffably *Brooklyn*. Everything, in fact, is hopelessly out of synch. (How Diane Arbus would have loved me!) I have created myself in the image of my fantasies, fantasies drawn from movies and novels of Bohemian life; I look like a child's energetic drawing of something he has never seen—crude, imaginative, and unfinished. The look on my face, bewildered but insanely grinning, is the look I have seen on men's faces two seconds before they've fully understood that their flies are open in public.

Everyone who grew up in the fifties will know something is missing in that picture: As it is my sixteenth birthday, I should be wearing a bouquet of sugar cubes and pink ribbons. But I was brought up in a fancy religion that frowned upon the frivolity of birthday celebrations; and my Sweet Sixteenth birthday came and went without sugar cubes, autograph books, sleep-over parties in baby-doll pajamas, and the exchange of girlish confidences over Going All the Way. It wasn't until I was twenty-one that I slipped out of the reins of parental authority and left my constricting religion—and made a beeline for Greenwich Village, the finishing school for my generation of energetic, imaginative, fantasy-bemused young women.

Now, this is the nice thing: My eccentric upbringing was in many ways a perfect preparation, and a passport, for my being alive-and-aware (we used the word aware a lot) in the Greenwich Village of the fifties. I fit as sweetly into that decade as a nut fits in its shell. Because the thing about the fifties was that everybody—everybody being the people one knew or emulated or loved—felt out of synch with his time, and glad of it. We all cherished our idiosyncrasies and our neuroses; we would have laughed at EST, AT, Esalen, and all the sixties/seventies psychic-smoosh therapies. In spite of the somewhat paradoxical fact that practically everyone one knew spent his or her lunch hour on the analyst's couch, we couldn't imagine where we'd be without our disfiguring—but *interesting*—neuroses. Narcissists worshipping our own singularity, we seldom thought that there might be public or group solutions to private problems. We had been teenagers during the McCarthy H.U.A.C. horror; but neither that cruel nightmare, nor the Cold War, nor the Korean War—so unlike the children of the sixties were we—served to "radicalize" or politicize us. Occasionally, it's true, we went to meetings of the Young Socialist Party, and we heaved sighs over our country's racism or America's intervention in the affairs of the banana republics, but mostly we took refuge in the rich interior lives we all believed we had; we did not know, or think to figure out, how our personal lives could mesh with public concerns. It was In to be an Outsider.

To be an Outsider was to be of the elect. We were generous enough to accept people at their own evaluation, and when grey-flannel drones from Madison Avenue invaded our turf and protested that they had poems in their heads and rebellion in their hearts, we believed them: If the Fat Lady could be Jesus Christ, why *couldn't* the man in the gray-flannel suit be a poet? We distrusted surfaces. This was, after all, the decade that had, without a hint of self-mockery, spawned a literary magazine called *The Noble Savage*. In our kindness and our condescension, we chose to believe in the nobility and the savage innocence of nine-to-fivers who paraded their nerves and sensitivity, their satchels full of unpublished manuscripts, in our bars and our coffeehouses. But in our heart of hearts, we knew that while everybody was "evolving," we were the people our generation really belonged to, we were more sensitive, more vulnerable, more risk-taking, more alive. Everybody was a rebel without a cause, but everybody living in the Village was a rebel where rebellion was *happening*. I think we thought we were holy. We thought everybody in pain was holy: When I had a love affair (my first) with a black jazz musician, and my best friend had an affair (her first) with an advertising executive, we quarreled over whose pain was greater— the pain of a black musician living on talent and no money and dope, or the pain of a man whose gray flannels covered quiet desperation and a yearning to "become." (Oh, those fifties words! No wonder Nichols and May were able to satirize us so adroitly.) Really we were having a quarrel over who was more holy.

Look at our heroes: Sinatra, Salinger, Camus, Brando. They were holy men.

Okay, on the face of it, Frank Sinatra seems an unlikely candidate for any pantheon of gods. But you have to think, not of the cold-eyed, paunchy, stale, and bullying Sinatra of the seventies, but of the tough-tender rakish reed from Hoboken, that sweet survivor. That Sinatra could crack your heart. Stubborn, defiant, proud, cocky, willful and winsome and wholly engaging, buffeted and boisterous and boyishly bashful, he did it his way then—and we loved him for it. And lonely. Of course we thought he was lonely, magnificently lonely, a golden-gloves fighter in the ring with the big bad pros, up against great odds, with nothing but his naive wit and his brashness to sustain him. He bucked the crowd, as heroes are meant to do. He was the Outsider who fought back and made it. That astonishing comeback: A has-been in the early fifties, an Academy Award winner in 1954 for his portrayal—drawn from life, we thought—of Maggio, the feisty rebel, friend-of-the-underdog, always-on-the-side-of-the-victim, wisecracking hero of *From Here to Eternity*. "Unless a man goes his own way, he ain't nuthin'," he might have been speaking for the Sinatra we loved, the Sinatra who had been written off in 1950 as a failure. In the fifties, failures, if they were flamboyant enough, endeared themselves to us; it was almost a mark of virtue to fail spectacularly, it meant that all the Insiders were against you. The crooner-idol of the forties, his marriage to Ava Gardner a disaster, his life a seemingly endless series of sullen set-tos with journalists, his career a whimper, was nothing if not a spectacular failure. (He had been reduced to the indignity of recording something called "Mama Will Bark" with dumb, busty Dagmar; poor thing, he growled and barked because Mitch Miller, Columbia's A and R man, thought novelty records sold.) When Sinatra once again achieved success—and with such showy grit—his past failures lent piquancy to his victory. What we loved was not so much his success as his persistence. What we admired in him was his rash, solitary courage. He has—this was the pre-*Godfather* myth—done it alone. To do it alone was the great thing.

That, surely, was the message we had drawn from Salinger and from Camus—the message that man had to carry the weight of his life alone. On the surface, the French existentialist author of *The Myth of Sisyphus* and *The Rebel* and the reclusive American ecstatic who wrote *Franny and Zooey* and *Catcher in the Rye* seem to be writers with vastly different sensibilities. Salinger had chosen, as it were, *against* the world: His characters' Christ-Zen-Vedanta, Kingdom-of-God-Is-Within mysticism transformed everyday occurrences into something holy. Camus, believing that death renders life

123

absurd, *accepted* the world in all its splendor and its futility. From both writers we imbibed the romance of the lonely struggle. (We learned to look for the marks of that struggle in our men.) Salinger wrote with an effervescent, painful ecstasy; it often seemed as if he were writing with his eyeballs, certainly with all his nerve endings exposed. It was his genius to appear to write, just as Sinatra appears to sing, to each of us alone. Camus wrote out of lucid despair. Both, in an ordered delirium, invited us to be both passionate and detached—or to value those qualities in our men. Salinger's poet-suicide hero, Seymour Glass (one of seven Glass siblings, all of whom we invariably preferred to our own prosaic brothers and sisters), says that his favorite word in the Bible is *watch*! Camus said that the hallmark of the absurd man is anguished awareness. It comes to the same thing. Both Camus and Salinger told us to drain life to its bitter end. And both men propelled us to the purest of joys—to feeling as opposed to thinking.

Camus said "a subclerk in the post office is the equal of a conqueror if consciousness is common to them"; Salinger said that the Fat Lady sitting on her porch in the unendurable heat, swatting flies, cancer eating at her insides, was Jesus Christ. Where one registered *God*, the other registered *human*; for both, everything was hallowed by one's awareness of it. They both inclined us to regard pain as a sacrament. (No wonder they used *terrible* and *beautiful* in the same sentence all the time.) Knowing, or feeling, that there were no victorious causes, both loved lost causes, causes that required "uncontaminated souls." Both conveyed the message that the discipline of awareness led, inevitably, to creation; poets and artists were the true see-ers, the only seers. Both seemed to be living on the dangerous edge of the world . . . And we said, "Whoopee! We'll go live there, too."

So we did. We went looking for terrible beauty and beautiful pain, in search of holy fools and noble absurd men.

And if, in our coffeeshops and bars and jazz clubs, we found, not poets and artists but dilettantes and poseurs, men who managed to be thoroughly absurd in the vulgar sense—that is, silly—without being at all noble, we did find plenty of lost causes. We found men, that is, who spoke the language of despair and the language of ecstasy, and we took them to our bosoms and our beds.

It is only on rereading Salinger and Camus that I realize how necessary women were to them as foils. Preferably long-legged, cool, innocent young women with undiscriminating hearts. Neither of our literary idols was a macho writer in the way that, say, Mailer is a macho writer, but both insisted upon the unspoiled beauty of women, to set off their ideal man's saintliness or heroism. Women were there to mediate between them and

124

the harsh world, to console. Mostly women were just there, like the ocean and the sky, to provide backdrops for their essential deeds. Men were the inspired lunatics, the lovers, the poets, and the anguished see-ers. Women held men to the things of the world—that was their value. Adorable in their sweet simplicity, women brought cups of consecrated chicken soup to sufferers. We could accept any damned nonsense from a man, provided it was haloed by poetic *feeling*. If our men were struggling and in pain—not to put too fine a point on it, if they were losers—we brought them cups of consecrated chicken soup.

It grieves me, it really does, to understand what we extrapolated from both Salinger and Camus was the message, perhaps unintended, that we were meant to be handmaidens to the gods. To the God-in-men. Camus regarded Don Juan as a great wise man who lives bravely without illusions of eternal love, a man for whom loving and possessing, conquering and consuming, were ways of knowing, means of provoking a nonexistent God. What good and earnest pupils we were! We invested every fast-talking faithless womanizer we knew with noble qualities. We lived to be loved, possessed, conquered, and consumed.

Once I sat on Frank Sinatra's lap. It was when I was living with a jazz musician. We'd left Birdland, it was three o'clock in the morning, and a voice—The Voice—hailed us from a cab. We piled in with alacrity. (Sinatra was, by the way, one of the few white musicians who had a good press among black musicians, most of whom insisted that white musicians couldn't swing because they didn't have soul—which is to say they hadn't suffered enough. White musicians were relatively low in the hierarchy of sufferers.) On the way to a Harlem after-hours club, I sat perched on Sinatra's bony knees, occasionally turning, heart in my mouth, to gaze. Though he was holding me, I felt as if I were holding something priceless and fragile, like a Greek urn. A small epiphany.

There were many such epiphanies—life was never boring—not all of them on a man's knees, most of them on a man's coattails. When I look back at my life, and my friends' lives, in the fifties, it seems to me we were always trying lives on. Another man, another life.

A devoted practitioner of serial monogamy, I went from man to man, believing each time, of course, that this was the only man, that all other loves had been delusions. Each time, not only did I take on the man, I acquired a whole new life (his), a new way of being.

When I lived with my musician, I became thoroughly immersed in the jazz world, and had, it must be said, faint scorn for anyone not privileged enough to be joined to that world of sufferers. It has been suggested that

125

we were the first groupies. Naturally, pleading True Love, I shrink from that label; but I see the point. At the time, I shared the musicians' contempt of female hangers-on who would attach themselves to any musician at all (not that their contempt precluded their availing themselves of the girls' services); I was in love with one musician, not the entire genre. Looking back, though, I can't be absolutely sure that I wasn't in love with the whole genre. G., my musician, was wonderfully appealing; he was witty, wry, self-ish, bitter, self-mocking, poor, married, a libertine who demanded total commitment from his women, a good and generous lover (when he was there). A perfect person with whom to break all the rules. His world was magic. I was literally transported to a hot, intense world where men took enormous risks, played their hearts out, blew their minds on drugs (at a time when marijuana was still called the Devil's weed), flirted with death, and lived permanently on the razor's edge of poverty. They were the inner circle of the Outsiders. Our proximity to them guaranteed us a place in that privileged circle. Our world was celebrated by the Beat poets; Paris had its existential chanteuses, we had the real thing, we lived next to the real cry of the heart. But I'm terribly afraid that, while those men used women to sustain them (both sexually and financially), we played our part in this dicey game. We objectified them by loving their suffering better than we loved them. The truth was, most jazz musicians wanted with all their hearts to become safe studio musicians and to live on Park Avenue with German maids. It was we, their romantic camp followers, who thought the secular equivalent of the Holy Grail could be found at the Five Spot or Mintons or Birdland, we who thought their poverty was a mark of their noble not-belonging. Told to drain life to its dregs, where better could we do it than in smoky clubs, illegal after-hours joints, with wounded men who had lovers in others towns? Everything in that world gratified our hunger for experience, it was like being plunged into pure feeling unsullied by thought. We were chained to men we regarded, not without reason, as rebels and mar-tyrs. The fact that these rebels and martyrs burned us up in the furnace of their own needs made everything all the more dangerous, hence all the more exciting.

The world was full of joy—those men were, after all, true creators, and they laughed a lot. But it was never really happy. To live exhilaratingly in and for the moment is deadly serious work, fun of the most exhausting sort. As Dorothy Parker once remarked, you can say *Live and laugh and love and lie . . . for tomorrow you must die* all you want, the sad truth is you don't die, you wake up with a hangover.

We were suckers for saints in the fifties, lovers of unsuccess. But there was one man who was a success, and still—restless and dissatisfied—out of synch with his time, a permanent Outsider, a man who stuck his tongue out at "them," even though, as Truman Capote said, he was "a young man sitting on a pile of candy."

There is a story that circulated about Marlon Brando. When he was quite little, his pet dog died. A neighbor lady attempted, with treacly sympathy, to console him. Brando looked her in the eye, said, "There's a bee on your nose," and punched her.

Brando despised Hollywood. Or so he said. We believed him. He sneered and sulked, he had all the fifties words: He questioned the point of being an actor if you didn't *evolve*; he wanted a life that *led* somewhere; endlessly introspective, he publicly doubted his ability to *love* or *relate* to anybody. It seems banal now, his Peck's-bad-boy/Yoga routine (more than one journalist interviewed him while he was standing on his head); it was potent then, potent enough for him to have been plagiarized by a generation of actors. Whether the stories were apocryphal or not, they struck a resounding chord. He'd flirted with the ministry, gone to military prep school, and, according to one story, gotten himself expelled for pissing on the floor of the math room. Marlon may have invented himself as he went along, to confound journalists, but whether or not he told the strict truth was beside the point; he was Hollywood's angry young man. There isn't a single story about him written in the fifties that doesn't have the word *vulnerable* in it, and very few that don't speak of his "terrible honesty." He said, to Capote: "Sensitive people are so vulnerable; they're so easily brutalized and hurt because they *are* sensitive." He was called the Valentino of the Bop generation. But we loved him because he kept impatiently shaking the stardust off. He was real, like the men we loved in real life, only more so. He was—it's an embarrassing word, but we used it then—authentic. Already in the fifties he was talking about making serious movies that dealt with "prejudice and hatred and discrimination." While his lofty stated aims seemed at times to be at odds with his behavior—he was making *Teahouse of the August Moon* and *Sayonara* while he was decrying Hollywood potboilers—if he didn't exactly bite the commercial hand that fed him, he snarled at it a lot, and that was enough to make us love him. We forgave him anything. Not least because of that world-stopping smile.

It's odd that, while he never stopped explaining himself, he seemed also to resist all attempts to enter his privacy. You always got the feeling that if you overstepped your bounds, he'd punch you in the nose. He was the Lonely Struggler incarnate.

His powerful screen persona (Elia Kazan called him the best actor in

127

the world) combined with his powerful offscreen persona to make him the paradigm of the fifties man: Uncouth and dignified, sensitive and rebellious, he was the poet-buried-in-the-animal. I'm willing to take bets that there isn't one woman in a thousand who saw *Streetcar* who didn't prefer Stanley Kowalski to Karl Malden's more sympathetic Mitch; there was poetry, as well as Method, in his savagery. Even at his most terrifyingly pugnacious—in *The Wild One*, for example—he was lyrical, and, he made you feel, redeemable.

Let's face it, there was something more than a little effete about the coffeehouse intellectuals who talked and talked and talked about life and death and God and happiness; they could make you long for a little healthy brutality. And as gorgeous as the physical, nonverbal world of the jazz clubs was, it was also ultimately stifling; in the fifties, we needed words for salvation, and that world had a limited vocabulary. With beautiful, brainy, muscled Brando, you got it all—Zen and Freud, talk and action, sex and sensibility, passion and detachment and romance. He was a tender man with authority, and he was irresistible.

Brando's beauty is ravaged now. And we've all moved on to other things. More or less. Some of us have gone in the direction Camus led us in: We've understood that in a world where there are victims and victimizers, we are obliged to take our stand with the victims. We have, that is to say, become political. Others have retreated into a Salingeresque privacy, hoping by that means to wash their hands of nonessentials. The most interesting problem for people of my age—people who grew up in the fifties—remains how to unite the personal and the political, how to be in the world and of it, but not to be bent out of shape by it.

As for the women I grew up with, a lot of them are still, with scant success, looking for the absurd man, the authentic man, the poet-in-the-animal. We're still carrying around those invisible cups of chicken soup.

I'm a (closet) Sinatra fan. Still. In spite of. (Fifties women are incredibly loyal: they don't forget.) I still think Brando is the best actor in the world. (I wish he wouldn't talk about Indians so much; I wish he'd smile more.)

They gave us a lot of grief, one way or another, our holy men and heroes. Still—this may just be nostalgia speaking, but I don't think so—if you have to have heroes at all, ours weren't all that bad. Tell, whom would you prefer: Sinatra-Brando-Salinger-Camus? Or Abby-Jerry-Rennie-Tom? I don't think there's any contest.

EXCERPTS FROM THE *MELBOURNE HERALD*,
Melbourne, Australia, January 1975

. . . the rudeness this entertainer displays in public should not be published. Reported filthy statements from the concert hall about the press (male and female) mark this aged crooner as a very poor ambassador for his country. . . .

. . . if Mr. Sinatra were 50 years younger, a good mouthwash with soap and a strong detergent would be advisable. As a public figure, Mr. Sinatra should represent his country as best he can. . . .

. . . while Mr. Sinatra's intemperate language cannot be condoned, nor yet the violence of his bodyguard, the blame for the recent unfortunate happenings at the Southern Cross must rest on the provocative actions of those TV reporters, whose behavior was disgraceful and no credit to the media. . . .

. . . I find it appalling that members of the press have the gall and the license to harass and persecute an artist of world standing such as Frank Sinatra. This man came out here to sing and entertain, and what right has the press to deprive the people of Australia the chance, possibly the last one ever, to see this great artist. . . .

. . . can we lower the curtain on this subject now. . . .

The Eighties:
OL' BLUE EYES

SINATRA: THE LEGEND LIVES
by Pete Hamill from *New York* magazine, April 1980

I. IN THE WEE SMALL HOURS

*O*ne rainy evening in the winter of 1974, I was home alone when the telephone rang. I picked up the receiver, looking out at the wet street, and heard one of the most familiar voices of the century.

It was Frank Sinatra.

"What are you doing?"

"Reading a book," I said.

"Read it tomorrow. We're at Jilly's. Come on over."

He hung up. I put the book down. I didn't know Sinatra well, but despite the rotten things I'd read about him, I liked him a lot and was sometimes touched by him. We'd met through Shirley MacLaine, who went back a long time with Sinatra. In 1958 Sinatra put her in *Some Came Running*, expanded her part to fit her talents, and made her a movie star. When they occasionally met, it was clear to me that Sinatra admired her relentless honesty, loved her in some complicated way, and was, like me, a little afraid of her.

I took a cab to Jilly's, a seedy time warp of a saloon at the Eighth Avenue end of Fifty-second Street. The long, dark bar was packed with the junior varsity of the mob; of all the Sinatra groupies, they were the most laughable. They were planted at the bar like blue-haired statues, gulping Jack Daniel's, occasionally glancing into the back room. A maître d' in a shiny tuxedo stood beside a red velvet rope that separated the back room from the Junior Apalachin conference at the bar.

"Yes, sir?" the maître d' said.

"Mr. Sinatra," I said. "He's expecting me."

He turned nervously, his eyes moving past the empty tables at the booths in the left-hand corner against the wall. Jilly Rizzo looked up from a booth and nodded, and I was let through. "Eh, Petey babe," Jilly said, coming around a table with his right hand out. Jilly has one glass eye, which gives him a perpetually blurry look. "Hey, Frank," he said, "look who's here."

"Hey, Peter, grab a seat!" Sinatra said brightly, half rising from the booth and shaking hands. He moves clumsily, a newly heavy man who hadn't learned yet to carry the extra weight with grace; he seemed swollen, rather than sleek. But the Sinatra face was—and is—an extraordinary assemblage. He has never been conventionally handsome: There are no clean planes, too many knobs of bone, scars from the forceps delivery he endured at birth. But the smile is open, easy, insouciant. And his blue eyes are the true focal point of the face. In the brief time I'd known him, I'd seen the eyes so disarmingly open that you felt you could peer all the way through them into every secret recess of the man; at other times they were cloudy with indifference, and when chilled by anger or resentment, they could become as opaque as cold-rolled steel.

"You eat yet?" he asked. "Well, then have a drink."

As always, there was a group with him, squashed into the worn Leatherette booths or on chairs against the tables. They had the back room to themselves and were eating chop suey and watching a Jets game on a TV set. Sinatra introduced Pat Henry, the comic who sometimes opens for him; Roone Arledge of ABC; Don Costa, one of Sinatra's favorite arrangers; a few other men; and some young women. Sinatra was with a thin blonde model in a black dress. He didn't introduce her.

The conversation stopped for the introductions, then started again. Sinatra leaned over, his eyes shifting to the TV screen, where Joe Namath was being shoved around.

"I don't get this team," he said. "They got the best arm in football and they won't give him any protection. Ah, *shit*!" Namath was on his back and getting up very slowly. "Oh, man. That ain't *right*!"

They cut to a commercial, and Sinatra lit a Marlboro and sipped a vodka. His eyes drifted to the bar. "Jesus, there's about 43 indictments right at the bar," he said loudly.

"Present company excluded," Pat Henry said, and everybody laughed.

"It better be," Sinatra said, and they all laughed again. The blonde smiled in a chilly way. The game was back on again, and Sinatra stared at the TV set but wasn't really watching the game. Then the game ended, and Jilly switched off the set. There was more talk and more drinking, and slowly the others began to leave.

"Hell, let's go," Sinatra said. He said something to Jilly, and then he and the blonde and I walked out. A photographer and a middle-aged autograph freak were waiting under the tattered awning.

"Do you mind, Mr. Sinatra?" the photographer asked.

"No, go ahead," he said. The flashbulbs popped. The blonde smiled. So did Sinatra. "Thanks for asking."

Then he signed the woman's autograph book. She had skin like grimy ivory, and sad brown eyes. "Thanks, dear," Sinatra said. We all got into the waiting limousine and drove down the rainy street, heading east.

"What do you think they do with those autographs?" he said. "Sell them? To who? Trade them? For *what*? How does it go? Two Elvis Presleys for one Frank Sinatra? Two Frank Sinatras for one Paul McCartney? I don't get it. I never did."

We drove awhile in silence. Then the chauffeur turned right on a street in the Sixties and pulled over to the curb. Sinatra and the blonde got out. He took her into the brightly lit vestibule. He waited for her to find a key, tapped her lightly on the elbow, and came back into the limo.

"You have to go home?"

"No."

He leaned forward to the driver. "Just drive around awhile."

"Yes, sir."

And so for more than an hour, on this rainy night in New York, we drove around the empty streets. Sinatra talked about Lennon and McCartney as songwriters ("That 'Yesterday' is the best song written in 30 years") and George Harrison ("His 'Something' is a beauty"), prizefighters ("Sugar Ray was the best I ever saw") and writers ("Murray Kempton is the best, isn't he? And I always loved Jimmy Cannon.") It wasn't an interview; Frank Sinatra just wanted to talk, in a city far from the bright scorched exile of Palm Springs.

"It's sure changed, this town," he said. "When I first came across that river, this was the greatest city in the whole goddamned world. It was like a big, beautiful lady. It's like a busted-down hooker now."

"Ah, well," I said. "Babe Ruth doesn't play for the Yankees anymore."

"And the Paramount's an office building," he said. "Stop. I'm gonna cry."

He laughed and settled back. We were crossing 96th Street now, heading for the park.

"You think some people are smart, and they turn out dumb," Sinatra was saying. "You think they're straight, they turn out crooked." This was, of course, the Watergate winter; the year before, Sinatra sat in an honored place at the second inauguration of Richard Nixon. "You like people, and they die on you. I go to too many goddamned funerals these days. And women," he said, exhaling, and chuckling again, "I don't know what the hell to make of them. Do you?"

"Every day I know less," I said.

"Maybe that's what it's all about," he said. "Maybe all that happens is you get older and you know less."

After a while, the limousine pulled up in front of the Waldorf, where Sinatra has an apartment. He told the driver to take me home.

"Stay in touch," he said, and got out, walking fast, his head down, his step jaunty, his hands deep in the pockets of his coat. I remember thinking that it was a desperately lonely life for a man who was a legend.

II. THE DARK LEGEND

At 64, Francis Albert Sinatra is one of that handful of Americans whose deaths would certainly unleash a river of tearful prose and much genuine grief. He has worked at his trade for almost half a century and goes on as if nothing at all had changed. He is currently in New York making his first feature film in ten years, *The First Deadly Sin*. His first new studio album in five years is in the record stores, a three-record set called *Trilogy*, and despite one astonishing lapse in taste (a self-aggrandizing "musical fantasy" written by banality master Gordon Jenkins), it reveals that what Sinatra called "my reed" is in better shape than it had been in since the 1960s. In concert halls and casinos he packs in the fans, and the intensity of their embrace remains scary. But his work and its public acceptance are now almost incidental to his stature. Frank Sinatra, from Hoboken, New Jersey, has forced his presence into American social history; when the story of how Americans in this century played, dreamed, hoped and loved is told, Frank Sinatra cannot be left out. He is more than a mere singer or actor. He is a legend. And the legend lives.

The legend has its own symmetries. Sinatra can be unbelievably generous and brutally vicious. He can display the grace and manners of a cultured man and turn suddenly into a vulgar two-bit comic. He can offer George Raft a blank check "up to one million dollars" to pay taxes owed to the IRS; he can then rage against one of his most important boosters, WNEW disc jockey Jonathan Schwartz, and help force him off the air. In his time, he has been a loyal Democrat and a shill for Richard Nixon; a defender of underdogs everywhere and then a spokesman for the Establishment; a man who fought racism in the music business and then became capable of tasteless jokes ("The Polacks are deboning the colored people," he said on the stage of Caesars Palace in 1974, "and using them for wet suits.") He has given magical performances and shoddy ones. He has treated women with elegance, sensitivity and charm, and then, in Lauren Bacall's phrase, "dropped the curtain" on them in the most callous way. He acts like royalty and is frequently treated that way, but he also comes on too often like a cheap hood. He is a good guy-bad guy, tough-tender, Jekyll-Hyde.

"Being an eighteen-karat manic-depressive," Sinatra said once, "I have an over acute capacity for sadness as well as elation."

Over the years, those wildly fluctuating emotions became a basic component of the Sinatra legend—accepted, even demanded by his audience. The audience is now largely Eastern, urban, and aging, with New York at the heart of the myth. The hard-core fans are Depression kids who matured in World War II, or part of the fifties generation who saw him as a role model. In some critical way, Sinatra validates their lives—as *individuals*. He sings *to* them, and *for* them, one at a time. These Americans were transformed by the Depression and the war into unwilling members of groups— "the masses" or "the poor" or "the infantry"—and their popular music was dominated by the big bands. Sinatra was the first star to step out of the tightly controlled ensembles of the white swing bands to work on his own. Yes, he was 4-F (punctured eardrum), but the overwhelming majority of Americans experienced World War II at home, and the 1940s Sinatra was a reminder that Americans were single human beings, not just the masses, the poor, or the infantry. Later, in the 1960s, when crowds once again shoved individuals off the stage of history, he was submerged by musical groups like the Beatles and Rolling Stones and in 1971 even went into a brief retirement. He came back later in the decade, when individual values were again dominant.

"I've seen them come and go, but Frank is still the king," a New Jersey grandmother said at one of Sinatra's weekend performances at Resorts International in Atlantic City. "He just goes on and on, and he's wonderful."

Indeed, Sinatra's endurance has become a rallying point for many people who feel that their sacrifices and hard work are no longer honored, their values demeaned, their musical tastes ignored and sneered at. They don't care that Sinatra moved from the New Deal to Ronald Reagan; many of them did the same thing, for the same basic reason: resentment at being ignored by the Democratic party. They had overcome poverty and survived two wars; they had educated their children and given them better lives; and sometimes even their children didn't care. But it should never be forgotten

137

that Frank Sinatra was the original working-class hero. Mick Jagger's fans bought records with their allowances; Sinatra's people bought them out of wages.

"There's just not enough of Frank's people around anymore to make him a monster record seller," says one Warner Communications executive. "Sinatra is a star. But he's not Fleetwood Mac. He's not Pink Floyd."

Sinatra has never been a big single seller (one gold record—more than a million sales—to twenty for the Beatles), but his albums continue to sell steadily. One reason: most radio stations don't play Sinatra, so that younger listeners never get to hear him and go on to buy his records. In New York, only WNEW-AM and WYNY-FM play Sinatra with any frequency. As a movie star, he had faded badly before vanishing completely with the lamentable *Dirty Dingus Magee* in 1970. Part of this could be blamed directly on Sinatra, because his insistence on one or two takes had led to careless, even shoddy productions. On his own, he was also not a strong TV performer; he needed Elvis Presley, or Bing Crosby, to get big ratings. Yet Sinatra remains a major star in the minds of most Americans, even those who despise him.

"What Sinatra has is beyond talent," director Billy Wilder once said. "It's some sort of magnetism that goes in higher revolutions than that of anybody else, anybody in the whole of show business. Wherever Frank is, there is a certain electricity permeating the air. It's like Mack the Knife is in town and the action is starting."

That electricity was in the air of Jilly's that night in 1974. But its effect was not restricted to a platoon of gumbahs. The other night, Sinatra came into Elaine's with his wife, Barbara, and another couple. It was after midnight, and Sinatra stayed for a couple of hours, drinking and talking and smoking cigarettes.

I was with some friends at another table. They were people who are good at their jobs and have seen much of the world. But their own natural styles were subtly altered by the addition of Sinatra to the room. They stole glances at him. They were aware that Sinatra's blue eyes were also checking out the room, and unconsciously they began to gesture too much, playing too hard at being casual, or clarifying themselves in a theatrical way. Somewhere underneath all of this, I'm sure, was the desire to want Frank Sinatra to like them.

I know how that worked, because I'd felt those emotions myself. When I first met Sinatra, I was bumping up against one of the crucial legends of my youth, and sure, I wanted him to like me. Growing up in Brooklyn in

138

the forties and fifties, it was impossible to avoid the figure of Frank Sinatra. He was armored with the tough-guy swagger of the streets, but in the songs he allowed room for tenderness, the sense of loss and abandonment, the acknowledgment of pain. Most of us felt that we had nothing to learn from cowboys or Cary Grant (we were wrong, of course). But thousands of us appropriated the pose of the Tender Tough Guy from Sinatra. We've out-grown a lot of things, but there are elements of that in all of us to this day, and when we see Sinatra perform, or listen to the records at night, the pose regains all of its old dangerous glamour.

And make no mistake: Danger is at the heart of the legend. At his best, Sinatra is an immensely gifted musical talent, admired by many jazz musicians. He is not a jazz singer, but he comes from the tradition. As a young band vocalist, he learned breath control from trombonist Tommy Dorsey; after work, he studied other singers, among them Louis Arm-strong, Lee Wiley, Mabel Mercer, and another performer who became a legend.

"It is Billie Holiday, whom I first heard in 52nd Street clubs in the early '30s, who was and still remains the greatest single musical influence on me," he wrote once, later telling *Daily News* columnist Kay Gardella that Lady Day taught him "matters of shading, phrasing, dark tones, light tones and bending notes." And in the saloons of the time, the young Sinatra learned a great secret of the trade: "The microphone is the singer's basic instrument, not the voice. You have to learn to play it like a saxophone." As he matured, Sinatra developed a unique white-blues style, supple enough to express the range of his own turbulent emotions. And like the great jazz artists, he took the banal tunes of Tin Pan Alley and transformed them into something personal by the sincerity of his performance; Sinatra actually seemed to *believe* the words he was singing. But Billy Wilder is correct: The Sinatra aura goes beyond talent and craft. He is not simply a fine popular singer. He emanated power and danger. And the reason is simple: You think he is tangled up with the mob.

"Some things I can't ever talk about," he said to me once, when we were discussing the mandatory contents of his book. He laughed and added, "Someone might come knockin' at my f—— door."

Sinatra is now writing that autobiography and preparing a film about his own life. Alas, neither form seems adequate to the full story; autobi-ographies are by definition only part of the story, the instinct being to prepare a brief for the defense and give yourself the best lines. And a two-hour movie can only skim the surface of a life that has gone on for six decades. Faulkner says somewhere that the best stories are the ones we are most thoroughly ashamed of; it could be that the best movies are the ones that can't be photographed. No, Sinatra deserves a novel.

The novelist, some combination of Balzac and Raymond Chandler, would recognize Sinatra as one of those rare public men to actually cast a shadow. The shadow is the mob, and who can tell what came first, the shadow or the act? A conventional autobiography will talk about the wives: Nancy Barbato, Ava Gardner, Mia Farrow, and Barbara Marx, one for each adult decade. It might mention, discreetly, all the other love affairs, passionate or glancing: Lana Turner, Juliet Prowse, Lauren Bacall, Kim Novak, Jill St. John, Lady Adele Beatty, Dorothy Provine, and the anonymous brigade of starlets, secretaries, models, stewardesses, and girls from the old neighborhood.

"I loved them all," Sinatra says now, smiling ruefully, reminding you that he is now a grandfather and all of that was long ago. "I really did."

But the novelist can come closer to the elusive truth than an autobiographer as courtly as Sinatra will ever allow himself to do. Both would deal with the public career, the rise, fall, rise again of Frank Sinatra. We can see the high school dropout watching Bing Crosby sing from the stage of Loew's Journal Square in Jersey City in 1933, vowing to become a singer. We can follow him, one of Balzac's provincial heroes, as he wins an amateur contest and crosses the river to appear for the first time on a New York stage at the Academy of Music (now the Palladium) on 14th Street the following year. The hero then sings with a group called the Hoboken Four on the *Major Bowes Amateur Hour* in 1935, plays local clubs, begs in the hallways of WNEW for the chance to sing for nothing on live remotes. And of course there will be the familiar story of the job at the Rustic Cabin on Route 9W in 1939, and how Harry James heard him late one night and gave him a job in the big time. And then how Sinatra went to work for Tommy Dorsey and played the Paramount and became a star.

And because this is a story with a hero, it must tell the story of The Fall. The hero hurtles into love with Ava Gardner, and his career becomes a shambles: He loses his voice, his wife, his children; he gets into public fights; he wins the love goddess; he loses her; he hits bottom. And then there is The Great Comeback: He pleads for the part of Maggio in *From Here to Eternity*, is paid $8,000, gives a stunning performance, wins the Academy Award, and comes all the way back. He leaves Columbia Records for Capitol, then starts his own company, Reprise, and makes his greatest records. At the same time he consolidates his power in Hollywood, investing his money brilliantly, producing his own films, using power with the instincts of a great politician. These are the years of the private jets, the meetings of the Clan on the stages of Las Vegas, the friendships with Jack Kennedy and other politicians, and the house at the top of Mulholland Drive, where the wounded hero heals his ruined heart with girls and whiskey and friends. It's a good story. A sentimental education or a cautionary tale.

But as autobiography it is not enough. We must have some understanding of the shadows. In *The Godfather* Mario Puzo used some of the elements in the singer he called Johnny Fontaine; other novels have used Sinatra-like figures in various ways; yet no fictional account has truly defined the man in all of his complexity. We only know that the mob runs through his story like an underground river. He is the most investigated American performer since John Wilkes Booth, and although he has never been indicted or convicted of any mob-connected crime, the connection is part of the legend. And to some extent, Sinatra exploits it. His opening acts feature comedians who tell jokes about Sinatra's sinister friendships; if you cross Frank, the jokes say, you could end up on a meat hook in a garage. In some circumstances Sinatra laughs at the implications; other times, he explodes into dark furies, accusing his accusers of slander and ethnic racism.

"If my name didn't end with a vowel," he said to me once, "I wouldn't have had all this trouble."

But the facts indicate that he did know some shady people. He was friendly with Jersey hoodlum Willie Moretti until the syphilitic gangster was shot to death. He was friendly with Joseph "Joe Fisher" Fischetti, traveled with him to Havana in 1947, where he spent time with Lucky Luciano. A nineteen-page Justice Department memorandum prepared in 1962 said that its surveillance placed Sinatra in contact with about ten of the country's top hoodlums. Some had Sinatra's unlisted number. He did favors for others.

"I was brought up to shake a man's hand when I am introduced to him, without first investigating his past," Sinatra said huffily during the Luciano uproar. The same could be said about the scandal over the photograph taken a few years ago with mob boss Carlo Gambino, backstage at the Westchester Premier Theater.

"Did I know those guys?" he said to me once. "Sure, I knew some of those guys. I spent a lot of time working in saloons. And saloons are not run by the Christian Brothers. There were a lot of guys around, and they came out of Prohibition, and they ran pretty good saloons. I was a kid. I worked in the places that were open. They paid you, and the checks didn't bounce. I didn't meet any Nobel prize winners in saloons. But if Francis of Assisi was a singer and worked in saloons, he would've met the same

141

guys. That doesn't make him part of something. They said hello, you said hello. They came backstage. They thanked you. You offered them a drink. That was it."

He paused. "And it doesn't matter any more, does it? Most of the guys I knew, or met, are dead."

One of them was Salvatore Giancana, sometimes known as Momo, or Mooney. A graduate of Joliet prison, he ducked World War II by doing a crazy act for the draft board, which labeled him "a constitutional psychopath." He rose through the wartime rackets to the leadership of the Chicago mob in the 1950s. During that period he and Sinatra became friends and were seen in various places together. The star-struck Momo later began a long love affair with singer Phyllis McGuire, and the friendship deepened. In 1962 Sinatra, Dean Martin and Sammy Davis played a special engagement at a Giancana joint called the Villa Venice, northwest of Chicago. When the FBI questioned the performers, Sinatra said he did it for a boyhood friend named Leo Olsen, who fronted the place for Momo. Sammy Davis was more to the point.

"Baby, let me say this," he told an FBI man. "I got one eye, and that one eye sees a lot of things that my brain tells me I shouldn't talk about. Because my brain says that if I do, my one eye might not be seeing *anything* after a while."

Sinatra's friendship with Sam Giancana was most severely tested in 1963, when the Nevada Gaming Control Board charged that the Chicago hoodlum had been a week-long guest at Sinatra's Cal-Neva Lodge in Lake Tahoe. His mere presence was enough to revoke the casino's gambling license, and Sinatra first said he would fight the charge. When Edward A. Olsen, then chairman of the gambling board, said that he didn't want to talk to Sinatra until he subpoenaed him, Olsen claims Sinatra shouted over the phone, "You subpoena me and you're going to get a big, fat, f——— surprise."

But when the crunch came two weeks later, Sinatra chose not to fight the revocation order. Apparently his friendship with Giancana was more important than his investment in Nevada, and he sold his interests for $3.5 million. In 1975 Giancana was shot to death in the basement of his Chicago home. Phyllis McGuire went to the funeral, but Sinatra didn't. Sinatra is again trying to get a gambling license in Nevada.

"It's ridiculous to think Sinatra's in the mob," said one New Yorker who has watched gangsters collect around Sinatra for more than 30 years. "He's too visible. He's too hot. But he likes them. He thinks they're funny.

142

In some ways he admires them. For him it's like they were characters in some movie."

That might be the key. Some people who know Sinatra believe that his attraction to gangsters—and their attraction to him—is sheer romanticism. The year that Sinatra was fifteen, Hollywood released W. R. Burnett's *Little Caesar*; more than 50 gangster films followed in the next eighteen months. And their view of gangsters was decidedly romantic. The hoodlums weren't cretins peddling heroin to children; they were Robin Hoods defying the unjust laws of Prohibition. Robert Wardshow defined the type in his essay "The Gangster as Tragic Hero":

> *The gangster is the man of the city, with the city's language and knowledge, with its queer and dishonest skills and its terrible daring, carrying his life in his hands like a placard, like a club. For everyone else, there is at least the theoretical possibility of another world—in that happier American culture which the gangster denies, the city does not really exist; it is only a more crowded and brightly lit country—but for the gangster there is only the city; he must inhabit it in order to personify it; not the real city, but that dangerous and sad city of the imagination which is so much more important, which is the modern world.*

143

That is almost a perfect description of Frank Sinatra, who still carries his life in his hands like a placard, or like a club. His novel might be a very simple one indeed: a symmetrical story about life imitating art.

III. THE PARTING GLASS

My son is like me. You cross him, he never forgets. —Dolly Sinatra

Somewhere deep within Frank Sinatra, there must still exist a scared little boy. He is standing alone on a street in Hoboken. His parents are nowhere to be seen. His father, Anthony Martin, is probably at the bar he runs when he is not working for the fire department; the father is a blue-eyed Sicilian, close-mouthed, passive, and, in his own way, tough. He once boxed as "Marty O'Brien" in the years when the Irish ran northern New Jersey. The boy's mother, Natalie, is not around either. The neighbors call her Dolly, and she sometimes works at the bar, which was bought with a loan from her mother, Rosa Garaventi, who runs a grocery store. Dolly Sinatra is also a Democratic ward leader. She has places to go, duties to perform, favors to deny or dispense. She has little time for traditional maternal duties. And besides, she didn't want a boy anyway.

"I wanted a girl and bought a lot of pink clothes," she once said. "When Frank was born, I didn't care. I dressed him in pink anyway. Later, I got my mother to make him Lord Fauntleroy suits."

Did the other kids laugh at the boy in the Lord Fauntleroy suits? Probably. It was a tough, working-class neighborhood. Working-class. Not poor. His mother, born in Genoa, raised in Hoboken, believed in work and education. When she wasn't around, the boy was taken care of by his grandmother Garaventi, or by Mrs. Goldberg, who lived on the block. "I'll never forget that kid," a neighbor said, "leaning against his grandmother's front door, staring into space. . . ."

Later the press agents would try to pass him off as a slum kid. Perhaps the most important thing to know about him is that he was an only child. Of Italian parents. And they spoiled him. From the beginning, the only child had money. He had a charge account at a local department store and a wardrobe so fancy that his friends called him "Slacksey." He had a secondhand car at fifteen. And in the depths of the Depression, after dropping out of high school, he had the ultimate luxury: a job unloading trucks at the *Jersey Observer*.

Such things were not enough; the boy also had fancy dreams. And the parents didn't approve. When he told his mother that he wanted to be a singer, she threw a shoe at him. "In your teens," he said later, "there's always someone to spit on your dreams." Still, the only child got what he wanted; eventually his mother bought him a $65 portable public-address system, complete with loudspeaker and microphone. She thus gave him his musical instrument and his life.

She also gave him some of her values. At home she dominated his father, in the streets she dominated the neighborhood through the uses of Democratic patronage. From adolescence on, Sinatra understood patronage. He could give his friends clothes, passes to Palisades Park, rides in his car, and they could give him friendship and loyalty. Power was all. And that insight lifted him above so many other talented performers of his generation. Vic Damone might have better pipes, Tony Bennett a more certain musical taste, but Sinatra had power.

Power attracts and repels; it functions as aphrodisiac and blackjack. Men of power recognize it in others; Sinatra has spent time with Franklin Roosevelt, Adlai Stevenson, Jack Kennedy, Richard Nixon, Walter Annenberg, Hugh Carey, Ronald Reagan; all wanted his approval, and he wanted, and obtained, theirs. He could raise millions for them at fund raisers; they would always take his calls. And the politicians had a lot of company. On the stage at Caesars Palace, or at an elegant East Side dinner party, Sinatra emanates power. Certainly the dark side of the legend accounts for some of that effect; the myth of the Mafia, after all, is not a myth of evil, but a myth of power.

But talent is essential, too. During the period of The Fall, when he had lost his voice, he panicked; he could accept anything except impotence. Without power he is returned to Monroe Street in Hoboken, a scared kid. That kid wants to be accepted by powerful men, so he shakes hands with the men of the mob. But the scared kid also understands loneliness, and he uses that knowledge as the engine of his talent. When he sings a ballad— listen again to "I'm a Fool to Want You"—his voice haunts, explores, suffers. Then, in up-tempo songs, it celebrates, it says that the worst can be put behind you, there is always another woman and another bright morning. The scared kid, easy in the world of women and power, also carries the scars of rejection. His mother was too busy. His father sent him away.

"He told me, 'Get out of the house and get a job,'" he said about his father in a rare TV interview with Bill Boggs as few years ago. "I was shocked. I didn't know where the hell to go. I remember the moment. We were having breakfast . . . This particular morning my father said to me, 'Why don't you get out of the house and go out on your own?' What he really said was 'Get out.' And I think the egg was stuck in there about twenty minutes, and I couldn't swallow it or get rid of it, in any way. My mother, of course, was nearly in tears, but we agreed that it might be a good thing, and then I packed up a small case that I had and came to New York."

He came to New York, all right, and all the great cities of the world. The scared kid, the only child, invented someone named Frank Sinatra and it was the greatest role he ever played. In some odd way he had become the role. There is a note of farewell in his recent performances. One gets a sense that he is now building his own mausoleum.

"Dyin' is a pain in the ass," he says.

Sinatra could be around for another twenty years, or he could be gone tomorrow, but the jagged symmetries of his legend would remain. For too many years the scared kid lashed out at enemies, real or imagined; he courted his inferiors, intoxicated by their power, he helped people and hurt people; he was willful, self-absorbed, and frivolous. But the talent survived

145

everything, and so did the fear, and when I see him around, I always imagine him as a boy on that Hoboken street in his Fauntleroy suit and remember him wandering the streets of New York half a century later, trying to figure out what it all meant.

THE MAJESTIC ARTISTRY OF FRANK SINATRA
by Mikal Gilmore from *Rolling Stone*, September 18, 1980

FRANK SINATRA
UNIVERSAL AMPHITHEATRE
UNIVERSAL CITY, CALIFORNIA
JULY 4, 1980

*H*e walked onstage with a brisk, matter-of-fact stride, wearing a crisp black tuxedo and a bright, cocksure expression. The audience reacted with a volley of cheers, whistles and squeals—just like bobby-soxers had done four decades earlier—and even if the acclamation came as no surprise, he appeared grateful for it, in that indomitable way of his. Then a crossweave of saxophones and violins wafted through the night breeze, and Frank Sinatra swung into Harold Arlen's "I've Got the World on a String," treating it as if it were tailor-written to illuminate his artistry. "I've got a song that I sing/I can make the rain go/Anytime I move my finger . . ."

It seemed like a fairly virile statement for a hoary pop singer, but in the next song, Cy Coleman's "The Best Is Yet to Come," Sinatra went one better. Escorted by a walking blues piano line, he entered the tune playfully, toying with syllables and phrases like a spry, sportive house cat pawing a ball. Then, with a squall of horns swelling behind him, he suddenly tenses his voice into a stealthy instrument and pounced on the middle verse with an awesome iambic roar: "The best is yet to come, and babe won't that be fine/You think you see the sun, but you ain't seen it shine."

With those two songs, Frank Sinatra not only made good on his reputation as America's pre-eminent romantic vocalist, but also served notice that he was making one final, high-reaching bid for artistic apotheosis. In a way, it was just an extension of the objective already set by his latest album, *Trilogy*: to make a monument out of one man's renaissance.

But Sinatra came closer to that goal onstage than on record, mainly because he *sang* better live. Which isn't to say there's anything flaccid about

147

his singing on *Trilogy*, indeed, it's probably better than he's committed to vinyl in more than fifteen years, deeper and rawer in his bass register, lighter and more inflective in the baritone range. In concert, though, the voice sounded impossibly big, animative, cunning, formidable. It was as if the presence of an audience somehow impelled him to renewed levels of ingenuity and intensity.

In fact, in a knockout tour de force like "I've Got You Under My Skin," Sinatra was plain stunning. He slugged out Cole Porter's lyrics with the wit and wallop of a superfine prizefighter, weaving rhythmic punches between the relentless strokes of baritone and alto saxophones, then hitting the last chorus with a blinding series of staccato jabs—"Don't you *know* you *fool*, you ain't *got* no way to win/Use your *men-tal-i-ty*/WAKE Up! STEP UP! to *re-al-i-ty*"—that cut between the fleet slashes of the cymbals.

Yet despite that display there was nothing showy about Sinatra's singing—none of the grandiloquent, instrumental-style "vocalese" that typifies such oral exhibitionists as Phoebe Snow, Al Jarreau or Rickie Lee Jones. In fact, just the opposite: Sinatra's delivery sounded guileless and "easy," even *colloquial*—meaning his phrasing and intonation seemed to spring as much from the rhythms of speech as from the cadences of melody. As a result, his vocalizing served to heighten the emotional and thematic intent of a song, and make its lyrics seem like nothing so much as a word between friends.

That air of intimacy worked to best effect in Sinatra's "saloon" medley, a thoughtful mating of Arlen and Gershwin's "The Gal That Got Away" and Rodgers and Hart's "It Never Entered My Mind." (Saloon songs, late-night, inebriated soliloquies of unrequited love, are a kind of Tin Pan Alley equivalent of the blues.) This was Sinatra at the full extent of his affecting interpretive power: prowling the shadowy fringes of the stage with cigarette in hand, letting the signs of age in his voice—the brandy-tone timbre, the grainy legato—infuse the lyric: "The night is bitter/The stars have lost their glitter/The winds grow colder/And suddenly you're older/And all because of a gal that got away."

For just a second there, Sinatra looked and sang like an old man, stripped of all conceits and most hopes. It didn't matter that the portrait was antithetical to everything we presume about the real Sinatra—it just mattered that Sinatra had the sensibility to make us believe it was real.

In other words, he sang the song like it was his, and his alone, to sing. I've seen maybe a handful of other singers who could pull off that trick so effectively: Bob Dylan, Van Morrison, Graham Parker, John Lydon—but then their songs, more or less, *were* theirs and theirs alone. What Sinatra did at the Universal was fundamentally different, but equally important: he took the songs of Porter, Gershwin, Arlen and others, and made them seem personal and imperative. It was an eloquent display of his paradoxical brand of artistry: tough yet sensitive, vain yet compassionate, grasping yet generous. And when Sinatra left the stage, we realized we might never witness artistry that big and that provocative, again.

DON COSTA—THANKS FOR THE MEMORIES
Warner Bros. Records Press Release, November 1981

*F*or Don Costa, the day he met Frank Sinatra is as vivid as if it had happened yesterday instead of nearly forty years ago. "I was a young kid," recalls the affable master arranger. "I didn't know how to read or write music, but I had perfect pitch and could pick out anything on the guitar. I had a job as a studio guitarist back in Boston at a radio station, WEI.

"Now, back then, Frank had a fifteen minute show that he'd do from wherever he was on the road. He'd bring his rhythm section in and use local guys to complete the complement. He was my favorite artist in the world and when I was hired to play for the broadcast, I was numb.

"Alex Stordahl—he was Frank's conductor and arranger back then— came up to me and said, 'You're doing great, kid. Just don't play too loud.' No chance of that; I was so stunned I don't think I even hit the strings!"

Costa laughs. "After that session, I went right out and bought some manuscript paper. I didn't even know which was the right way up, but I was determined to learn. After all, I'd been with the best—Sinatra, Stordahl, my heroes."

It takes one to know one. A gentle, self-effacing man whose energy, sense of humor and creative capacities place him firmly in the "ageless" category, Don is one of the few certifiable legends in pop music history: over 280 chart records in more than 30 years; producer, arranger and friend to a galaxy of musical luminaries including Paul Anka, Dinah Washington, Sarah Vaughan, Johnny Mathis, Tony Bennett, Steve and Eydie, Trini Lopez, Ferrante and Teicher and a literal host of others—including the ineffable Mr. Sinatra.

As producer of Sinatra's latest Reprise release, *She Shot Me Down,* the astonishing magic of Costa/Sinatra has once more been brought to bear on vinyl.

"Frank had always wanted to do an album of what he would call saloon songs," explains Don. A round man with neatly trimmed salt-and-pepper goatee and expressive gestures that reveal his Italian heritage, he reveals how this latest fruit of a long-standing partnership came to pass. "He'd had this segment of his live show for a long time that he called the saloon spot, in which he sang a lot of his favorite tunes about lost love. For a while he even used a wheel-on bar as a prop. That and a cigarette, of course. We'd talked about the idea, and when he finally decided to do it last summer, he already had most of the material in mind.''

The material included two tunes, "A Long Night" and "South to a Warmer Place," penned especially for the singer by the late composer Alec Wilder. Also selected was "I Loved Her" written by arranger and conductor Gordon Jenkins, as well as the Sonny Bono classic "Bang Bang (My Baby Shot Me Down)".

"I wrote one tune for the album as well," continues Don, "It's called 'Monday Morning Quarterback.' I liked that for a title and when I suggested it to a songwriter I know named Pamela Phillips, she wrote the words and I filled in the melody.

"Frank really should get coproduction credit," comments Don. "I told him that, but he said 'It's not my department.' "

Resuming his tale of earlier days, Don says "I didn't see Frank at all after that night in Boston. A couple of years later I went on the road with the Vaughan Monroe band. I'd taught myself to write and arrange by that time, and I did a lot of both for Vaughan."

There followed a period of building a reputation that highlighted work with a fledgling duo by the name of Steve Lawrence and Eydie Gorme, as well as accomplished jazz vocalists Sarah Vaughan and Dinah Washington.

"When I finally met up with Frank again, it was when he called me in to do the arranging and conducting on an album called *Sinatra and Strings.* I think that's still my favorite album of all time.

"Right after the *Strings* project, we planned to do another album called *The Italian Songbook.* I did a lot of research on that one, had my mother sing into a tape recorder, the whole bit. I did all the arrangements and I even have the jacket slick, that's how far it went. But it was a real on-again, off-again deal, and I'll tell you, there was a lot of olive oil and garlic in those arrangements! After we finished work on *She Shot Me Down*, I brought it up to Frank again. 'If you don't do it,' I said, 'I'll take it to Tony Bennett.' " He laughs. "I'm still waiting to hear."

Sinatra and Strings was one of many hits Don enjoyed in the 1960s, hit after hit with such artists as Johnny Mathis, Tony Bennett, Ferrante and Teicher and a struggling singer/songwriter called Paul Anka. "Paul and I worked together. We came up with seventeen straight hits." Don recalls the time he switched jobs as A&R chief at ABC/Paramount to the same position at United Artists. "I'd had a good run at ABC, and when I made

152

the move to U.A., they took out a big ad in the trade papers saying something like 'Welcome Hitmaker.' I tell you, for eight months I couldn't get arrested with a record. It was embarrassing; I'd hide under my desk.

"Finally, one day at the end of some session I was working on, I decided to try out this idea. I had to make an instrumental version of Johnny Cash's 'I Walk The Line.' I played the guitar and we did it in two takes, with seven minutes of studio time left. It was nothing great, but it made the charts and it finally broke the ice for me."

Don subsequently discovered and signed Trini Lopez to Sinatra's infant Reprise label. "If I Had a Hammer," produced by Don Costa, became the company's first hit. Shortly thereafter he returned to the studio with Sinatra for what was to become a long series of highly acclaimed LP's, starting with *Cycles* ("the only time Frank ever gave me three hours on one song") and including *Some Nice Things I've Missed, Ol' Blue Eyes Is Back,* and *The Main Event.*

"Frank is an impatient guy sometimes. He's demanding, but only about things being just right. He may work fast, but he'll never let anything go with a bad reading."

A respected conductor in his own right, Don is currently working on a project in Italy to be known as the Don Costa Orchestra. And there is no sign that the Costa magic is diminishing. Nikki Costa, his youngest daughter, recently scored a number one single in Italy, Brazil and Argentina with the tune "On My Own" from the film *Fame,* produced by none other than Daddy Costa.

"I have a lot of fun," Don sums it up, "and I love what I'm doing. I'm really lucky."

153

*B*ing Crosby and Frank Sinatra were the two most popular American singers of the 1930's and 1940's. Mr. Crosby dominated the former decade, although his fame lasted beyond it; Mr. Sinatra began recording in the late 30's, came into his own with the Tommy Dorsey band in the early 40's, and erupted into matinee idol celebrity right after World War II.

The two men's popularity has never really abated—especially that of Mr. Sinatra, who of course is still with us, cultivating his legend. In fact, he will be cultivating it in person between September 13 and 23 at Carnegie Hall. And now two record releases serve to document both singers' early years. MCA has issued a single disk of recordings made by Mr. Crosby on the Brunswick label in 1930 and 1931 (MCA 1502) and three two-disk albums comprising the complete 83 songs Mr. Sinatra recorded with the Tommy Dorsey Orchestra between 1940 and 1942 (CPL2 4334, 4335 and 4336).

With Mr. Crosby's ultimate evolution into a foggy-bottomed bass-baritone "crooner," and Mr. Sinatra's steady extension of stylistic breadth into every corner of American popular song, the two singers grew apart. But at the beginning, they had much in common. Both were light baritones who produced their voices in an unpressured way and phrased with a relaxed sensuality. Their singing eschewed operatic rhetoric in favor of an intimate, conversational approach that owed much to the technical improvement of the microphone and electronic amplification.

In addition, both represented white adaptations of black styles. Mr. Crosby, born in 1904, was a jazz singer in Spokane before he sang with Paul Whiteman's Orchestra between 1926 and 1930. His use of easy ornamental slurs and sexily understated portamentos was a domestication and extension of black vocal traits as surely as rock-and-roll was later on.

Mr. Sinatra, too, who was born in 1915, had jazz in his background, and it was only accentuated during his stint with the Dorsey band. Tommy Dorsey was a good deal more jazz-oriented than his brother Jimmy, who took over their joint band after the two split in 1935. Tommy Dorsey had a lively interest in Dixieland jazz, although his own band gradually evolved into a smoother swing-style, big-band dance orchestra by the late 40's. The band included a number of notable jazz musicians (Bud Freeman, Bunny Berigan, Buddy Rich, et al.). And Mr. Sinatra himself later attested to the way his own phrasing grew in imitation of Mr. Dorsey's sinuous trombone lines.

"There were many trombone men who could play in the soft, long phrase sort of style, but none of them could play as relaxed as Dorsey," Mr. Sinatra recalled. "Compared to him, everybody played nervously. I figured that if he could do that phrasing with his horn, I could do it with my voice."

In the 30's and 40's, jazz and pop were much closer together than they are today, when pop aspires unashamedly to the commercial (new-wave rock apart) and jazz to the artistic. When Mr. Crosby and Mr. Sinatra were singing, there was a similar range, but the extremes were less widely separated, and jazz commonly borrowed pop songs as themes. Tommy Dorsey's band may have seemed more jazzish than that of Jimmy Dorsey, but it sounds often frothily pop to us today, no more serious than the songs on Mr. Crosby's album. Indeed, the material that both men recorded— prized by pre-rock pop defenders of today as the result of a golden age of sophisticated songwriting—is often ludicrously kitschy, anticipating the nadir of Tin Pan Alley songs of the early 50's, which triggered the rock rebellion. Still, there are good songs on all seven disks here.

The Crosby and Sinatra reissues come at slightly different stages of their careers. Mr. Crosby's Brunswick disks were cut just after he had left the Whiteman band and had embarked as a solo artist. In 1931 he began the nationwide radio appearances that were to seal his success. His theme song in those years was "Where the Blue of the Night Meets the Gold of the Day," and it leads off side 2 of the MCA disk.

With the Dorsey band in the early 40's, Mr. Sinatra was on the verge of his solo success, but had still not achieved it. The first Sinatra recordings with the band merely listed the title "with vocal refrain," but Mr. Sinatra soon managed to get his proper credit. The breakthrough was "I'll Never Smile Again," which topped the *Hit Parade* for two months.

The RCA albums, a postscript to the seven volumes (14 LP's) the company has thus far issued of the complete Tommy Dorsey sessions from 1935 through 1938, are an obvious discographical labor of love. They are arranged chronologically, with complete personnel information. The masters have been used with no artificial sonic updating, although in a few cases actual records borrowed from collectors have stood in for lost masters.

155

Any student of American popular song must hear these records, and they should trigger powerful memories for those who danced to this band 40 years ago. But you don't have to be student or a nostalgist to enjoy this music. Great popular artistry transcends fashion, and even the stigma of commercial popularity. Frank Sinatra's singing—and Bing Crosby's too—is as "classical" as anything American music has yet produced.

AT HOME WITH THE PALM SPRINGS SINATRAS
by Jody Jacobs from the *Los Angeles Times,* March 27, 1983

*R*ANCHO MIRAGE—The doormat leading out to the tennis court says it best: "Ol' Blue Eyes and Barbara."

This is the spacious desert compound where Francis Albert and Barbara Sinatra spend their happiest and most relaxed days.

Togetherness is spelled out everywhere.

There are "his" and "hers" cactus gardens. (She's worried about hers—two cacti have died.) In front of the rambling house are mats monogrammed BAS (for her) and FAS (for him).

And over the bar, the Sinatras have a sign that might sum up their life style: "Living well is the best revenge."

That living well includes such touches as a vegetable patch where the basilico, the herb that's so important in his Italian-style cooking, is grown behind a wire mesh fence to protect it from their dogs. There's a swimming pool and tennis court, guest houses and green spaces and a projection room in an old railroad caboose where he also keeps his collection of model trains.

NEW YORK APARTMENT

Besides the desert estate, they also have an apartment in New York's chic Waldorf Towers and a home in Los Angeles (another house in Idyllwild was donated to St. John's Medical Center to be used as a retreat and a vacation place), but it's here in Rancho Mirage where they feel most at ease. It's where their relationship blossomed from friendship to love and marriage. (She had for many years lived across the Tamarisk Country Club golf course from the compound with her then-husband, Zeppo Marx.) The desert is "definitely home," Barbara Sinatra says. "We love it here. We're real desert rats."

During the hottest months of the year they escape. This year, he'll be singing again at Sun City in Africa, and then Mrs. Sinatra adds, "We're going to Monte Carlo." Sinatra and Sammy Davis Jr. will be the entertainers at the Monte Carlo Red Cross Gala, the little municipality's most important social gathering. "It will be difficult this year," Mrs. Sinatra said, "because it was Princess Grace's favorite charity and I've heard people say it will not be the same without her. So he (Frank Sinatra) was the first to offer to do it." This year, Prince Albert, son of the late Princess Grace and Prince Rainier, will take over as head of the Red Cross and its benefit.

Between short and long trips, benefits and concerts, the Sinatras find peace and relaxation here. "We usually like to have some very close friends over, and family. (The Sinatras' family includes her son by her first marriage, Robert Marx, a law student at Fordham University; her parents, who live in Southern California; Sinatra's children Nancy, Tina and Frank Jr.; Nancy's husband Hugh Lambert and their two daughters.)

"My husband will usually cook. He likes his cooking; I like his cooking and so does everybody else. And we like to stay home. We show movies and mainly just let down. I guess that's the main thing. And I have my dogs and my girlfriends."

TENNIS AND CHARITIES

She plays tennis, and she works for her charities, which in the desert include the Desert and Eisenhower hospitals, the desert museum (she's on its board), a group that works with children on kidney-dialysis machines (she's working on a rodeo fund-raiser for them), and most recently the Sexually Abused Children's Program, part of the Family Counseling Service of the Coachella Valley.

She's also involved with the City of Hope in Duarte; New York's Sloane-Kettering Hospital and its cancer research program; St. John's Medical Center in Santa Monica; the World Mercy Fund, an organization that provides medical, educational and technical assistance for communities in West Africa; and the American Cancer Society.

Last Sunday night, she received the Hebrew University of Jerusalem's Scopus Award (her husband received it a few years ago) at a dinner hosted by the Palm Springs Chapter of the American Friends of the University. Barbara Sinatra scholarships have been set up at the university. And between hops to Las Vegas with her husband, she is helping to organize the Barbara Sinatra Art Auction, which takes place April 9 at the Sheraton Plaza-Palm Springs to benefit the Abused Children Program. Among the celebrity amateur and professional painters she has recruited is Francis Albert himself. One of his paintings will go on the block.

*   *   *

It is what desert lovers say is a typical weekend. The sun is shining, the weather is balmy and at the Sinatra compound there are 18 houseguests, most of them famous. At 7:30 A.M. on this morning a few weeks ago, Sammy Davis Jr. phoned the kitchen for steak and eggs. Now it is almost time for lunch and one of the staff is passing by carrying the breakfast tray for Ed and Victoria McMahon, who haven't yet surfaced.

Competing fiercely on the tennis court or simply lounging about, watching the games protected from the glare by a canopy and dark glasses, are Jimmy and Gloria Stewart, Veronique and Gregory Peck, Angie Dickinson, Cynthia and Glenn Ford, Altovise Davis (husband Sammy already is in town rehearsing with Dean Martin). Neighbors Mrs. Sidney Korshak and Danny Schwartz are there for the exercise. Schwartz's wife Natalie arrives in time for the buffet luncheon. All of them will add to the celebrity quotient later that day at Sinatra's Love-In II, a fund-raiser (the take is more than $1 million) for the Desert Hospital.

DEFINITELY A STAR

Barbara Sinatra already has played her game of tennis and now she's greeting a guest. She looks cool, collected and very pretty wearing a red turtleneck sweater, white pleated tennis skirt, immaculately white tennis shoes. The long, shapely legs are tanned. Not a blonde hair on her head is out of place. Her makeup is discreet. Her lipstick is bright. She's a friendly woman, a warm hostess and a calming influence on her husband.

He's on his way out, passing through the living room wearing a navy windbreaker and a USS *Nimitz* cap. "C'mon Nero," he says to the large, black Rottweiler as he holds the screen door open. Nero pays no attention. "He went to school, eh," Sinatra says mock seriously to his wife. She answers with a smile. "For only a week." And then, turning to her guest, she fills in the statistics. "He's only 4 months old, he's a baby. But when he's grown, his chest will be enormous and he'll have a thrust of about 1500 pounds. Nero," she mentions as the dog finally follows his master, "is definitely a star, no doubt about it."

No doubt about it, Barbara Sinatra is an animal lover. At the Rancho Mirage compound there are eight dogs including Nero—a cuddly ruby-colored Cavalier King Charles spaniel called Caroline acquired in London; an Afghan called "Miss Hollywood because she doesn't walk, she just floats and her hair just bounces and she's kind of above it all." One dog lives in the Los Angeles house, seven more at the Rancho Mirage stables.

The stables, a three-minute drive from the compound, are on land "given to me by my husband." Her four horses—a colt called Straw Dancer, an Appaloosa, a Peruvian Paso and an Arabian that was a gift from Wayne Newton—are kept there. "I helped deliver that one (the Arabian) and he named her after me. Then he raised her and broke her and got her ready and then gave her to me for Christmas." Pals Bernice Korshak, wife of the Los Angeles attorney, and Susy Johnson also board their horses there.

The desert compound was totally redecorated after Barbara Marx married Frank Sinatra on July 11, 1976. Accompanied by Mrs. Korshak, she visited wholesale showrooms in Los Angeles, bought new furniture and accessories, changed colors (it's *café au lait* canvas covering for the upholstered pieces in the living room.) "We really gave Los Angeles hell," she recalls. "Bernice has a decorator's license and she does it more or less as a hobby, not as a profession, so she helped me do all this. There have been quite a few changes," she grins. There is still a little bit of work to be done on "the back house," one of four guest cottages, before her project is completed, but the rest of it is "pretty much together now."

At the moment, including the celebrities and the Sinatras' friend Father Tom Rooney, there are 18 guests housed in the compound in four cottages furnished with white wicker furniture. They, too, were refurbished and renamed. "When I married Frank," she said, "the rooms were named after friends of his who had stayed there. It was the Romanoff (named for the late Prince Mike Romanoff), the Brisson (named for producer Freddie and his late wife Rosalind Russell), the Hornblow room. But most of those friends weren't living anymore and if the widows or widowers came back, then it kind of brought up some bad memories."

NAMED AFTER HIS HITS

"Frank was away and I was trying to find names and finally we decided to name them after his hits. This (the main house) is 'The House I Live In' and his office is 'My Way' and the theater is 'Send in the Clowns' and that guest house is 'High Hopes' and the other one 'Young at Heart'. We don't have a 'New York, New York' yet, but I may use that for the back house." There are four bedrooms in the back house and two in each of the other guest cottages.

Hosting so many people poses no problems for her. "I guess it's because I'm really well-organized and we plan ahead and a staff comes in and gets things ready. We have a wonderful staff here."

Except when an important charity event keeps her in Palm Springs, Barbara Sinatra goes where her husband goes. "I travel with him, that's really our life." The statement is matter-of-fact. "We're really on the road most of the time, and a plane is almost our home or a hotel or whatever. He starts out each year with a small schedule and somehow it just seems to get filled up. I think he's really happier working. I think it keeps his juices going and he likes it. I think he'd be very unhappy if he really retired totally.

"So in order to try to make some kind of normalcy out of it, out of that crazy kind of life, I travel with him and make it as comfortable as possible."

Barbara Sinatra was born in Missouri. "I'm a Midwesterner," she says. "I lived there for a while and then I moved to Wichita, Kansas, the big city. I was there during the second World War and then right after that I moved to Long Beach and I've considered California my home since then."

She still was in Long Beach running a modeling school when the Miss Universe pageant began and "I was the beauty consultant for the pageant. It was really fun meeting the girls from all over the world." There was also a brief 8-month stint as a Las Vegas showgirl and some modeling for fashion designers in Los Angeles.

The Sinatras visit New York "five or six times a year," and she loves the city now, but when she first moved there, after Long Beach, "I didn't like it at all. All I did was work (as a model). It was like six o'clock in the morning until eight o'clock at night and I was dead tired all the time and I hated it." She pauses. "I must say, to go as Frank's wife and with him, well it's like an entirely different New York than I knew. I love the people and all the social events and I love the shopping and the art museums and there is always something to do. I love everything," she enthuses. "The plays, the shows. It's just a terribly exciting city."

To work on the Love-In, Barbara Sinatra had returned from Las Vegas a few days ahead of her husband. She'd helped with the seating, a tricky problem for a party that included a former President (Ford), a couple of former ambassadors (both Walter Annenberg and Leonard Firestone), a studio head (Marvin Davis of 20th Century–Fox), a large segment of the Hollywood entertainment scene and big philanthropists. She'd worked on

161

the decorations, the menu and a lot more. One thing she hadn't touched. The entertainment. Her husband had seen to that.

Flashing her winning smile, she reveals one secret for keeping a perfect balance in her marriage. "There's room for only one star in this marriage."

*F*rank Sinatra has long been acclaimed as the world's leading performer of popular music, the artist who set the mold for all others to fill. He is, of course, more than a singer—he is also an actor, recording artist, cabaret and concert star, radio and television personality and, on occasion, a producer, director and conductor. His career, which includes acting roles in more than 50 films, some of which he produced and directed, is studded with accolades: Oscars, Grammys, Emmys, Peabody Awards. A dedicated humanitarian, he has received numerous honors and awards in appreciation of his charitable endeavors.

An entertainer for 44 years, he shows no signs of slowing down. His career in recent years has been marked by prodigious activity in films, recordings, concerts and cabaret appearances. He returned to the screen in *The First Deadly Sin,* released two blockbuster albums, the three-record *Trilogy* and *She Shot Me Down,* performed in Rio de Janeiro before the largest audience (175,000 people) ever to attend a concert by a soloist— the event is recorded in the *Guinness Book of World Records*—and served as producer and director of entertainment for President Reagan's Inaugural Gala.

He also appeared in three successive annual engagements at Carnegie Hall, each surpassing the previous year in critical acclaim and box office success. Indeed, Mr. Sinatra has established several box office records at the Hall.

During his career, he has acquired such famous nicknames as Chairman of the Board, the Voice, the Greatest Roman of Them All, and, of course, as virtually the entire world knows him, Ol' Blue Eyes. The whole world also knows that he was born Francis Albert Sinatra in Hoboken, N.J. As a youngster, he had visions of a sportswriting career and he worked briefly as a copy boy for a local newspaper. However, that ambition was short-lived once he heard the music of Billie Holiday and Bing Crosby. (Years later, Crosby co-starred with Mr. Sinatra in the film *High Society.*) He decided to pursue a singing career himself and he started with a local group called the Hoboken Four. It didn't last very long, and when the quartet broke up, the young singer took the solo route and toured the vaudeville circuit. Eventually he landed a job as a singing MC at the Rustic Cabin, a roadhouse across the river in Englewood, N.J. His talent attracted Harry James, who hired him as a band vocalist. It was 1939, the heyday of the big bands, and Frank Sinatra was on his way. A year later, he joined Tommy Dorsey and began recording with the band's vocal group, the fondly remembered Pied Pipers.

Mr. Sinatra later struck out on his own and appeared on radio's *Your Hit Parade* and his own show, *Songs By Sinatra*. Then, in late 1942, he appeared at the old Paramount Theatre on Times Square. The headliner on the bill was Benny Goodman and when the bandleader introduced Mr. Sinatra, the audience erupted and cheered itself hoarse. There was dancing in the aisles, whistling, whooping and shrieking and it was the beginning of a long love affair between the singer and his fans. It was one of the most spectacular events in show business history and Frank Sinatra's career went soaring.

The next year, he made his movie debut and he went on to appear in such notable films as *Anchors Aweigh, On the Town, The Man with the Golden Arm, Pal Joey, The Manchurian Candidate, The Detective,* and, of course, *From Here to Eternity,* the motion picture which brought him an Academy Award as Best Supporting Actor. He also received a special Oscar for *The House I Live In,* the documentary that made an eloquent plea for an end to prejudice. During the 1960's, Mr. Sinatra established his own recording company, Reprise Records, and came out with a number of well-remembered hit albums. During those years, he also starred in several award-winning one-man TV specials. In 1971, he took time out to relax but in less than two years, he was back in the performing spotlight.

His return was marked by a number of highlights: an album, *Ol' Blue Eyes Is Back,* which was followed by a TV special of the same name; the film *That's Entertainment* in which he appeared as one of the narrators who recounted the glories of the great MGM musicals, many of which he starred in; a Madison Square Garden concert that was televised live as a special on ABC-TV; several concert tours, including a seven-nation swing through Europe; an engagement with old friends Count Basie and Ella Fitzgerald at the Uris Theatre, where the trio broke all box office records for a Broadway theatre. On television, he starred in the NBC movie, *Contract on Cherry Street,* the specials, *Sinatra and Friends, John Denver and Friend,* and a *Dean Martin Roast,* with Ol' Blue Eyes as the roastee.

In 1978, he went to Israel for the dedication of the Frank Sinatra

164

International Student Centre at the Mount Scopus campus of the Hebrew University (another building in Israel named for him is the Frank Sinatra Youth Centre in Nazareth). The following year he returned to the Middle East, performing a benefit concert in Egypt at the request of Madame Sadat for her favorite charity. At the end of the year he celebrated his 40th anniversary as an entertainer. At a huge party at Caesar's Palace in Las Vegas, he was honored by more than 1,000 friends and colleagues. At the celebration, which was taped and later aired as an NBC-TV special, he received special awards from the American Society of Composers, Authors and Publishers and the National Academy of Recording Arts and Sciences. In 1981, he appeared at the Sun City Hotel-Casino in Bophuthatswana, southern Africa, and then went to South America for concerts in Argentina and Brazil. Then came his NBC-TV special, *Sinatra—The Man and His Music*, which was cheered by critics and viewers alike, and his new album, *She Shot Me Down*, which received wide acclaim by reviewers.

In 1982, he recorded "To Love a Child," the theme song of the Foster Grandparents Program, the favorite subject of President Reagan's wife Nancy and the title of a book she has written. Proceeds from the record, which he dedicated to the First Lady, go to the program.

In 1983, he received two honors of distinction. Variety Clubs International, the show business charity, saluted him for his achievements as an entertainer and a humanitarian. The event, which was attended by scores of Sinatra's celebrity friends, was a CBS-TV special. As a tribute to him, the Sinatra Family Children's Unit for the Chronically Ill, was established at the Seattle Children's Orthopedic Hospital and Medical Center.

In addition, Sinatra was one of five distinguished honorees—the others were Jimmy Stewart, Elia Kazan, Virgil Thompson and Katherine Dunham—of the 1983 Kennedy Center Honors. On that occasion, Mr. Thompson noted, " . . . one of my fellow honorees, the one I'm proudest to be with, is Frank Sinatra. He's a truly great vocalist. His vocal line is like a tube full of air, it never collapses. The proof of his eminence in his field is that he's the model most other pop singers follow; they all try to emulate his pure delivery . . ." This event, too, was a CBS-TV special with a guest list headed by President and Mrs. Reagan.

Currently in the planning stages is *The Frank Sinatra Story*, a film biography which will dramatize his life and career, covering the years between his youth in Hoboken and 1953, the year he won the Academy Award for *From Here to Eternity*.

165

by Alex Heard from *The New Republic,* February 11, 1985

"Listen, I want to tell you something," Frank Sinatra told *Entertainment Tonight* reporter Barbara Howar at a Convention Center inaugural gala rehearsal Thursday night. "You read the *Post* this afternoon? You're all dead, every one of you. You're all dead."

". . . I was very benign," Howar said. "I'm a 120-pound entertainment reporter, right? I'm not paparazzi."
—*The Washington Post*

*T*here is no word for the phenomenon in English, but I'm certain most Americans have experienced that strange sensation produced by exposure to certain entertainers—a mixture of hatred, disgust, embarrassment, and pathos. Sometimes, if the performer is sufficiently schlocko or self-congratulatory, this feeling intensifies to a point at which, suddenly, through an epiphanous psychic alchemy, it becomes highly pleasurable. If you've ever heard Phil Harris sing "It Was a Very Good Year" you know what I mean. (Richard Harris's version of "MacArthur Park" and Paul Anka's "You're Havin' My Baby" work too.) For many, watching Jerry Lewis "take on his critics" during the waning hours of the Labor Day Telethon arouses this emotion; as does Sammy Davis Jr.'s "Mr. Bojangles" routine. Let's call the feeling "hathos." Other highly hathotic people include Merv Griffin, Gene Rayburn, Bert Convy, Buddy Hackett, Alan Alda, John Ritter, Ricky Schroder, Webster, and any of the 253 little red-haired girls who have played "Annie."

But for me, the chairman of the Hathos Board has always been no other than Old Rheum Eyes himself, Mr. Frank Sinatra. So you can imagine how much I enjoyed being in Washington the week before the inauguration. "The Pope" was in town—bringing with him "Dino," Sammy, Merv, Liz, Lou, "Bobbie" Wagner, Pearl Bailey ("The Ambassador of Love"), and many, many other giants from the "entertainment industry." And I was able to follow it all in the pages of the *Post* style section, on *Entertain-*

ment Tonight, and on the local news. What a week—I haven't had that many hathos surges since *Sammy & Company* went off the air. At times, taken with the already-rich Style section offerings on inaugural preparations, gowns, and parties, it all seemed somehow . . . *too good.*

There was Dino being interviewed on the evening news: "He's our president and we're here to honor him. And he was our governor. Now he's our president." There was the song Donna Summer would sing with the U.S. Naval Academy Glee Club at Sinatra's "Presidential Galas," as printed in the *Post*: "You're living in America/You're living in the land of the free/[repeat]/A country of the people by the people for the people/ Just make it what you want it to be."

And best of all there were the breathless daily reports in Style on what Frank was doing, all written with maximum toadification. It was almost as if the Style section reporters had agreed in advance: "Frank hates the press—let's show him that we can be *neat!*" There was, for example, a special report on Frank buying an overcoat at Brooks Brothers: "Old Blue Eyes Warms to Washington." And a sarcasm-free account of radio talk-show host Larry King's decision to accept a pre-taped interview with Frank: "Ron Nessen, Mutual Radio's vice-president for news and special programs, said, 'The only other person I can think of we would agree to pre-tape would be a president.' " There were glowing preview stories on rehearsals for the God-awful inaugural entertainment galas:

"Sinatra: 'He's the most powerful man in the world.' "

"Martin: 'Aw, you're just being humble.' "

"This will undoubtedly provoke galas of laughter tonight and tomorrow . . ." (The day after the second gala came the inevitable comment: "Ronald Reagan was the guest of honor . . . but it was producer Frank Sinatra's show. They did it his way.")

And then there was the Frank "dinner beat." "Here's the inside skinny on Frank Sinatra at the Italian Embassy Thursday: he sat between Maria Pia Fanfani, wife of Italy's former prime minister, and Ginny Milner, of the California contingent, at the table presided over by Ambassador Rinaldo Petrignani." (That left me wanting to know *more*. Did Frank's chair wobble? Did he throw butter pats at the ceiling? Did he load the prongs of his fork with lima beans?)

But by Thursday it was already too late—this attempt to woo Frank was a bust. On Thursday Style had run the infamous article on the "Rat Pack"—Frank, Dino, Sammy, Joey, Peter Lawford, and "honorary member John F. Kennedy"—that made Frank threaten to stop punching reporters and start killing them. The millions of people who saw Frank's outburst on

167

Entertainment Tonight surely must have thought, "Gee, that Style section article really must have frosted 'The Pope' and the Rat Pack."

Actually, no. Aside from a few brief lines about extreme boozing and misogyny, the article contained 67 more inches of Frank-worship written by Style's new movie reviewer, Paul Attansio. Attansio must be puzzled, because the article was quite favorable, and it credited the Rat Pack movies with a seriousness of purpose that Frank probably hadn't realized was there: "Joey Bishop functions as the Fool to Sinatra's Lear, a motif representing the Pope's own self-pity (Sinatra is famously put-upon), and a reminder of his humble origins."

The article also argues that the Rat Pack is back, and how: "What's fascinating is that Rat Pack style has also resurfaced, simultaneously, at the very center of national life—in the person of Ronald Reagan. . . . When Reagan sought to alchemize certain elements of the Kennedy elegance as his own, he inevitably adopted the Rat Pack aesthetic as well.

"With this inaugural, Reagan emerges as a seventh member of the Rat Pack, the first since Kennedy . . . who is not a foil, but Sinatra's equal."

And this is because—better sit down—Sinatra and Ron are very much alike: "And most important, both have subsumed their personal contradictions beneath individual panache. . . . Together, Sinatra and Reagan have designed attractive personas that effortlessly complement each other, stylized myths of guilt and innocence, sin and expiation, corruption and Kiwanis."

Wow. Maybe I understand why Frank went berserk after all. The idea of a 1950s-era Ronald Reagan being admitted to the Rat Pack . . . Personally I'll always be grateful to Attansio for that image. Think of it:

The Pack is lounging around a hotel suite, drinking, smokin' cigs, flipping playing cards into a fedora. From one of the bedrooms we hear the staccato coos of a dame being riveted. Ron runs in, carrying a football and wearing a letter sweater. "Hey, Frank! You know when sex is best? In the afternoon, right after I get out of the shower!"

"That's good Ron. Now be a good Clyde and go get us some more ice."

One mystery remains. It's not yet clear whether Frank plans to rub out all journalists—right down to the guy who marks up the *Federal Register* for the Corrugated Pipe Manufacturers Association newsletter—or *just* show-biz writers. (A suggestion: First, kill all the "120 pound entertainment reporters.") Either way, this is probably not the safest time to launch the "Complete-the-Frank-Sinatra-Joke-Contest" this magazine has been planning for months. But . . . well, here goes.

Q. "What's the difference between Frank Sinatra and a 180-pound Luganeghe (pork, link) sausage with jug ears that is dressed in a tuxedo?"

(Note: Someone has already thought of, "Because of his religious beliefs, Sammy Davis Jr. cannot worship the sausage.") Send all entries to this magazine c/o "The Pope." The winner—and all runners-up—will also be rubbed out by Frank Sinatra.

BUT SERIOUSLY, COMRADES
—PRESENTING THE SINATRA DOCTRINE
by Bruce McCall from the *Los Angeles Times,* November 1989

Whether you like it or not, history is on our side. We will bury you.
—Nikita Sergeyevich Khrushchev, talking about capitalist states, at a Polish Embassy reception in Moscow, November 18, 1956.

You're all dead, every one of you. You're all dead.
—Francis Albert Sinatra, to reporter Barbara Howar and assembled press at a rehearsal for Ronald Reagan's inaugural gala in Washington, January 17, 1985.

Soviet Foreign Ministry spokesman Gennadi I. Gerasimov said on Oct. 25 that the Soviet Union had adopted the "Sinatra Doctrine" in its policy toward Warsaw Pact nations. "He has a song, '(I Did It) My Way,'" Gerasimov explained. "So every country decides on its own which road to take."

Now, a speech allegedly delivered by Soviet President Mikhail S. Gorbachev, has come to light.

*C*omrades, delegates to the 43rd Plenum, observers from the friendly socialist camp, hero veterans of the Great Patriotic War, ladies and germs.

What *is* the Sinatra Doctrine? I will explain. The interpretation of Marx—whereby *we* got Karl . . . and *Frank* . . . got Barbara! (Rim shot.)

Speaking of mistakes, Frank never would have sung "Come Fly with Me" if he had to fly Aeroflot! (Prolonged applause.)

We keep Aeroflot's crashes a state secret, of course. Also what they put in their *flight meals*! (Rim shot.)

When Comrade Eduard Shevardnadze spoke in Helsinki of the Sinatra Doctrine, certain stooge elements of the kept Western press interpreted it as mere "My Way-ism."

What *is* the Sinatra Doctrine? Is it a sacred right to consort unmolested with hooligans and goon elements whenever one chooses, without accountability to anyone? *We like to think so*! (Rim shot.) Although Frank never got bear-hugged by Kadafi!

We interpret the Sinatra Doctrine to guarantee the freedom to crush, like a Baltic independence parade, any parasitical journalist muckraker who dares deviate from the correct sycophancy and puffery line. As we were recently forced to do in the case of the criminally unsycophantic Vladislav Starkov, soon to be ex-editor of the pestilential tabloid rag, *Argumenty i Fakty*. This one's for you, Ol' Blue Eyes!

And let us just see Kitty Kell—er, Vladislav A. Starkov—Argumenty with *that* Fakty!

Does the Sinatra Doctrine place its practitioner somehow above the law? Whenever possible: Let us postulate that we are beating a man senseless in a restaurant in retaliation for a mildly critical comment, while our bodyguards hold him down. Applying this to a nation such as Afghanistan or Angola, anyone can see the dramatic possibilities of the Sinatra Doctrine for world peace. If not, our bodyguards—in this case the Red Army—will elucidate the situation for them.

The Sinatra Doctrine encourages 180-degree U-turns in political direction, as the Chairman of the Board has achieved in moving from the liberal Kennedy Democrat to the hard-line conservative Republican, and as we have done in moving from Lubyanka-bound KGB apparatchik to globe-trotting, glad-handing *perestroika* flack.

The Sinatra Doctrine means the solidarity of the Rat Pack, nodding like puppets at everything you say and rubber-stamping your every decision.

But it's a quarter to three, there's no one in the Hall of Delegates except you and me. So set 'em up, Arkady, I got a little Five Year Plan you oughta know. (Rim shot.) Thank you comrades. You're a beautiful bunch of Communists. Safe home. Shooby dooby doo . . ."

(Red Army Cocktail orchestra begins "New York, New York.")

The Nineties:

THE LEGEND

THE PATRON SAINT OF ATTITUDE
by Kimberly Ball

*A*ttitude is all. I became aware of this truth while slogging my way towards a bachelor's degree in philosophy. Such wisdom might have been gleaned from Descartes or Schopenhauer, I suppose. But, no, it took Frank Sinatra to enlighten me.

Attitude is how you maintain basic human dignity under inhumane conditions. When people sneer or roll their eyes or otherwise question your right to exist, the best of all possible antidotes is complete disregard, cool self-assurance and "What's it to ya, copper?" invincibility.

Frank Sinatra is the patron saint of Attitude. Just listen to his music. He's great, and he knows it. He doesn't merely sing a song, he swaggers through it. Add to this the imposing grandeur of his reputation: the mob ties, the drunken brawls, the general intolerance for any guff; throw in a few finger-snaps and "Jack!"'s, and the result is truly inspiring. It matters not whether The Legend at all coincides with the reality; Frank Sinatra is an archetype.

I discovered Frank Sinatra one day at the bottom of a discount bin and bought him on a whim. Later, even while musing over the sexist implications of "You'd Be So Nice to Come Home To," I found myself enjoying Frank. Here was a great singer, yes; but here too was an Attitude, an Attitude so huge, so absolutely overblown, it positively seeped through the recording. When Frank sang, you believed that no matter how down he got, no matter how hung-over, no matter how many lovers had left him to sing the Blues in the Night, he still had the World on a String. And what's more, you felt like that string could just as easily be around your finger.

I was hooked. It was a lonely addiction, met, for the most part, with glassy incomprehension by my peers. And then a newfound friend, a fellow devotée, stumbled upon the tape in my glovebox and asked breathlessly, not daring to hope, "You like Frank?"

From that moment forward, we were Frank buddies. We were both philosophy students, and there seemed no fitter restorative after a day of earnestly probing the ultimate questions than a single malt on the rocks, a fat Honduran, and a hefty dose of Ol' Blue Eyes. Inspired by Frank, we reveled in the decadent pleasures of Attitude. We would saunter along the boulevard smoking cigars, lost in an aromatic haze. We commanded the sidewalk. This was probably due to the mass flight from our toxic fumes, but we felt power. Nothing gives that feeling of capitalist-robber-baron satisfaction quite so abundantly as smoking a cigar in public. Nothing inspires one to the heights of Attitude required for such obnoxious behavior quite so upliftingly as Frank Sinatra. To a couple of impoverished students, these feelings were intoxicating.

One day, my friend proposed a pilgrimage: Sinatra in concert. Vegas was our Mecca and Frank was the muezzin calling us to worship. Sinatra was celebrating his seventy-fifth birthday, and we wanted to seize the opportunity to see him while he yet walked upon the earth. Unable to procure Dad's crumbling yet noble Lincoln Towncar for the journey—big enough to make you feel like a Vegas mobster, and *air conditioned*—we threw our cigars into the Honda, and headed for the Sands.

After an open-windowed trip across the desert, we stumbled haggardly into the Sands lobby with an hour to spare before the show. Fording the churning sea of casino, we had a brief but harrowing encounter with some official-looking thugs who seemed deeply concerned that we would actually try to enter a Sinatra show in our defiled state. "Deez damn kids," the looks on their faces seemed to say.

But they had us all wrong. Our respect for Frank was far too great. Once we had transformed ourselves, we were, if anything, overdressed for the event. All around us, aging Palm Springians were garbed in loud Hawaiian shirts and polyester leisure wear. As we sipped our weak drinks, the lights dimmed and a hush fell over the bright orange hula-dancers and pink palm trees. "Ladies and gentlemen, Mr. Frank Sinatra!" The moment of transcendent union had arrived.

We were initially dismayed at the short, grayed, impeccably dressed, bellied figure who bowed graciously to us from the stage. After all, how could any mere physical entity possibly live up to our grandiose expectations? But we needn't have worried, and we were not disappointed.

Over the course of the evening Frank sang, with his trademark phrasing, all of our guilty pleasures. He snapped his fingers, tinkled his ice cubes, bantered with the audience, and generally projected that certain joie de vivre, esprit de corps, or other je ne sais quoi that we shall herein term Attitude. Whatever it is, it was in full force that night. He introduced the audience to his son, who also happened to be his band leader, at three separate junctures, summoning him up from the pit so that the audience could have a look at him.

"He's my son," Frank would say each time. "Hell. We had to find some way to keep him out of trouble." Sinatra, Jr. looked more and more sheepish with each new entrée onto the stage, but, loyal to the last, entrée he did. At the time, my companion and I attributed this repetition to the contents (or former contents) of Frank's tumbler. But, on further reflection, he probably did it because, hell, he felt like it.

One of the more memorable moments from that evening came when Frank took a sip from the aforementioned tumbler and, gasping somewhat, remarked, "Now, that's a drink. That's the way Dean used to make 'em." At this point, all the power in the theatre went out, and Frank, mikeless, rasped, "Sorry, Dean. Just a joke." The power returned in a minute and, after the eerie specter of incorporeal visitation by the spirit of Dean Martin had lifted somewhat, the swinging resumed. But my most cherished memory from that concert was when Frank, gearing up to perform "Mack the Knife," announced that he was now about to sing a song written by "some Kraut." The sheer Attitude awes me to this day.

Until that night, I had only experienced The Voice on recordings, and of course, Frank Live was an entirely other fish to fry. Listening to his old records, one is transported back to the yesteryears of The Voice That Is Thrilling Millions. But in person, one must face Frank from the modern perspective: Vegas performer and retirement community heartthrob. Furthermore, I don't know why, but there's always something very unsettling about seeing a member of one's parents' generation (or beyond) groove— and that's exactly what Frank did. But once the initial shock wore off, I could rest easy in the knowledge that Frank still had it. The simple fact that he was still going strong, still packing them in, and that women in the audience were still screaming his name rhapsodically spoke volumes.

Even as the cheesy, glittering "New York, New York" backdrop appeared behind him for the final number and he began to belt, "Start spreadin' the news," it was clearly evident that Frank's Attitude, and all that it implies, is undeniably intact.

177

1958: *Only the Lonely* wins for Best Cover Art.

1959: *Come Dance with Me* wins Album of the Year and Best Male Vocal.

1965: *September of My Years* wins Album of the Year; "It Was a Very Good Year" wins Best Male Performance. Sinatra also received NARAS' Lifetime Achievement Award "for his unswerving faith and devotion to the beauty of music."

1966: *Sinatra: A Man and His Music* is named Album of the Year. "Strangers in the Night" wins Record of the Year and Best Male Vocal Performance.

1979: Wins the Trustees Award "in acknowledgment of his lifetime of devotion to the high standards of recording artistry."

1994: The Grammy Legend Award

ALSO RANS

1958: "Witchcraft" loses Song of the Year and Record of the Year awards to Domenico Modungo's "Nel Blu Di Pinto Di Blu (Volare)." Both *Come Fly with Me* and *Only the Lonely* lose Album of the Year to Henry Mancini's *Theme from Peter Gunn*.

1959: "High Hopes" loses Record of the Year to Bobby Darin's "Mack the Knife."

1960: "Nice 'n' Easy" loses Record of the Year to "Theme from *A Summer Place*" by Percy Faith. The *Nice 'n' Easy* album loses Album of the Year to Bob Newhart's comedy LP, *The Button Down Mind Of . . .*

1980: "Theme from *New York, New York*" loses Song of the Year and Record of the Year to "Sailing" by Christopher Cross.

A PERFECT SINGER, EVER SINCE HE BEGAN THE BEGUINE

by Harry Connick, Jr. from *The New York Times*, December 9, 1990

This week Frank Sinatra celebrates his 75th birthday and begins a yearlong world tour with concerts Tuesday and Wednesday at the Brendan Byrne Arena in East Rutherford, N.J. In this article Harry Connick Jr., the 23-year-old singer who has just concluded his own show on Broadway, analyzes Mr. Sinatra's prowess as a singer and describes the older man's musical influence on the younger performer.

As of today, I've only met Frank Sinatra once. I was about 9 years old, and my father took me and my sister to Al Hirt's club in the French Quarter of New Orleans, where Sinatra was performing, so we could meet him.

After my father introduced us, Sinatra patted me on the shoulder and said, "Hello, young man." Then he signed his *All the Way* album for my sister. I had no idea that I had met the man who would shape my whole approach to music.

I believe Sinatra to be the greatest male singer of American popular song. He is accessible to people who know nothing about music.

For one thing, Sinatra is a total master of vocal technique. He was the first to do so many things—hanging over the bar with phrases and holding phrases out for such a long time, sliding from note to note. The way he can get vibrato on the high notes—it's amazing. Then there is his breath control, the way he can hold phrases for 20 or 25 seconds. The best example is on "Old Man River" from the *Concert Sinatra* album. He must have an extra set of lungs; I wish he kept them in my chest.

People always try to analyze his sound. It's got something to do with the way his jaw is shaped, I think. He has very little air in his tone; every note he sings, whether soft or loud, is all sound.

Sinatra is also a musician. He sings every note perfectly. And he does things musicians do. I remember listening to the outtakes on some re-releases and hearing him say things like "On the downbeat I need more viola," or "Give me more of a crescendo."

He surprises me every time he changes melodies, when he sings "no" eleven times on "Mood Indigo," for example, or stretches "e-e-ev-vr-vry" on "I Love Paris." He understands everything a musician understands—and he can articulate it because he is dealing with words, not merely sounds. Musically, I trust him implicitly.

When I was about 13, Al Hirt told me about Sinatra. "Phrasing, phrasing, phrasing . . ." he said. I didn't know what he meant then, but I do now. Everybody who listens to Sinatra talks about his phrasing, whether or not they know anything about music. Sinatra swings like no one else. He knows where to put the words. He can take liberties; he never gets lost.

There is no way to notate authentic swing; there is no way to teach it, either. But one can develop it if he or she has the potential. Sinatra redefined swing for the American popular singer. Even when he sang "Begin the Beguine" with Tommy Dorsey in the early 40's, his phrasing displayed the purest of swing. On the *Trilogy* album, some 45 years later, "It Had to Be You" swings with an elegance and wisdom that I don't even begin to understand. The way he phrases the first five words—"It . . . had . . . to be you"—perfect triplets. He just knows it. I'm still trying to figure it out.

180

UNDER MY SKIN
A LIFETIME OF LISTENING TO SINATRA—HIS SOUND, HIS CADENCE, HIS TUNES, HIM

by William Kennedy from *The New York Times Magazine,* October 1990

So Frank is 75 this year, and what does that mean? I remember what it meant when he was 68 in June 1984. He was at Carnegie Hall singing "Pennies from Heaven" and "Fly Me to the Moon" and he was in great voice. When he did "Come Rain or Come Shine," a woman in a box called out to him, "Frankie, baby, you're the best."

Frank asked her name and she said it was Angie and he said to her, "You ain't so bad yourself, Angie, you know what I mean?"

"I just wanted to warn you that I love you," Angie said.

"Is that a threat or a request?" Frank inquired.

"I'm leaving my husband for you," she said.

"I think we gotta talk that over a little bit," Frank said.

Angie turned to the audience below to tell us: "I'm gonna wash his underwear, too. I don't care."

"I'm gettin' scared now," Frank said raising his glass of whisky. "I'll drink to you."

"You're still 25 to me," Angie said.

I'd bumped into Jilly Rizzo, a friend of Frank's, in a New York saloon a few weeks earlier and we talked about the upcoming Carnegie Hall concert, for which tickets were scarce. Jilly said he could get me two, and what's more he'd introduce me to Frank backstage, and would I like that? I said that'd be a little bit of all right, and so there we were (Jilly, my wife, Dana, and me) in Frank's backstage parlor where half a dozen others were bending his ear.

It was intermission between acts. Buddy Rich and his band, the opening act, had just concluded a hot session and Frank was on next. A roving waiter brought us a drink and I tried to imagine what you could possibly say to Frank. You couldn't gush. You couldn't say you'd been a fan for 48 years. Also, you had no friends in common you knew of. Yes, it's true you were in love with Ava 35 years ago and once watched her dance barefoot in Puerto Rico, but you couldn't bring that up, and you didn't know his wife or kids.

Jilly broke the ice by telling Frank I traveled with tapes, meaning, of course, Frank's tapes. So I talked then about my Pluperfect Sinatra tapes, which a friend and I had concocted to take the best of Sinatra from forever forward to right now and tape them, leaving out all songs that do not make you climb the wall.

Frank listened to my Pluperfect story without much surprise, for his record producers had been doing this for him all his life: *Frank Sinatra's Greatest Hits* and *Sinatra's Sinatra*. for example. But I have to say that nobody ever put together seven tapes such as the Pluperfects, in which you climb the wall every time out.

In one sense, the conversation was good practice for writing this memoir on behalf of Frank's 75th birthday disks, for I climb the wall more often with these Reprise tunes than I ever did before, given this many choices. There are certain exceptions we will not go into, and even if I am tortured I will not mention their titles, for this is not the critic's corner. This is a story of listening to Frank for 48 years, maybe 49, and finding out what it means that he is now turning 75.

So I told Frank how I planned to be a drummer in 1942, and when I saw Buddy Rich in a movie playing a tom-tom solo called "Not So Quiet Please" I went out and bought the record before I had a phonograph. I would set it on top of my dresser and let my eyes be the needle and I listened to that solo for six months before I came up with enough cash to buy a friend's used phonograph. Frank remembered the solo. It was in a movie called *Ship Ahoy,* with Eleanor Powell and Red Skelton and Tommy Dorsey and guess who else: Frank. You knew that. . . .

The other significant thing that happened at Carnegie Hall was my wife. She had been a tepid Sinatra fan, growing, if not fond of, then at least used to him as I played his tapes. She knew him as an actor before I came along but not really as a singer and here I was clogging her brain with him on every trip we took. She would sometimes look at me and say, quietly, "Overdose," and I'd then have to put on the Kiri Te Kanawa tape.

But unbeknownst, Frank had been growing on her ever since she'd heard him do "Lonely Town" better than anybody else had ever done it, and then here he was singing "Mack the Knife" and "Luck Be a Lady" and swinging everybody's brain from the highest trapeze and even dancing (which also got to her, for she'd been both a ballerina, and a gypsy on Broadway), and suddenly there she was on her feet like everybody else when he wound up with "New York, New York": Dana, a convert, no longer susceptible to overdose.

That is the remarkable thing about Sinatra recordings: that you can

182

listen to them not only forever, but also at great length without overdosing, once you have been infected. I say this not only on my own behalf but on behalf of the entire set in which I move, and which I have helped infect to the point that Frank is now a common denominator among this group of seriously disparate ages and types. I am the Methuselah of the set and can remember not only Frank's hits with Tommy Dorsey's orchestra when they were new—"I'll Never Smile Again" and "There Are Such Things"—but also tunes that never quite made it—"Everything Happens to Me," for instance, which I knew by heart in 1943 and still remember from that era when listening to records was what you did with your friends when the baseball diamond was a major mud puddle.

In the 1950's, there came *In the Wee Small Hours,* which conditioned your life, especially with a young woman with lush blond hair who used to put the record on and pray to Frank for a lover. All that perfumed hair, and it came undone. That certainly was a good year, but it remained for another album, *Swing Easy,* to teach you how to play a record 12 times in one night, which was merely a warm-up for 1983 when you listened to *New York, New York* for the first time seriously and then played it 60 times until 5 A.M., also calling your friends in New York and San Juan and Aspen and permitting them to stop sleeping and get out of bed and listen along.

The true thing about this phenomenon is that you do not have to have Frank on video, or in a movie or TV show, or even invent conversation in person with this fellow who is a stranger. You really don't need those presences. All you need is the music the man has made and that has been with you all your life, and which is even better now because you have all the songs of his maturity. He was new in the 40's and still growing in the 50's into such masterpieces as "Drinking Again" (1967), by Johnny Mercer, the greatest of all torch songs Frank ever sang, and also such breakouts as "I've Got You under My Skin" (1966) and "The Lady Is a Tramp" (1974) that put earlier white-bread versions out in the backyard. Of course, these views are open to argument but, even so, I will brook none of it here. This is my memoir.

There is another superb thing Sinatra does, which is Irving Berlin's schmaltziest work—"All Alone," and "What'll I Do?" among others—shameless, cornball, wonderful throwbacks to the Tin Pan Alley time when schmaltz was a Number One, King of the Hill.

It was the schmaltz and also too many trumpets that turned off my son, Brendan, when I played Frank in the car. (He once listened to a Bing Crosby and the Rhythm Boys tape from 1929, and decided the music was prehistoric.) We would fight over tape time in the car, he opting for the

183

Police, me for guess who? This was 1983 and Bren was 13. Now he's in college and last month he told me, "We were at a party and this horrible music was on and this girl and I put on a tape of Frank and danced until somebody shut him off."

Two weeks ago he asked my advice on dance tunes and I recommended *Swing Easy* and the albums with Ellington and Jobim, and so now Brendan also travels with Frank tapes, in case of emergency dancing.

The finale of all this is that Frank turned up in our hometown, Albany, as the opening act for the brand new Knickerbocker Arena, with 17,000 seats. Would Albany turn out for him in any numbers? Word had gone out, as it always does with these myth-making events, that Frank wasn't well, might not show up, that Liza Minnelli was standing by to go on if he crumpled. What's more, Ava had just died and so maybe this was not one of those very good years.

And yet here he came on Jan. 30, six years older than when I'd last seen him, looking smaller and—how not?—older, his 75th year just barely under way. He's wearing his single-breasted tux with an orange pocket handkerchief, his hair totally silver, adding to his years. Then he opens his mouth. "Come fly with me," he sings and a cheer goes up from the yes, 17,000 who have packed the place to hear and see this legendary character who only *seems* to grow old.

A lifetime of staying young at center stage: how can anybody be so good for so long? You listen and know that this is not Frank in his best voice ever but it doesn't matter. It's *his* sound, *his* cadence, *his* tunes, *him*, and it's as good as it can be and that's still very, very good. He moseys to the improvised bar on stage with the Jack Daniel's and the ice bucket and he sits on the bar stool and says: "I think it's about time to have a drink. I don't drink a lot, but I don't drink a little either." And then he opens his mouth again: "It's quarter to three . . ." and the crowd roars and he calms them with his old torch.

And then, finally, he segues into "New York, New York" and the spotlights circle the crowd, which is stomping, and Frank is making love to all here. He opens his arms, points to everybody . . . "It's up to you, New York, New York. . . ."

Then it's over and the spots cross on him, and the aging bobby-soxers, having come full circle from 48 years gone, reach up to shake his hand, and he fades down the stairs and out, and you follow him with your eyes because he is carrying the sound of your youth, the songs of your middle age. And then you think, the song is you, pal, the song is you.

184

"Why is Frank Sinatra the most potent figure of popular culture who ever lived?" So asks author David McClintick in the liner notes for *The Reprise Collection*, an 81 song retrospective of Frank Sinatra's best work over the last 30 years. And McClintick doesn't stop there. He boldly claims that no performer—not Bing Crosby or Elvis Presley or Charlie Chaplin or Marlon Brando—has captivated so large an audience for so long. He notes that Sinatra, who is a jazz singer only in the broadest sense, has been identified as a favorite by everyone from Miles Davis and Duke Ellington to Benny Goodman and Andre Previn. He even cites literary figures such as Wilfrid Sheed, Frank Conroy, Murray Kempton and Albany Pulitzer Prize–winner William Kennedy (whose monograph also appears in *The Reprise Collection*), who all find intellectual reasons for declaring Sinatra the Chairman of the Board.

But as convincing as McClintick's argument is, there's just one problem: It doesn't go far enough. The swinging, ring-a-ding-dinging, morose, melancholy, egocentric genius featured in Reprise's box set isn't simply more compelling than the other greats of music and film. He's more compelling than just about anyone who ever drew breath.

The reasons are so many and so varied that they cannot be contained in a single article, or even in a 26-volume set of the *Encyclopedia Britannica* devoted entirely to Sinatra. Space will allow only a few modest comparisons between the Voice and the greats of human civilization. If the answers to the questions below don't prove our point, nothing will.

WHY IS SINATRA BETTER THAN WINSTON CHURCHILL?

Because he made World War II a more enjoyable time for all of us. While Churchill was busy sending fighting men into the jaws of the Nazi beast, Sinatra was here at home, giving the largely female work force something to live for. The box set's masterful "Without a Song," a mature rerecording of a song Sinatra sang with the Tommy Dorsey Orchestra during the early Forties, amply demonstrates why women of the period loved him and suggests that this love may have inspired them to build more of the tanks, bombs and artillery that eventually helped us to victory. Without Sinatra, we could be wearing jackboots and funny mustaches to this very day.

WHY IS SINATRA BETTER THAN DON JUAN?

Because Don Juan only made women want to sleep with *him*, while Sinatra's singing makes everybody want to sleep with *everybody*. His voice is the aural definition of seduction, yet his supreme self-confidence prevents this gift from seeming contrived. The collection's "All Alone," from 1962, is so pitiful, and yet so majestic, that no woman within earshot could resist comforting the nearest man, and no man in the area could prevent himself from showering the nearest woman with a Sinatra-esque dose of masculine sensitivity. Christ, even the dreadful "Send in the Clowns" sounds as if it were meant to provide a tender backdrop for boinking when it comes out of Sinatra's mouth. Don, eat your heart out.

187

WHY IS SINATRA BETTER THAN ALBERT EINSTEIN?

Because the nuclear energy made possible by Einstein's theories is not nearly as powerful as Sinatra's primary weapon: swing. It's all but impossible to listen to *The Reprise Collection's* "My Kind of Town" or "New York, New York," or even a mid-tempo bossa nova such as "Oh, You Crazy Moon" without snapping your fingers and wagging your body back and forth to that hipster beat and raising your eyebrows and lowering your lids until you resemble a member of the Rat Pack. The power this more-than-middle-aged man packs into the live, Nelson Riddle arranged "I've Got You under My Skin" and "Zing! Went the Strings of My Heart," just one of the many unreleased rarities contained herein, is enough to make a terrorist salivate. When Ol' Blue Eyes drops the big one, it stays dropped.

WHY IS SINATRA BETTER THAN MAHATMA GANDHI?

Because he doesn't believe in any of that live-and-let-live crap. He's a scrappy mug from Jersey, and his style seems to say that if he hears any guff coming out of your yap, the only thing you'll be having for lunch is a knuckle sandwich (thrown by one of his retinue, no doubt; that's what they're there for). His 1962 version of "I Get a Kick out of You" is tough enough to kick back, and even "Mack the Knife," with a vocal recorded when Sinatra was 71, does some serious damage.

How he has managed to combine these thuggish, never-back-down qualities with a brooding, romantic empathy that makes him irresistible to listeners of every sexual predilection is a mystery *The Reprise Collection* can't answer, but it does provide some incredibly enjoyable clues. And one thing's for sure: Gandhi couldn't lick him in a fistfight.

WHY ISN'T SINATRA BETTER THAN POPE JOHN PAUL II?

Because he wouldn't want to be. He has too much class.
That's potency for you.

*B*ruce Janu, a high school teacher from Riverside. Illinois, has a novel punishment for punishing misbehaving students . . . students whose taste, he assumes, runs mainly to rap and metal. He sentences them to listen to Sinatra records.

After an hour of the Frank Sinatra Detention Club, one student moaned "I couldn't stand it!" and promised to turn his life around.

189

CHAIRMAN OF THE BOARD STILL BOSS
AS HE TURNS SEVENTY-FIVE

by Tony Gieske from *The Hollywood Reporter,* December 12, 1990

"*O*ne doesn't easily leave Frank Sinatra," said his pal, songwriter Jule Styne. "Sometimes the privilege of departure seems reserved for Mr. Sinatra."

The spiffy little singer with diamonds in his eyes and silk in his voice has made almost as many departures as he has comebacks, and while he was trying to make up his mind, we've had almost half a century of Sinatra, a star among stars, looking over his shoulder and passing through the spotlight pools into the darkness, like Jimmy Durante.

But he always comes back. Mr. Sinatra, 75 today. Frankie. The Voice. The Crooner. II Padrone. Ol' Blue Eyes. The Chairman of the Board.

When he finally does leave, it's going to make a mighty big hole in 20th-century music, maybe the biggest one of all: Bigger, surely, than his old idol Bing Crosby, or Elvis Presley, or the Beatles, or even Duke Ellington or Charlie Parker.

Because when you add it all up, it's only Sinatra who speaks to everybody, who touches a little place in everybody's heart—young, old, black, white, male, female, rock fans and opera lovers.

Thus he feeds that deepest of all American hungers, the hunger for identity, the unacknowledged wish for something everyone can feel, some feeling that links us all.

Sinatra found that feeling months back when he played the Greek Theater, the voice now more tweed than silk, but the impact pretty much the same. When he sings a song, you seem to be able to see right into his heart. Hey, no big thing, the performance seems to say, his heart is just like yours (and here's what makes it fun), *rich and sinful and powerful and successful as he is.*

This communicative gift was his great talent when he first sidled into the American big time in the Good War years, riding the tail end of the big band era as a vocalist with Harry James and Tommy Dorsey, clinging to a microphone on the stage of the Paramount Theater.

All or nothing at all.

Half a love never appealed to me.

He was a male Edith Piaf, a waif with an all-too-believable tenderness in that nonetheless masculine voice, a muted yet throbbing conviction, a veiled but distinct signal of sexual desire, all or nothing at all—the bobbysoxers, now pushing 70, fell before his amplified sweet nothings as though poleaxed.

Of course, they quickly rose again, on their feet and ready to faint anew for Eddie Fisher, Perry Como, Vic Damone, Frankie Laine, Billy Eckstine, Guy Mitchell. And it wasn't long before their daughters were falling for Elvis, Buddy Holly, the Beatles and all the now-departed pillars of the rock era.

Sinatra was not ready to depart, despite the flood of rock that washed out many another pop icon. The immediate postwar years, when as a rising young film star he began to define la dolce vita from his mansion in Toluca Lake, Calif., were interrupted briefly by his downslide of the early 1950s, when he pursued his great love, Ava Gardner.

For a brief moment there, marked by the making of "Mama Will Bark," a recording with Dagmar on which he barked like a dog, it seemed that the curtain might have fallen. The disc sold 30,000 copies. The maestro's mind was not on his work.

But then came *From Here to Eternity*, which won Sinatra his best supporting actor Oscar in 1953, remade him as a movie star, and brought back the musical magic, too.

It took him a long time to get over Gardner, his pals all agree.

But while he carried the torch, the long-playing record era dawned and he made a series of them for Capitol that are still selling in the second-hand bins and on CD reissues, still being taught as examples of American popular song at the top of its form: *Songs for Young Lovers* (1954); *In the Wee Small Hours* (1955); *Songs for Swingin' Lovers* (1956); *A Swingin' Affair* (1957); *Only the Lonely* (1958); *Come Dance with Me* (1959); and *Nice and Easy* (1960).

These records are still spinning, but, oddly, when Gardner was buried not long ago in North Carolina, Sinatra was not at the grave, and no real tear fell on the earth that covered his old flame.

Perhaps the passion had gone into the Capitol series, in which he covered dozens and dozens of the great ballads in American popular music— no rock or R&B—floating along on these hovering arrangements played by Nelson Riddle and Axel Stordahl and Billy May. Sinatra's place at the summit of pop music would be secure had he never done anything else.

But he still had at least 20 years to go.

191

First came the stirring 1960s sides with Ellington and Basie for his own label, Reprise, where he showed he could stand right up there with guys like Joe Williams or Al Hibbler, the dyed-in-the-wool jazzmen. And there were five more LPs in the 1970s, after his Los Angeles Music Center "retirement" in 1971, a retirement that ended early in 1974 with an appearance at Caesar's Palace in Las Vegas. And even in the 1980s, when the sultan of the 1960s entered his 70's, there were a half-dozen more including *Trilogy, She Shot Me Down,* and *L.A. Is My Lady.*

And during all this time, in addition to the saloons he had to play, the whiskey he had to drink, the bets he had to lay, the enemies he had to deck, the friends he had to bless and the women he had to woo, there were the films he had to make: 58 of them in all, from *Las Vegas Nights* in 1941 to *Cannonball Run II* in 1985.

Through it all, the boulevardier who was a duke to his buddies was not immune himself to hero worship. He took Jackie Kennedy out, he was pals with JFK and LBJ and Nixon and Reagan and Agnew and Humphrey.

But it was a night in 1966 that says something worth knowing about his integrity as a musician, a night when his table at Jilly's was empty while he dined at the Cote Basque. Midway through the evening, the immaculately tailored Sinatra rose from his table and crossed the room with a folded piece of paper in his hand.

He stopped at a table occupied by an elegant little man in horn-rimmed glasses. Sinatra held out the paper and asked politely if he could have the man's autograph. The man complied.

It was the author of *The Rake's Progress,* Igor Stravinsky.

ARE YOU READY, BOOTS? START TALKIN'
—NANCY SINATRA ON FRANK (AND NANCY) SINATRA
by Jeff Tamarkin from *Goldmine* magazine, March 22, 1991

What most people who bought "These Boots Are Made for Walking" didn't know was that it was far from being Nancy Sinatra's debut single. In fact, there had been nearly a dozen Reprise singles preceding it, all of them flops.

Nancy Sinatra signed to her father's label in 1961, at its inception—her first single on the label, "Cuff Links and a Tie Clip," was only the 17th record released by Reprise. She was anything but a runaway success; not a single one of her records even hit the charts in the U.S. until the one preceding "Boots" in 1965, "So Long Babe." And it only made #86.

Nancy Sinatra claims that she didn't get her record deal because she was a Sinatra, that she had to work for it. This may be true, but chances are she got to keep it because she was a Sinatra; it's difficult to imagine any record company would hold onto an artist whose first 15 singles failed to make the charts.

Nancy Sandra Sinatra was born June 8, 1940 in Jersey City, New Jersey, about a 10-minute drive from Hoboken. Her mother had married the struggling singer only a year before—he wouldn't even make his first record, as an uncredited member of the Harry James orchestra, until after they wed. Before his daughter could walk or talk, Frank Sinatra had gone from being virtually unknown to being swooned at by millions. He was an unprecedented entertainment phenomenon.

After the birth of her brother, Franklin Wayne Emmanuel (Frank Jr.) in 1944, the family packed up for Los Angeles. Nancy's younger sister, Christina, known as Tina, was born in L.A. in 1948. Of course, the Sinatras quickly became part of the Hollywood celebrity elite—the children grew up in a home where movie and recording stars regularly dropped by, which makes it less surprising that she chose to enter the entertainment field herself.

Although she took acting, voice, dance and piano lessons as a child, her most important lessons were learned from the best in the business. From early childhood, her father would bring Nancy and his other two children to the recording studio to watch him make records.

Nancy made her national TV debut on "The Frank Sinatra Timex Special" on May 12, 1960, a show highlighted by a segment featuring Frank Sinatra and Elvis Presley singing one another's hits. The same year, she married actor/singer Tommy Sands.

In 1961, Reprise chief executive Mo Ostin set Nancy up with producer Tutti Camarata, who had produced all of Annette Funicello's records. Ostin, not believing that rock 'n' roll was here to stay, felt that a novelty direction was best, and Nancy's first single was "Cuff Links and a Tie Clip," which she describes today as "bubblegum." It went nowhere.

Nancy's subsequent singles also failed to attract any attention in the U.S., although several did moderate business in Italy, South Africa and Japan. She felt her failure at home was due to her company's refusal to let her rock—she protested the lightweight material and the babyish voice in which she was asked to sing.

Meanwhile, she appeared in films: *For Those Who Think Young*, with James Darren and Dean Martin's daughter, Claudia; *Get Yourself a College Girl*, featuring Mary Ann Mobley and Chad Everett; *Marriage on the Rocks*, with her father and Dean Martin, a difficult experience for her in light of the recent failure of her own marriage.

In 1965, Reprise decided it was time to either get her a hit or get rid of her. Ostin assigned producer Jimmy Bowen to Nancy, and they came up with a version of Cole Porter's "True Love." It, too, was unsuccessful. All along, Nancy had been telling Reprise to give her some material with guts and a punch. Bowen agreed he wasn't the man to do that, and recommended Lee Hazelwood.

When Hazelwood played Nancy the unfinished song "These Boots Are Made for Walkin'," he didn't think it was right for a female singer. But she liked it—and so did her dad, who heard it from the next room. As they worked on it, Hazelwood felt that Sinatra was singing the lyrics too innocently. "For crissake, you were a married woman, Nasty"—he called her "Nasty"—"you're not a virgin any more. Let's do one for the truck drivers!"

"These Boots are Made for Walkin'" became the second Reprise #1 (Dean Martin's "Everybody Loves Somebody" was the first) and put Nancy Sinatra on the map. The *Boots* album reached #5, the highest-charting of her albums. On the cover, purchasers saw a Nancy with piercingly seductive, heavily mascara-ed eyes, a half-smile/half-pout on her lips, stylish blonde hair and a Mod mini-skirt and matching red boots. Frank Sinatra's daughter epitomized the hip style of L.A.'s rockin' and rollin' Sunset Strip at its peak in the mid-'60s.

All of her photos from this era were equally sexy: Nancy in skimpy

white bikini; Nancy in low-cut white shirt and go-go boots; Nancy decked
out in biker black hanging onto Peter Fonda in the 1966 film *The Wild
Angels.* She was doing to teenaged boys what her father had done to their
mothers a generation earlier.

By late 1967, the Sinatra Invasion was winding down. She recorded a
series of singles with producer Hazelwood in the summer of '67: They'd
already cut "Summer Wine" for the B-side of Nancy's "Sugar Town," and
subsequent duets included "Jackson," a Billy Edd Wheeler country tune
that Johnny Cash and wife June Carter Cash had been singing, and the
haunting "Some Velvet Morning," which reached #26 in early 1968. An
album collecting the pair's recordings was released that year; it reached #13.
They reunited in 1972 to make another album, this time for RCA, but it
did not chart.

In 1970, Nancy married choreographer Hugh Lambert, with whom she
had worked in Las Vegas. Although she cut a handful of singles for RCA in
1972 and '73, and another batch for Private Stock Records in 1975-77, she ba-
sically retired from show business after 1974 to be with her husband and raise
the couple's two daughters, Angela and Amanda. (Unfortunately, her familial
bliss was shattered when husband Hugh died in the 1980s.)

Nancy Sinatra made one last stab at reentering the recording world in
1981, when she cut an album with country music's Mel Tillis. *Mel & Nancy*
was released on Elektra Records and two country chart singles came out of it,
"Texas Cowboy Night" and "Play Me or Trade Me." But lately, Nancy has
been fooling around in the studio and is considering launching a full-scale return to recording after her daughters are old enough to be on their own.

She turned 50 last year, but with her dad celebrating his 75th—more
than 50 of those spent performing—growing older would appear to be no
great obstacle to this family. It would not be a surprise to see those boots
come out of mothballs before the century is over.

Would you agree that your father reached his artistic peak while at Capitol?
Well, it's possibly the finest recorded Sinatra, but there's so much to
be said for the Reprise stuff in terms of growth and awareness and knowledge, the aging process. There is such a big story in his voice from '63 to
L.A. Is My Lady (1984). That's a lot of growth in a human being. A lot of
growth in a nation. He always reflects what's going on in our lives.

You've mentioned that In the Wee Small Hours *(1955) is your personal
favorite Sinatra album.*
Absolutely. Without a doubt.

The record that followed, Songs for Swingin' Lovers, *seems to have gained a more legendary status.*

I love those songs, and I love to see him perform those live. But *In the Wee Small Hours* is just as profound as far as I'm concerned. It was a great marriage of a label [Capitol], arranger [Nelson Riddle], vocalist and producer [Voyle Gilmore].

There's nothing today in a recording studio that equals the electricity that was in the air at those sessions. The live spontaneity, the anticipation of the end result—which you could hear instantly in the playback, you didn't have to wait months for the overdubbing.

In your book, you describe your father as a greatly misunderstood man. How did the public's image of him come to differ so much from the man you describe?

The other night I was at a bookstore, and I overheard a college-age girl saying to her male friend, 'Oh, that's the book that talks about Frank Sinatra's connection to the Mafia.' I don't even know which book she was talking about; there have been so many. I let it go for a couple of beats, because I was so shocked to hear it, and then I said 'Wait a minute.' I could feel the steam coming out of my ears. I turned to her and I said 'Frank Sinatra is not connected to the Mafia, and I'm so tired of hearing people like you say this. And I wish you would stop it.'

She couldn't come back with anything, she was so stunned. I don't think she recognized me—people don't recognize me now, I look different than when I was performing. This is a younger generation now, and one of the things they hear about is that he's connected to the Mafia, which is total bullshit. I'm so sick of it I don't know what to do. It's part of the myth, part of the legend.

When did it start?

As far as I know—and I have the FBI files—it came from a feud between Dad and [newspaper magnate] William Randolph Hearst. The Hearst Syndicate was Republican. My father, with his young, skinny looks and his sweet voice and his bobbysoxers falling all over him, was staunch FDR, and came out to say so publicly. As far as I know, the Hearst people went out to get him.

He [Sinatra] made a trip to Cuba, which my family did a lot, and a lot of people did. It was like Las Vegas then. And the Hearst papers printed that he was going to see Lucky Luciano. Now, whether or not he saw Lucky Luciano, I don't know. In those days, the underworld guys pretty much owned all of the nightclubs. I mean, I worked for them too when I started singing 20 years later. We all did, and guilt by association is a very dangerous thought process.

Fortunately, Frank Sinatra had been big enough, talented enough and strong enough to survive it. There are people who are not, who are destroyed by this kind of garbage. Anyway, the rumors were printed, and the innuendoes were printed again in movie magazines. And again and again. And then, because of appearing in clubs owned by these people, and having photographs taken with them and so on, he suddenly became a member of the Mafia, which is so stupid. All the other guys—Tony Bennett, Vic Damone, all of those guys—worked for the same people, but the Hearst people went after my dad.

After a number of years of these rumors, people began to drop words like "alleged" and just let them slip by. He was seen with so-and-so and therefore he must be pushing drugs. This is a man who never takes an aspirin! Until recently, when he's had to take prescribed medication, he hadn't his whole life.

When someone gets to that level of celebrity, they have no control over what's said about them.

Nothing. And it's something, by God, I'm gonna fight until the day I die. I tried to get Alan Dershowitz, who is a constitutional lawyer, a professor at Harvard. I said "You don't know me and I apologize for intruding on your life, but we need help here. We are dealing with a situation that is unfair. Our rights are being abused. We're being lied about and my children are affected. My father got upset when his children were affected, and now his grandchildren are affected. What can we do?"

The law doesn't take into consideration the change in technology, the speed of communication. That if someone writes something nasty, they can also go on television and say it. A lot of people's minds are made up simply because Bryant Gumbel invites someone on his show and gives credibility to someone who's lying. There's got to be new precedent made. I wish I had gone to law school just so I could be involved in getting this thing a little more in our favor.

Nobody wants to hurt the First Amendment. I mean, you know what a patriot my father is. He would never, in a million years, want to go up against the Bill of Rights in any way. What we need is some kind of ethical committee that polices the press. Somebody should be calling these people on the carpet. Other reporters. There should be limits.

The tabloids pay lawyers to keep suits dragging on for years; eventually the celebrity gets tired of pursuing it.

The law is very specific about what you may sue about. He [Sinatra] won the one where they said he was going to Switzerland for injections of unborn lamb placenta.

Where do they get this stuff!?

I don't know, but I was on a talk show with Robert Cummings, and he said, "I get those shots; they're wonderful. You ought to tell him to go!"

It must have been difficult in many ways, having Frank Sinatra for a father. Didn't you want to rebel like most teenagers?

No, it was never a problem. His relationship with his kids is pretty much known; we've always been close. There's never been that kind of trouble. That's all the more reason that people shouldn't believe this nonsense.

Has he given up on trying?

His philosophy always was "I don't want to sell more books or newspapers. I'm not gonna dignify this by getting into it. If you argue with an idiot, people will wonder which one is the idiot." But it is driving me crazy!

When did you start going in to watch your father work?

We always attended things as little kids, but as soon as I got my driver's license at 16 I was able to propel myself to these record sessions, and I did. I can't tell you how exciting it was to be there. It was tangible. Everybody walked in with a smile and standing about 6 inches taller.

What was a typical Sinatra session like?

There were three to five songs recorded at a session, and they zipped through them. The musicians were on the ball, the crew in the booth was on the ball. There's nothing else that's as instantly creative and fulfilling, unless it's a Polaroid picture.

Did he take the initiative in sessions, or would he defer to Nelson Riddle or whoever was producing or arranging?

He always deferred. If something didn't fit, he'd ask for the tempo to be changed, or whatever. Occasionally the song or the arrangement didn't work, and it was set aside. Some of those were songs that my sister and I asked that Capitol remove from the collection. You don't put forward second-rate material in a collection.

Your brother chose the same musical direction as your father. You gravitated toward rock 'n' roll. How did that happen? Was it difficult, as the daughter of Frank Sinatra, to become a rock 'n' roll singer?

No, not at all. I did try to get my dad interested in it, but he would never change. He did venture forth with Don Costa and Ernie Freeman on a few things with Jimmy Bowen producing, and he did come up with "Strangers in the Night"—which he hates.

You were friends with Elvis, who was to kids what Frank Sinatra was to their parents. Did you feel caught in the middle?

No, never. My father is the one who booked Elvis on that TV special. I was the one who met Elvis when he got out of the Army at Fort Dix, in the worst blizzard. I greeted him on behalf of my father and the Timex people [who sponsored the show].

I'd spoken to Col. Parker prior to that and said I wanted to bring Elvis a gift. He said, "He'd like one of those ruffled tuxedo shirts," so I went and got a couple of those and brought them to him at the press reception.

What did Frank think of Elvis' music?

I think he had great respect for Elvis and what he did. Elvis was possibly one of the best blues singers who ever lived, and he [Frank] realized that, although it was not what he does. He did say many years later that Elvis never grew as a musician, unfortunately. We discussed this and we felt that perhaps it was a combination of the people who were guiding his career and the fact that his fans really wanted the same old stuff.

My favorite recording was his favorite, a Bob Dylan song called "Tomorrow is a Long Time." And I loved his religious songs. I have every Elvis album. We were like family. I miss him a lot. I didn't believe it when he died. I still don't believe it.

Did Frank have any input into your records?

As fate would have it, I was living at my mother's house because my marriage [to Tommy Sands] had dissolved. I wasn't quite ready to go back to my house where I'd lived with my husband. It was too sad.

Jimmy Bowen, who was then head of A&R [artists and repertoires] at Reprise came over with a strange, deep-voiced guy named Lee Hazelwood. My father happened to be there that evening, and Lee and Jimmy and I were in the den. My dad and the rest of the family were in the living room.

Lee was auditioning material for me because Reprise was about to dump me. I hadn't had a hit, even in another country, in a couple of years. I was fighting the material being given to me. I wanted to be a grown-up and they didn't know what to do with me. I'm what I call a freak—there are a lot of us freaks who are difficult to place. We're freaks for numbers of reasons, in my case being Frank Sinatra's daughter.

Would it have been different if your name had been Nancy Jones?

Oh, of course. In fact, Lee named me "Nasty Jones." Anyway, Lee was auditioning material for me that night. Mo Ostin was giving me one more chance. Lee went to Mo and said "I promise I will have a chart record for her the first time out of the box." And while Lee was auditioning material, my dad was in the other room reading the newspaper—I would see him out of the corner of my eye. Lee got to "Boots" and I said, "That's it, that's the one."

Lee said, "Nah, I only have two verses, it's not long enough and, besides, it's not a song for a girl. I just thought you might like to hear it." So we dropped it because it wasn't completed. But that night, as he was leaving, my dad said, "That one about the boots, I like that one."

You knew it was a hit?

I *knew* it was a hit. Don't ask me why you know something is a hit but when you hear it you know. One was "Boots," and the other was "Something Stupid."

Are you thinking about making music again?

After my kids are grown, we'll see. To support myself and my kids, we have a company called Design and Build. We design homes and build them, and we do remodels. That's what I'm doing now.

Your brother works as your father's orchestra leader. Do you have any interest in joining the team?

If my dad ever needs me and I'm able to travel, yes, of course I'd do that. But I want him to get off the road. I want him to stop.

Do you think he ever will?

I don't know. He likes getting out where the people are. It's his only forum.

FRANK SINATRA—THE REPRISE COLLECTION II
by Steven McDonald from *Video Online*, a cyberspace magazine, May 1991

*F*rank Sinatra has assumed an almost mythological status in America, thanks to his image, his career and his music. For some he's the essence of a purely American art form—the saloon singer (and at one point in this set he describes himself as just a saloon singer who made good.) For others he's the epitome of schmaltz, described and dismissed in one shot with "My Way," glorified and vilified all at once with a punk rock parody executed by the late Sid Vicious. At one time he was an idol to millions of women; these days he's more of an icon, a symbol like the American flag, like Walter Cronkite, like Bob Hope (who was once described as "that upstart Yorkshireman" by one wag, amused at another round of Hope being charitably patriotic.)

202

The three shows in this box set depict Sinatra settling into that status of icon and symbol. By now most of the acting days are done with, and so are the days of challenge. What's left is hardly Sinatra the artiste; the Reprise years, the sixties changes and the seventies doldrums have taken their toll, leaving us with Sinatra the showman, Sinatra the icon. It doesn't matter that he's testy and somewhat offkey in "The Main Event," an hour-long special originally telecast live from Madison Square Garden in 1974. In the black and white "Sinatra" (1969) he's uncomfortable at times, a little too stiff, too fixated by the camera eye, but still working hard to give his best, and doing so smoothly. The Voice, perhaps, isn't quite there anymore, the resonance slipping away with age, and the game has changed, too, in baffling way—here he's Sinatra as Entertainer but still not quite adjusted away from the saloon singer, Rat Pack leader, relaxed balladeer.

By the last show, the 1971 "Sinatra in Concert at the Royal Festival Hall," he's completely adjusted, completely at ease, the Voice back in shape. He commands the stage, actually awes the late Princess Grace (herself beautiful indeed, and in fine voice) and closes with a rousing rendition of "My Way." This is once again the man in command of his instrument, and he might as well be back in a saloon someplace, with only a piano player, because that's the way he plays it—as much as he holds in reserve to himself, he gives himself to the audience: a well-defended vulnerability, perhaps. Sure, he does the standards and executes string-laden variations on modern popular songs. But he puts them across so well and leaves the audience uncomplaining. No flashy stage show, no dry ice, no girls in skimpy tight outfits. Just him and the orchestra, not always the most visually appealing stuff, but possessing interesting dynamics.

This is good stuff to watch, entertaining and undemanding, showmanship at its best. Sinatra has created a remarkable library of material over the years, from his days at Columbia to his time with Reprise. The three tapes in this box set are a small snippet of that. Check it out.

A total of 39 obscure punk bands, ranging from Jawbox to Zonic Shockum, have recorded a two-CD homage to Frank Sinatra called *Chairman of the Bored*. The bands do thrash interpretations of Rodgers and Hart, Jimmy Van Heusen and Cole Porter.

SECRETS OF SINATRA: INSIDE TALES OF HIS LIFE AND CAREER

by Budd Schulberg from *New Choices for Retirement Living,*
December 1993/January 1994

*I*t's 50 years later, but it doesn't seem that long ago to Ria Del Bene as she takes five in the beauty shop she opened in Westhampton Beach, New York, in the early 1940s. A beautician who shows no signs of letting up as she works into her 70's, she doesn't mind the interruption because it involves a favorite subject: Frank Sinatra.

"I can't believe he's going to be 78 this December," Ria was saying to me in her landmark beauty salon the other day. "I mean, when I think of Sinatra, I'm back there standing in line at the Paramount Theatre on Broadway. I was an apprentice beautician, and when I saw he was coming to the Paramount I took the day off—every girl I knew took the day off. Thirty thousand bobby-soxers crazy in love with Frankie!"

Once a graceful Italian child of the Bronx, Ria has a matronly figure now, but she still sings "Young at Heart" along with her idol as she relives the day she saw the "Hoboken Heartthrob" for the first time. "Did I mind waiting on that line for hours? We were too excited to mind. Nothing mattered except to get into the theatre, and when we did, it was mesmerizing. My parents loved Caruso . . . and now this little kid with the big voice, he was our Caruso. He had a special way of putting himself into a song that made every one of us feel he's singing it to me—he's telling me it's got to be 'All or Nothing at All.' "

Ria didn't swoon as Frankie wooed her and wowed her from the stage of the Paramount, but bobby-soxers around her actually fell out of their seats and fainted into the aisles. Sinatra-bashers spread rumors that Frank's press agent, George Evans, triggered the hysteria by planting ringers in the audience to scream on cue and parking ambulances in front of the theatre, ready to carry off the swooners. But the Sinatra explosion at the Paramount in '42, encored in '43 and '44, was an unprecedented happening. It began unexpectedly with Benny Goodman—supposedly the main attraction— winding up one of his fireworks clarinet solos with four simple words: "And now Frank Sinatra." The ear-piercing audience reaction caught Benny so completely by surprise that he wheeled around and said, "What the hell was that?"

Years later when I was having lunch with Goodman in Mexico City before a jazz concert there, he still remembered the unexpected screams that seemed to rise up from the soles of 5,000 saddleshoes. Until that moment Goodman assumed that he was the star and Sinatra was simply an "added attraction." But Frankie fanatics in the balcony were seized with such acrobatic acclamation that the theatre manager seriously feared the shaking balcony would collapse into the orchestra below.

Success in America—the lightning speed with which it strikes and the sudden blackout into which it often disappears—is a subject that has fascinated me all my life, and Sinatra's is a prime example. In very quick dissolves, we see the skinny teenager from Hoboken on *Major Bowes Amateur Hour* with the forgettable Hoboken Four, moving on to a $25-a-week gig at a Jersey roadhouse where he's discovered by band leader Harry James, and soon moving up to vocalist with the Tommy Dorsey Orchestra.

More than a famous bandleader, Tommy Dorsey was our greatest lyric trombonist, his smooth "singing" style due to incredible breath control. Sinatra listened and learned. Hence his unique ability to sing a ballad so slowly—his operatic breath control enabling him to sustain the musical line without interruption. A natural from his *Amateur Hour* days onward, he was put down by detractors as a sex symbol of the war years who would fade like Dick Haymes and other meteors, but his real strength lay in his musicianship.

A high-school dropout, Sinatra learned all he needed to know on 52nd Street, when 52nd was wall-to-wall jazz greats. Soon he'd be swinging with jazz hall of famers like Count Basie and Duke Ellington, Ella Fitzgerald and Sarah Vaughan. When the inimitable Lester Young—that quiet giant of the tenor sax—said, "My man is Frank Sinatra," the musician in Frank Sinatra knew it was an honor worth a brace of Grammys.

What Sinatra learned from Tommy Dorsey he was quick to make his own, but what he does with the lyrics is what gifted poets do when they read their own works. Having listened to poets as varied as Robert Frost, Dylan Thomas and Yevgeny Yevtushenko, I put Sinatra in their class. Before you snicker, listen to his *kick* in "I get a kick out of you," or *luck* in "Luck be a lady tonight." In "I've Got the World on a String," listen hard to "Got the string around my fiiingerr" and feel that string tightening around your own. His trademark is not just biting into the notes and the words. Strong on music and diction, he has an uncanny ability to convince you he's telling you something he believes.

Wearing your heart on your sleeve may be a cliché's cliché, but let's dust it off for Sinatra with this variation: He wears his song on his sleeve, the first (and best) of the pop singers to sing the words with a feeling for the story they're telling. On his emotional roller-coaster with Ava Gardner—whom he wed in 1951 and, after a tumultuous on-again, off-again marriage, finally divorced in '57—the master of the torch song was also our most publicized torch carrier. He didn't seem able to live with her or without her.

In the fishbowl tabloids, we followed him to Africa on that desperate trip to the location where Ava was shooting *Mogambo* with Clark Gable, and to Spain, where he impulsively chartered a plane in another quixotic attempt to win back the elusive vixen with a temper to match his own. Listen to the album (*Frank Sinatra Sings for*) *Only the Lonely*, recorded a year after the divorce—listen to the sad, slow numbers like "It's a Lonesome Old Town" and "Willow Weep for Me"—and you can't help thinking of Frank the woebegone loser pining for love forever lost and singing loneliness as no one except the great black blues singers had ever sung it before. On that album is my own lifelong favorite, "One for My Baby (and One More for the Road)."

From the day he almost literally brought down the balcony of the Paramount Theatre in 1942, nobody climbed the golden ladder faster than Frank Sinatra, and in the love-hate relationship the American public has with success, no one hit rock bottom with a sicker thud than the Sinatra of '52. The Ava Gardner knock-down drag-out had finally gotten to him. Whenever I hear him sing "Each time I find myself flat on my face, I pick myself up and get back in the race—that's life!" I remember a time when it looked as if he might finally stay down for the count.

If he always seemed to be singing his own autobiography, 1952 was not a very good year. A return engagement at the Paramount had proved a box-office disappointment. The postwar kids were swooning for "Cryin' " Johnny Ray and Frankie Laine. Sinatra's recent movies, *Double Dynamite* and *Meet Danny Wilson*, did nothing to restore his waning popularity. His continuing melodramatics with Ava were the wrong kind of publicity, and in the insult-to-injury department, even the prestigious Hollywood talent agency MCA walked out on him.

One night in the fall of '52, I happened to catch him at what must have been the nadir of his career. I was in Philadelphia to cover the Rocky Marciano-Jersey Joe Walcott heavyweight title fight and heard that Sinatra was working some second-rate joint in town. The room was less than half full and openly hostile because "The Voice" wasn't there anymore. There had been rumors and nasty column items about Frank's emotional upsets and artistic failures eroding that easy baritone. And they hadn't exaggerated. Yesterday's "All" was "Nothing at All"—a pathetic burnout. A heckler told him to shut up and go home. A few other lushes seconded the motion. Frank may have lost his voice but not the combativeness he had brought with him from the streets of Hoboken. "I'm doing one more number," he threatened, "and then I'll be happy to pass among you—with a baseball bat."

That was the level of desperation to which Sinatra had fallen when James Jones' powerful army novel *From Here to Eternity* was announced as a forthcoming Hollywood film. Half a dozen Hollywood friends (including my cousin Roz, whose husband, Henry Rogers, handled Sinatra's public relations) tell the same story of Sinatra's obsession with winning the role of Maggio, the feisty little Italian underdog who stands up to the bullying M.P. played by Ernest Borgnine.

It was a juicy part, and the best character actors in Hollywood were begging to play it. A 100-to-1 shot against an actor's actor like Eli Wallach, Sinatra hounded studio head Harry Cohn around the clock, insisting "I am Maggio!" and offering to play the part for next to nothing. Ava Gardner (whom Cohn wanted for a biblical picture she wanted no part of), though cats-and-dogs with Frank, put in a good word for him in that loyal down-home way of hers: "That s.o.b. I'm married to—he's perfect for it."

Sinatra was in Africa trying to talk Ava back into the marriage again when word came from Cohn: "If you want a screen test, be here tomorrow." Sinatra almost didn't need a plane to get back to Hollywood. Hard-nosed Harry watched the test once and then ran it again. I knew Harry Cohn. Both my producer father and my talent-agent mother had worked for him. He wouldn't give a blind man a nickel. He liked to kick people, especially when they were down. But Harry wasn't one of those corporate executives who hold the reins in Hollywood today—he was a movie man. "The bleepin' truth is, I had no use for the little s.o.b.," Cohn told me. "I knew he was a pain. . . . But the bleepin' test told me something: He was on the money. He outacted the actors. He *was* Maggio. And I got him for peanuts."

The Academy Award that Sinatra won for playing the living hell out of Maggio in *From Here to Eternity* turned those peanuts into golden nuggets. After falling flat on his face, he was not only back in the race but ahead of the pack. It was one of filmdom's most memorable performances, and it led to other serious roles that convinced his most cynical critics that "the little s.o.b." was as effective an actor as he had been a ballad singer before the debacle of '52.

My old friend Nelson Algren, the truth-telling Chicago novelist, leery of Hollywood and afraid of what they would do to his classic *The Man with the Golden Arm*, was won over by Sinatra's interpretation of Frankie Machine, his heroin addict going cold turkey. "I was afraid nobody out there could play it and that Preminger (the director) would crap it up. But Sinatra was Frankie Machine, just the way I wrote him in the book." In *The Manchurian Candidate*, in comedies like *The Tender Trap* and *A Hole in the Head*, Sinatra proved that his Oscar for Maggio was no fluke. If he had wanted to make film-acting a serious full-time career, he might have given Brando, the nonpareil, a run for his money.

In fact, he came *this close* to playing Brando's now-classic Terry Malloy role in *On the Waterfront*. This is exactly how it happened: When I finished the script, director Elia Kazan's first choice for the role of the scrappy young "contendah" was Marlon Brando, whom he had helped develop in the Actors Studio. For reasons only Marlon knows, he sent the script back. I was convinced he hadn't read it. The pages seemed untouched. Then Kazan and I thought of Sinatra. We remembered that under the polished troubadour beat the tough little heart of the kid from Hoboken, where we planned to shoot the picture. Together Kazan and I phoned Sinatra and described the part; he sounded excited.

"I can do it with Frank," said Kazan, one of the keenest judges of performers I've ever known. Then producer Sam Spiegel (*The African Queen*) came into the picture. Worried that he couldn't raise enough money on Sinatra's name and facing the challenge of doing a nitty-gritty New York film that the major studios were rejecting, Spiegel wined and dined Brando and finally talked him into it.

I was in the room when Sam Spiegel held a screaming match with Sinatra's agent, who was charging him with breach of contract. Spiegel was red in the face and literally shaking with rage. Or was it guilt? Truth is, both Kazan and I felt guilty because we had in good faith offered Frank the part. Spiegel's argument was that he was the producer and that Kazan and I had no authority to commit to Sinatra. In time, the messy thing was settled out of court.

Marlon, as we all know now, made Terry Malloy his very own, deserved his Oscar and left behind him a parade of imitators. But if you can get Marlon's Terry out of your mind—not easy to do—Sinatra would have been his own Terry Malloy. No, he wasn't a method actor, he had little patience with rehearsals and even less with retakes—unlike his perfectionism in recording sessions. But as he compared the two professions: "Actors aren't necessarily singers, but good singers are essentially actors. If we don't believe what we're singing, if we don't feel the story-song we're telling, we're just making a lot of pretty sounds."

A winner again in the mid-'50s, Frank Sinatra faced emotional turmoil but no more professional disaster. New musical fads and trends—bebop, soft rock, hard rock, punk, rap, hip-hop—come and go, but somehow the Sinatra show that exploded half a century ago beats on into the '90s. Most of the stars he worked with have passed on or surrendered to inactivity: Sammy Davis, Gene Kelly, Dean Martin. The gifted generation that came of age in the '40s is history now. But Frank Sinatra is out there, the voice a little hoarser but still on the beat or subtly just behind it, singing the old Gershwins and Porters along with such contemporary songs as Stephen Sondheim's "Send in the Clowns."

Sinatra has more than his share of enemies. Unauthorized biographer Kitty Kelley filled a 575-page book with their accusations. But the front ranks of the pro-Frank lobby are filled with lyric writers: Sammy Cahn, Frank Loesser and Johnny Mercer among them. The gifted poets of Tin Pan Alley embraced him as their favorite interpreter, and Sinatra always repaid the compliment, going out of his way to remind his audience who wrote the songs that he chose for their meaning along with their music.

On a personal level, his generosity has taken other forms. I was talking to Dr. Michael DeBakey at the Methodist Hospital in Houston, Texas, the other day, and the famous heart surgeon took time between operations to rebuke the Sinatra-bashers. "Of all the people I've known, I think he's the most unique human being I've ever met," he said. "I first met him when I took care of his father down here. I saw the way he kissed his father.

"I can't tell you how much money he's given to our work—it runs into the hundreds of thousands. Like Joe Louis. When Joe had his stroke, Frank sent him to me. I'm not sure he'd want people to know this, but he said: 'Take care of him and just send me the bills'—not just mine but the hospital's, which ran to thousands and thousands of dollars. None of the people who made money off Joe Louis when he was fighting were there for him. Only Frank. That's the way he is. 'I don't care what it costs,' he said. 'He's my champion and I owe it to him.'"

I've heard that Sinatra did much the same thing for one of our greatest character actors, Lee J. Cobb. When Lee was fighting a critical heart attack, Frank reportedly went to see him at the Cedars of Lebanon Hospital in Los Angeles. Lee was surprised because, while they had worked together in *The Miracle of the Bells*, they had never been close friends. He was even more astonished when he heard, after Frank left, that Sinatra had quietly arranged to pay his medical bills.

To my surprise, Dr. DeBakey called me back after completing an operation to underscore his point about Sinatra: "I know I sound like someone mesmerized, but I simply love the man. People who put him down don't understand him. The stream of humanitarianism runs deep in him, like his music. It's all of one piece."

If Dr. DeBakey is known literally as a life-saver and a yea-sayer, Don Rickles has made his reputation as a naysayer, the master of the vicious putdown who's been described as ready to cut his own mother down, if it would get a laugh. "I've worked a lot of rooms with a lot of famous people, but never anyone like Frank," Rickles said to me as he got ready to shoot his TV series, *Daddy Dearest*. "When he walks into a room, everything stops. It's dumbfounding. I love working with him because you feel the electricity. What's his magic? It's the personal intensity he puts into every song he sings. Everyone else his age is in wheelchairs or taking rest cures—and here's Frank still singing his heart out. He's on the Boardwalk. He's in Vegas. Berlin. Chicago. Mexico City. Never stops. I can't wait to do the Nassau Coliseum gig with him. Me, I make my living putting people down. But Frank is something else. Him, you've got to put *up*."

Come February, Ol' Blue Eyes will preside over the Frank Sinatra Celebrity Golf Tournament, the annual fund-raiser for his current wife's treatment center for victims of sexual abuse, the Barbara Sinatra Children's Center. The '94 theme is "My Funny Valentine" and, Barbara says, "Frank will be singing it at the gala with special feeling for all the kids who need our help."

Back in Westhampton, I called Ria Del Bene's beauty salon to give her my progress report on Frank. From Barbara, I had also learned that, "he's just finished the most fabulous album, *Duets*, with Barbra Streisand, Liza Minnelli, Charles Aznavour, Aretha Franklin, Natalie Cole, Kenny G and others."

"That'll make 47 in my collection," Ria Del Bene said, "and I play one of my LPs every day. I start with *A Man and His Music* and go all the way through to *Frank Sinatra—Like Never Before*."

The bobby-soxers may be grandmas now but, like Sinatra himself, they never lost that Paramount passion that possessed them 50 swinging years ago.

They've still got him under their skin. As The Voice keeps reassuring them, "The best is yet to come. . . . "

211

SINATRA GOES MULTI-PLATINUM

*T*he Recording Industry Association of America awarded Frank Sinatra his first multi-platinum record in a 55-year career, for 2 million units sold of the all-star vocal collection *Duets*.

While this is Sinatra's first multi-platinum LP, he had scored platinum with *Strangers in the Night* in 1966 and *Greatest Hits!* in 1968.

Sinatra has also racked up 21 gold albums in his career.

212

INTRODUCTION: LIFETIME ACHIEVEMENT AWARD
by Paul "Bono" Hewson from the Grammy Awards telecast, 1994

*F*rank never did like rock 'n'roll. And he's not crazy about guys wearing earrings, either. But he doesn't hold it against me in any way. The feeling is not mutual.

Rock 'n' roll people love Frank Sinatra because Frank Sinatra has got what we want: swagger and attitude. He's big on attitude. Serious attitude. Bad attitude. Frank's the Chairman of the Bad. Rock 'n' roll plays at being tough but this guy, well, he's the boss. The boss of bosses. The Man. The Big Bang of Pop. I'm not going to mess with him. Are you?

Who's this guy that every city in America wants to claim as their own? This painter who lives in the desert, this first-rate, first-take actor? This singer who makes other men poets, boxing clever with every word, talking like America: fast, straight-up, in headlines, coming through with the big shtick, the aside, the quiet compliment—good cop/bad cop, all in the same breath. You know his story, because it's your story. Frank Sinatra walks like America: cocksure.

It's 1945 and the U.S. Cavalry are trying to get their asses out of Europe. But they never really do. They're part of another kind of invasion: AFR, American Forces Radio. Broadcasting a music that'll curl the stiff upper lip of England and the rest of the world, paving the way for rock 'n' roll with jazz, Duke Ellington, the big bands, Tommy Dorsey and the right-out-in-front Frank Sinatra.

His voice, tight as a fist, opening at the end of a bar, not on the beat, over it—playing with it, splitting it. Like a jazzman, like Miles Davis. Turning on the right phrase in the right song, which is where he lives, where he lets go, where he reveals himself. His songs are his home, and he lets you in.

But you know, to sing like that you've got to have lost a couple of fights. To know tenderness and romance, you've got to have your heart broken.

People say Frank Sinatra hasn't talked to the press. They want to know who he is, what's on his mind. But you know Sinatra's out there more nights than most punk bands, selling his story through his songs. Telling and articulate in the choice of those songs. Private thoughts on a public address system. Generous.

This is the conundrum of Sinatra. Left and right brain hardly talking: Boxer and painter, actor and singer, lover and father, band man and lover, troubleshooter and troublemaker. The champ who'd rather show you his scars than his medals. He may be putty in Barbara's hands, but I'm not going to mess with him, are you?

Ladies and gentlemen, are you ready to welcome a man heavier than the Empire State, more connected than the Twin Towers, as recognizable as the Statue of Liberty—and living proof that God is a Catholic? Will you welcome the King of New York City—Francis Albert Sinatra!

FRANK SINATRA DUETS II
by Bill Zehme,
liner notes, 1994

*E*ven now he watches the dawn. He has broken more dawns than most mortals. Those hours belong to him. "Look at the colors!" he will say, even now, pointing a bleary friend toward the horizon. "What kind of blue would you call that?" he will ask, full of wonder. He is a poet and this is what a poet does. He sleeps only when he is ready, knowing he will preside over dawns for as long as dawns will break. That is his legacy.

The nights are also his, always were. He teaches at night. He is there for anyone who wants to learn life. Once—and only because somebody asked—he said, "I think my real ambition is to pass on to others what I know. You know, it took me a long, long time to learn what I now know, and I don't want that to die with me. I'd like to pass that on to younger people." What he knows he has sung, and what he has sung is wisdom, the hard and timeless stuff that gets you through the night, that which no book contains. (For instance, it is only through his work that men understand women and women understand men, if but for the duration of one song at a time.) He remains young in order to teach us old lessons, lessons-learned-rough. He fights on the side of youth, availing himself to each new generation, there when we need him, there when we are ready for him. He is always ready for us. For seven decades of singing, of learning, of teaching, he has been ready for us. We are his legacy.

Further proof, new evidence, these duets, more duets: songs and alliances, worlds not colliding so much as embracing, there but for the grace of Sinatra. Because he is not presumptuous, we know well that we have all sung with him. (Somewhere, at this moment, it is happening again.) Last summer, in Dodger Stadium, with the world watching, three tenors—the gods of all tenors—sang "My Way" their way, directly to one man, *the* man, who sat down-front, his way, listening, eyes glistening. Afterward, they blew him kisses. He stood and the world roared.

"Rock and roll people love Frank Sinatra," said Bono, on another night, "because Frank Sinatra has got what we want—swagger and attitude." This was Grammy night at Radio City, a palace only one man can render intimate as a saloon. (Such is the power of penultimate swagger.) Bono, a duet partner of the previous season, shared further that which was under his skin, explaining to contemporaries the importance of being Frank ("This singer who makes other men poets, boxing clever with every word, talking like America . . ."). Bono presented the rare Legend Award to the Legend himself, who really wanted no other honor that night but to sing. "You mean I don't have to sing?" he said backstage. "Can't I do just one for them?" Here was Zeus, fresh from Olympus, offering to sing for his supper, as always preferring to give than to get. Humbled, he simply spoke: "I hope we do this again from time to time," he told all present out front. "That I get to see you and get to know some of you is important to me, very important." Also he said, "I'm not leaving you yet."

He has never left, not really, not for long. And now the end is nowhere near. Born December 12, 1915, Francis Albert Sinatra has work to do. Because a Chairman's work is never done. He must be Frank because no one else can be, will be. Forever he has played solitaire, in public, on-stage, in studios. Nowadays he hosts duets, these duets, and his guests approach timidly at first, but are at once welcomed warmly. Still, they jitter: "Phil, he's never heard of me," said Luther Vandross last time around, incredulous upon getting the call. "Of course he has," said Phil Ramone, *Duets* producer. "He listens, he knows." It is said that Tony Bennett giggled before his turn at-bat and Aretha Franklin swooned. This time, Patti LaBelle asked for a glass of wine to calm herself, assured that FS would approve. Thus, history mixes the second time around and new and different flavors emerge.

If Part One was event and spectacle, Part Two is document and chronicle. The pairings bode sentiment, importance, nice surprise: "Francis, let's fly!" beckons old friend Antonio Carlos Jobim, down from the mountain, back at the lunar launch-pad for "Fly Me to the Moon." (Exactly twenty-five years ago, Neil Armstrong carried the tune aboard Apollo XI, blaring Sinatra in space. Said the singer shortly thereafter: "I watched three men fly to the moon and imagine their surprise when they found out I was there two nights ahead of them!" There are other unions and reunions, swinging fierce or murmuring low—fine and disparate company kept with Willie Nelson, Stevie Wonder, Gladys Knight, Linda Ronstadt, Lorrie Morgan, Jimmy Buffett. With elegant Lena Horne, fragile winter love is hereafter made eternal ("Embraceable You"). With Chrissie Hynde, the dice are blown with formidable sass ("Luck Be a Lady"). In Chicago, father meets son, miraculously, for sweet home posterity ("My Kind of Town"). Steve and Eydie, Lawrence and Gorme, pave a sunning, skitting path fit only for one seasoned traveler, whom they know as few other do ("Where or When").

Latin boy-wonders, Jon Secada and Luis Miguel, get a load of raw manhood, in separate helpings, by dint of the Hoboken boy-wonder emeritus ("The Best Is Yet to Come" and "Come Fly with Me"). And then there is Neil Diamond sharing the heroic drama of American dreams, never sung more poignantly or with greater resonance than right here, right now ("The House I Live In").

In from the desert, in from the road, he is back in the studio, back in the music, down deep inside, deeper than ever, flexing the reed, telling the truth, wiser than ever. "The reed feels all right tonight," he will say. Then: "Shoot!" he will say, whereupon his friends, the musicians, begin at once, as in immediately. You do not wait for him and he does wait for you and that is how business is done. "You got it?" he says afterward, not a question really, for he is famously a man of few takes, especially when one take will suffice to make history. Further, he does not go back to fix a note here, a phrase there: it is, as they say, all or nothing at all. For him, a song is not a sum of parts, but a living whole. And a life must be full, like his own, not fragmented, never isolated. "What's next?" he will then say, not a question really.

For every rule he makes, he breaks ten, even now. Back in Hollywood, back at Capitol, Studios A and B, where it happened then and it happens again now, right now, he stands firm, smack in the middle of his players, so that he feels them just as they feel him, begetting raucous energy unheard in this segregated age of pristine production. He does not hide behind a glass booth, for he is not supposed to be contained. He is to be experienced, up close. He sets his own tempo, tapping trigger finger against thigh, in full view of his conductor, Pat Williams, who conducts and cooks accordingly. In this fashion, the night moves briskly and life-lessons are recorded, as put forth by the prize-fighter who holds all the secrets. "How was that?" he will say, knowing exactly what he has wrought, not waiting for an answer. Ol' blue orbs twinkling, heart soaring in kind, he pronounces, "If you don't like that, you don't like ice-cream!"

Then: "Next!" And another generation gets smarter.

Kind permission has been granted to reprint the following and can be considered an extension of the copyright page:

"He Can't Read a Note but He's Dethroning Bing." *and* "Frank Sinatra Is 'Wunnerful to the Gals'"
(From *Newsweek,* March 22, 1943. © 1943, Newsweek, Inc. All rights reserved. Reprinted by permission.)

"Sweet Dreams and Dynamite" by Jack Long
(From *The American Magazine,* September, 1943.)

"The Voice"
(From *Newsweek,* December 20, 1943. © 1943. Newsweek, Inc. All rights reserved. Reprinted by permission.)

"My Bow Tie" and "The Little Things, An Appreciation" from the collection of Gary L. Doctor. Reproduced with permission.

"Phenomenon, Parts I and II" by E. J. Kahn, Jr.
(Reprinted by permission; © 1946, 1974 E. J. Kahn, Jr. Originally in *The New Yorker.* All rights reserved.)

"Star-Spangled Octopus" by David G. Wittels
(Reprinted from the *Saturday Evening Post,* © 1946. With permission.)

"The Nine Lives of Frank Sinatra" by Adela Rogers St. Johns
(From *Cosmopolitan,* 1956.)

"When Old Blue Eyes Was 'Red'" by Jon Wiener
(Reprinted by permission of *The New Republic,* © 1986, The New Republic, Inc.)

"Daddy-O!" by Louella O. Parsons
(Excerpted from *Tell It to Louella* by Louella O. Parsons, G. P. Putnam's Sons, 1961)

"Watching Sinatra Tape a Show" by Peter Levinson
(From *New York Herald Tribune,* January, 1961; © 1961, New York Herald Tribune Inc. All rights reserved. Reprinted by permission.)

"*Playboy* Interviews: Frank Sinatra"
(From the *Playboy* interview: Frank Sinatra, *Playboy* magazine. Copyright © 1963 by Playboy. Used with permission. All rights reserved.)

"Sinatra Means a Jumping Jilly's" by Gay Talese
(© 1965 by The New York Times Company. Reprinted by permission.)

"Protecting Sinatra Against the Big Beef Story" by Christopher Buckley
(From *New York* magazine, 1971. Reprinted by kind permission of the author.)

"Sinatra: An American Classic" by Rosalind Russell
(© 1973, Meredith Corporation. All rights reserved. Reprinted with permission from *Ladies' Home Journal* magazine.)

"Sinatra: Still Got the World on a String" by Michael Watts
(From *Melody Maker* [U.K.], November 9, 1974. © 1974 by IPC Magazines Ltd. Reprinted with permission.)

"Oh, How We Worshipped the Gods of the Fifties" by Barbara G. Harrison.
(Copyright © 1976 by Barbara G. Harrison. Reprinted by permission of Georges Borchardt, Inc. for the author.)

"Sinatra: The Legend Lives" by Pete Hamill
(From *New York* magazine, April 28, 1980. Reprinted with permission of International Creative Management, Inc. Copyright © 1980 by Pete Hamill.)

"The Majestic Artistry of Frank Sinatra" by Mikal Gilmore
(From *Rolling Stone*, September 18, 1980. © 1980 by Straight Arrow Publishers. All rights reserved. Reprinted by permission.)

"An Homage to the 'Classical' Crooners" by John Rockwell
(© 1982 by The New York Times Company. Reprinted by permission.)

"At Home with the Palm Springs Sinatras" by Jody Jacobs
(Copyright 1983, *Los Angeles Times*. Reprinted by permission.)

"Frankie and Ronnie" by Alex Heard
(Reprinted by permission of *The New Republic*, © 1985, The New Republic, Inc.)

"But Seriously, Comrades—Presenting the Sinatra Doctrine" by Bruce McCall
(From the *Los Angeles Times*, November 1989. Reprinted by kind permission of the author)

"A Perfect Singer, Ever Since He Began the Beguine" by Harry Connick, Jr.
(© 1990 by The New York Times Company. Reprinted by permission.)

"Under My Skin" by William Kennedy
(From *The New York Times Magazine*, October 7, 1990. © 1990 by William Kennedy. Reprinted by kind permission of the author.)

"Frankly, My Dear" by Michael Roberts
(Appeared in *Westword* magazine, December 5-11, 1990. Reprinted by kind permission of the author.)

"Chairman of the Board Still Boss As He Turns Seventy-Five" by Tony Gieske
(Reprinted by permission from *The Hollywood Reporter*, December 12, 1990.)

"Are You Ready, Boots? Start Talkin'—Nancy Sinatra on Frank (and
 Nancy) Sinatra" by Jeff Tamarkin
 (Excerpted from *Goldmine* magazine, Iola, Wisconsin, March 22, 1991.
 Reprinted by permission.)
"Frank Sinatra—The Reprise Collection II" by Steven McDonald
 (From *Video Online,* May 30, 1991. Reprinted by permission of the au-
 thor.)
"Secrets of Sinatra—Inside Tales of His Life and Career" by Budd Schulberg
 (From *New Choices for Retirement Living.* Reprinted by kind permission
 of Budd Schulberg, © 1993.)
"Introduction: Lifetime Achievement Award" by Paul "Bono" Hewson
 (Grammy Awards, 1994. Reprinted by permission of NARAS.)

*All possible care has been taken to trace the ownership of every selection
included and to make full acknowledgment for its use. If any errors have
occurred, they will be corrected in subsequent editions provided notification is
sent to the publisher.*

*E*thlie Ann Vare is known as both a music journalist and historian. Her book *Mothers of Invention: From the Bra to the Bomb, Forgotten Women and Their Unforgettable Ideas* (William Morrow) won the American Library Association's Best Books for Young Adults award in 1988; *Adventurous Spirit: A Story About Ellen Swallow Richards* (Carolrhoda, 1992) received the Public Library Association's Top Titles for New Adult Readers award.

At the same time, she was honored for her work as Executive Editor of the iconoclastic *Rock* magazine, and her syndicated newspaper column, *Rock On*—which ran in up to 1,700 newspapers nationwide from 1979-1990—was the Number 1 popular music column in the U.S.

Ms. Vare is currently a music critic for *The Hollywood Reporter*, the Hollywood correspondent for *Shout* magazine in the U.K.; and film critic for *Countdown* magazine in New Zealand. Her other books include biographies of film stars Harrison Ford and Martin Sheen, and rock stars Stevie Nicks and Ozzy Osbourne. Her most recent book reunites her with *Mothers of Invention* coauthor, Greg Ptacek: *Women Inventors and Their Discoveries* (Oliver Press, 1993).

She frequently speaks at college campuses on the topic of women who changed the world.